Religious Education in the Secondary School

Religious Education in the Secondary School is a comprehensive, straightforward introduction to the effective teaching of Religious Education in the secondary classroom. Acknowledging the highly valuable yet often misunderstood contribution of RE, this text shows how the subject can be taught in a way that explores the impact of religion on the lives of people and society, engaging pupils and preparing them to become individuals who celebrate and respect diversity.

It is illustrated throughout with ideas for teaching at different key stages and offers expert chapters introducing you to both the World Religions and the core aspects of effective teaching and learning. With an emphasis on developing an understanding of the importance – and different ways – of meeting the learning needs of all pupils, key chapters cover:

- understanding different pedagogies of RE;
- spirituality and RE;
- tips on effective planning and assessment;
- an approach to teaching across the Key Stages;
- core subject knowledge in Buddhism, Christianity, Hinduism, Islam, Judaism and Sikhism.

Written by an experienced teacher, teacher educator and examiner, *Religious Education in the Secondary School* is a succinct compendium and has a real classroom applicability offering all trainee RE teachers, as well as those teaching Religious Education as specialists or non-specialists, a wealth of support and inspiration.

James D. Holt is Senior Lecturer in Religious Education at the University of Chester, UK.

Religious Education in the Secondary School

An introduction to teaching, learning and the World Religions

James D. Holt

Routledge
Taylor & Francis Group

LONDON AND NEW YORK

First published 2015
by Routledge
2 Park Square, Milton Park, Abingdon, Oxon OX14 4RN

and by Routledge
711 Third Avenue, New York, NY 10017

Routledge is an imprint of the Taylor & Francis Group, an informa business

British Library Cataloguing in Publication Data
A catalogue record for this book is available from the British Library

Library of Congress Cataloging in Publication Data
Holt, James.
Religious education in the secondary school : an introduction to teaching, learning and the world religions / James Holt.
ISBN 978-1-138-01899-0 (hardback) -- ISBN 978-1-138-01900-3 (paperback) -- ISBN 978-1-315-77919-5 (e-book) 1. Religious education. 2. Religions--Study and teaching (Secondary) 3. Religion in the public schools. I. Title.
LC331.H65 2014
207'.5--dc23
2014019984

ISBN: 978-1-138-01899-0 (hbk)
ISBN: 978-1-138-01900-3 (pbk)
ISBN: 978-1-315-77919-5 (ebk)

Typeset in Bembo
by Saxon Graphics Ltd, Derby

Printed and bound in the United States of America by Publishers Graphics, LLC on sustainably sourced paper.

Dedicated to three remarkable teachers in my life:
Eric Starkey who inspired me to teach.
Ted Banks who made that inspiration focused on RE.
Cliff Shortell who was a great teacher, mentor, guide and friend.

Contents

List of figures and tables

Figures

Tables

Foreword

In May 2009 I made the hardest decision of my life to leave the school classroom and move into the world of University teaching. I love teaching, and there is nothing better than standing in front of a class of pupils and discovering learning together. Religious Education is my passion; I come alive when I am with classes of pupils discussing the most important subject in the world. Why then was I leaving all that I loved? I was having an impact on the pupils I taught but I was aware through various aspects of my work that RE was not everyone's favourite subject, it was sometimes, and perhaps often, taught badly. I thought that going to work with people training to become teachers would enable me to have an impact on the way that RE is taught. Five years have passed, and I still feel, perhaps arrogantly, that I have a contribution to make. As such, this book is the wisdom of all of my experiences condensed into an approach to teaching. I do not pretend to have all of the answers but the principles outlined herein have worked for me and many others as we have striven to make RE come alive in the classroom and have an impact on the wider world.

Various approaches are suggested, and then followed by an introduction to the six major world religions. Reading the book will be one step on a long journey of discovering what approach to RE a person wishes to take, but I hope that people find it useful. Hopefully the passion I have for RE will come through the pages of this book, it really is the greatest subject in the curriculum.

Acknowledgements

There are many people who have helped in the formulation of this book. It is based on my experiences as a pupil, teacher, AST and latterly as a University lecturer. During that time I have been inspired by many teachers and pupils who have all helped shape the approach advanced in this book. Thanks are due to the staff and pupils of Egerton Park High School (1997–2004); Parrs Wood High School (2004–2009); and colleagues and students in the Education Faculty of the University of Chester. Particular examples of excellent teachers and friends are Mark Crashley, Sarah Walsh, Lisa Humphries, Jay Patel, Stephen Henry, Emily Teague, Andrew Wallace, Cassie Meller and Natalie Daniels. Students are too numerous to name, but thank you to all of you. The lively discussions with Diane Kolka, Diane Spradbery, Emma Milbourn, Christine Paul, Sally Hunter, Ranvir Singh, Duncan Johnson and Stephen Darlington have all contributed to my love of RE; thank you.

It would be remiss of me not to thank Mark Peace, Helen Stedman and Claire Fletcher who allowed me to pick their brains and utilise aspects of those conversations in specific areas of this book. Thanks also to Emma Davies for being a sounding board, John Rudge for being well, amazing, Geoff Teece for his encouragement and my mum for not placing any limits on my ambitions.

Huge thanks are due to my wife Ruth and our four gorgeous children Eleanor, Abi, Gideon and Martha who are my everything and were patient with me while I took time to write this book.

Finally, I would be nothing without my Heavenly Father, His Son Jesus Christ and the Holy Ghost. Thank you for forgiving my imperfections and sustaining me every step of the way.

PART I

Introduction to Religious Education

Chapter 1

What is Religious Education?

The nature and purpose of Religious Education

Religious Education (RE)[1] is an incredibly valuable subject within the curriculum but is often misunderstood or even denigrated. Teachers of Religious Education (whether specifically trained or a non-specialist teacher) should have an understanding of what they are trying to achieve through the subject; this will then help pupils, parents and school leaders understand the contribution RE can make to their lives, children, school and society. The lack of understanding about the nature and purpose of RE has been shown by leaders in society, and if shown by them, this view will also be shared by others. One example is the then School's Minister, Nick Gibb, when he spoke to the RE Council of England and Wales in 2012. He spoke positively of religion as a 'Rosetta stone' to help understand different subjects. Then, to exemplify his point he continued:

> A pupil who understands the religious context can walk into a nation's great art collections and appreciate the nuanced iconography of paintings by men like Giotto and El Greco. A pupil who understands the restrained faith of the Quakers can appreciate the growth of London today as a financial powerhouse. A pupil who understands the great mathematical advances and discoveries under the Caliphs can appreciate how the first great European explorers navigated to new worlds.
>
> (p. 1)

This all sounds very positive, and was echoed somewhat by Michael Gove, who was then Secretary of State for Education:

> Without doubt the constructive working and mutual understanding between faiths in this country is one of our greatest strengths. Educating children about different faiths is of immense importance in leading children to understand the history that has helped shape the values and traditions of this country, and of other countries and cultures.
>
> (Linden, 2012)

Both Michael Gove and Nick Gibb miss the point about the purpose of RE. While recognising its value, they do so on the basis of a flawed assumption. This assumption is that RE's greatest contribution is to help people to understand their own and other people's culture, history and countries. If RE is pursued on that basis then it becomes a purely academic exercise with no attempt to understand people; and for the most part with no attempt to make it relevant to the pupils' own experiences. It may be that the painting of the above approach to RE is simplistic and an extreme caricature; but the resultant actions that the understanding above caused suggest that RE's immediate importance and applicability in the world was lost.

If RE is purely about understanding culture and history, the resultant RE lessons could be vibrant and evocative, but the telos, or the end point, which teachers would be working towards would be knowledge focused rather than any reference to other elements that it could be argued are central to good RE. Ofsted, in their 2010 publication *Transforming RE*, suggested that the purpose of the teacher is important:

> There is uncertainty among many teachers of RE about what they are trying to achieve in the subject resulting in a lack of well-structured and sequenced teaching and learning, substantial weaknesses in the quality of assessment and a limited use of higher order thinking skills to promote greater challenge.
>
> (Ofsted, 2010, p. 6)

This continued to be the case in *Realising the Potential* (Ofsted, 2014). It is for this reason that each individual teacher should undertake an exercise to construct their own aims for teaching Religious Education. They should do this not on the basis of a whim or what they think but by exploring what other people have said and synthesising this into aims that will underpin their approach to RE. Of course, there are stated aims in national guidance, and also in the Agreed Syllabi but going through this process will help the teacher make the aims of the classroom belong to them, and also help integrate with the aims of the curricula they follow. This chapter will explore various aims that have been put forward, and suggest that good RE focuses on a number of shared aims that can be reflected upon and developed by individual teachers.

The aims of Religious Education

In developing aims for RE it is important for a teacher to critically examine statements that could be found in an individual's approach to, and understanding of, RE. It might be useful for the reader to consider their own positive and negative responses to the stimulus aims below before reading the associated commentary. It must be said that not all of the stimulus aims listed below are appropriate and each of these aims is deliberately vague, and in some cases provocative, in order to enable a teacher to explore their initial thoughts about the nature of, and approach to, teaching RE.

1 RE is bringing children up to be true to their own religion and culture.
2 RE is helping children to develop their own ideas and values.
3 RE is teaching children about the major religions of the world.
4 RE is teaching children morals.
5 RE is helping children to be tolerant in a multi-cultural society.
6 RE is teaching children to accept Christian beliefs and values.

I RE is bringing children up to be true to their own religion and culture

At first glance this may seem to be an inappropriate aim of RE in a state secondary school. RE in schools should be non-denominational. John Hull suggests that any approach to RE should be 'a syllabus which can be taught by any well trained and well informed teacher, regardless of his faith, to any pupil whose interest can be caught, regardless of his faith' (1984, p. 179). It is hoped that the teacher would have a positive neutrality: 'It does not mean that the teacher does not care but that he cares for them all, accepting them as they are' (p. 181). To enable a child to be 'true' to their own religion and culture suggests that the purpose of RE is to foster faith; and while this may be appropriate in a school with a faith basis, in a state school this is not appropriate.

However, to argue that RE can be neutral also suggests that it cannot be positive about existing faith. As a subject that engages with pupils' own beliefs, it is important that pupils feel that their contributions are valued and that their beliefs (or lack of) are taken seriously. Also, in RE the teacher must be careful that nothing is done that might require a child to contravene their own religion or culture. This does not mean that questions are not asked, rather that practices that might be deemed to be wrong or offensive are avoided. Simple examples might include not having children portray the Prophet Muhammad; or utilising material that might unquestioningly present a perception of a faith that is out of step with the traditional understanding of that faith. Consider, for example, the following passage from a GCSE mark scheme:

> Other candidates might offer examples of denominations which have additional texts or which give different weight to existing texts, such as the Mormons who describe themselves as Christian but who give scriptural status to the Book of Mormon over the Bible.
>
> (OCR, 2012, p. 38)

While seemingly objective, there are elements that would question a Mormon child's understanding of their own faith. First, the Book of Mormon is given equal weight to the Bible, however, the sentence that suggests 'Mormons describe themselves as Christian *but* give ...' causes issues as it suggests that they might think of themselves in this way, but they cannot be because .... . A better way to phrase it might be 'such as the Mormons who describe themselves as Christian, a claim that is disputed by others ...'. This does not mean that RE is not challenging, but it is respectful of a faith's self-understanding.

2 RE is helping children to develop their own ideas and values

The National Curriculum guidance for RE (2007) suggests that RE:

> encourages pupils to learn from different religions, beliefs, values and traditions while exploring their own beliefs and questions of meaning. It challenges pupils to reflect on, consider, analyse, interpret and evaluate issues of truth, belief, faith and ethics and to communicate their responses.
>
> (p. 275)

In this way RE can be seen to help pupils develop their own ideas and, based on their exploration of other people's views, to develop their own values, which might mean responses to questions of meaning and moral and social issues. In a multi-faith society, which can also be described as secular, or post-religious, it is important for everybody to develop reasoned responses to their identity that will include ideas and values. For some, these will be religious, but for other pupils they might well use a reflection on others' experiences to develop their own views.

This approach comes with a potential danger that needs to be acknowledged. A large number of faiths, and perhaps those from a non-religious worldview, would see this pick-and-mix approach to the development of ideas and values as seriously flawed; that certain of the ideas are meaningless without a basis in the faith. RE is also, in being as objective as possible, not the approach that has sometimes been 'referred to as "market place religion" – the idea that children are given an objective description of a variety of religions and then encouraged to choose one for themselves' (Read et al., 1998, p. 5). In agreement with Hull it should be recognised that:

> truly educational teaching is directed to all pupils alike, since no distinction is made in divergent education between Christian pupils, Jewish pupils and pupils of no religious affiliation. … It does not mean that the teacher does not care but that he cares for them all, accepting them as they are.
>
> (1984, p. 181)

It also raises the question as to whose values are the pupils exposed to? Should the RE teacher be the person who encourages the development of values, or is this better done in the home?

3 RE is teaching children about the major religions of the world

Having come a long way from the days of 'Religious Instruction' where the tenets of Christianity were the focus of education, most people would agree that this is one of the fundamental principles of the RE classroom. In most faith schools the curriculum is not limited to the parent faith; it is widely recognised that religious understanding, and what some have termed 'religious literacy' (Prothero, 2008), is crucial in today's society. The major world religions of Buddhism, Christianity, Hinduism, Islam, Judaism, and Sikhism account for the majority of people's faiths that are found within the United Kingdom. Even in areas where there is not a large amount of religious diversity, people of all ages are still exposed to varieties of religious expression and experience:

A few decades ago the terms Buddhist, Hindu, mosque, Sikh, pagoda, and synagogue were unfamiliar labels filled with mystery. Today, however, the world is a close neighbourhood – few societies or religions are any longer distant or foreign. The study of the religions of the world is no longer a matter of reading about exotic lands to which only the most intrepid travellers have voyaged. Almost any faith from anywhere is a presence in our lives – and an immediate option.

(Palmer, 1997, p. 8)

As such, the restriction of RE to any one perspective could be detrimental to the development of a pupil's own perspective of their place within society.

There are, however, at least two problems with statement 3, even though it has just been suggested that this is a laudable approach to RE. First, the phrase 'about the major religions of the world'. If all RE is concerned with is learning about religions, then all pupils will be prepared for a pub quiz but not much else within society. It is doubtful that those who teach RE would limit themselves to a recitation of facts, but it is possible that some observers would see this as the primary purpose. Consider, for example, the change from the aims of the 2007 National Curriculum, which wanted pupils to develop into 'responsible citizens', while the 2014 National Curriculum seeks 'educated citizens'. Although not a part of the 2014 National Curriculum (except to say it needs to be taught) the implications of this for RE are dangerous. People who are educated do not automatically have the understanding and attitudes to respect those of other faiths and none; nor do they automatically understand the impact that faith has on the life of the believer. RE should, therefore, maintain the goal of responsible citizens based on the ability to empathise; to learn from the religious and non-religious experiences of others. RE should provide the opportunity for all pupils to appreciate 'You never really understand a person until you consider things from his point of view … until you climb into his skin and walk around in it' (Lee, 1988, p. 30).[2]

The second concern with teaching about the major religions of the world is the possibility that the RE taught could be limited to the 'Big Six'. There are minority religions and also non-faith worldviews that have a significant local or national presence that, when included in RE, could give pupils a wider understanding and experience of Religious Education. The *Review of Religious Education in England* (hereafter *RE Review*) suggests that the aims of RE should include helping children to 'Know about and understand a range of religions and worldviews'. It then footnotes what is meant by the phrase 'religions and worldviews':

[It] is used in this document to refer to Christianity, other principal religions represented in Britain, smaller religious communities and non-religious worldviews such as Humanism. The phrase is meant to be inclusive, and its precise meaning depends on the context in which it occurs, eg in terms of belief, practice or identity.

(RE Council of England and Wales, 2013, p. 14)

It has been argued that the 'major focus of RE is the study of diversity of religion and belief in the UK and how this influences national life' (DCSF, 2010, p. 8). As such, the inclusion of fewer large world religions, and also non-religious worldviews, could be seen to prepare children in a better way for life in the United Kingdom. Indeed, Miller suggests:

I'm convinced that RE has to move away from the 'safe six' and be far more adventurous in what is included in RE – and NRMs are so much more obvious in society than some of the religions they study that we owe it to children to help them develop an informed understanding of Jehovah's Witnesses, Latter-day Saints, Hare Krishnas and all the others they encounter – literally – on the streets.

(in Holt, 2010, pp. 80–81)

It has been argued that there are reasons why teachers might feel justified in excluding smaller religions from the RE classroom (see Holt, 2010), but these reasons and concerns are outweighed by the need to be religiously inclusive and sensitive to the pupils' own worldviews:

The most persuasive argument for the inclusion of NRMs is in those environments where they may constitute the pupils' own world views. The good teacher builds upon the experiences of those pupils. The bad teacher would dismiss a child's faith as not relevant or else would have an erroneous understanding of that faith, upsetting and confusing the child and their family.

(Holt, 2010, p. 85)

Arguments could similarly be made against the inclusion of non-religious worldviews in the RE classroom; after all it is Religious Education. However, it could be argued that as the UK becomes generally more of a secular and post-religious society that non-religious (not necessarily, though possibly, atheistic) worldviews are becoming more of a norm within secondary schools. There is still a Christian underpinning of society, not the least of which is evident in the laws and celebrations of the country, but it is not unusual to find children who are agnostic, atheist or who consider themselves religious but not affiliated to any particular group. Although the main focus of RE should be religious beliefs, teachers need to be aware of the pupils they teach, and also the wider society in which their schools function.

4 RE is teaching children morals

The immediate question that arises with this statement is 'Whose morals?' It cannot and should not be an aim of RE in the state secondary school to promote a particular morality as the accepted norm. If a Christian's morality should be taught then it would be in conflict with other forms of religious and non-religious codes of morality. Similarly, any religious code of morality, or even secular morality, could find itself at odds with the morality of individuals and religious groups. As such, an RE teacher should be positively neutral when it comes to issues of morality. This means ensuring that morals are taught about, and when they are that they are contextualised and challenged positively and negatively so that a pupil is able to develop their own ideas and values.

However, if teachers feel it is not their place to teach morality then they are in the wrong profession. There is an accepted morality that is taught in every school; it is encompassed in the rules and the ethos of the school. To teach that bullying and racism are wrong entails every teacher to become a teacher of morals. It is interesting for a teacher to consider where societal morals stop and which areas they do not want to approach. For example, while every teacher should recognise the importance of challenging homophobia in whatever guise they find it within the classroom, this does not mean that children should not be able to express their opposition to gay marriage. This is a very fine line of demarcation, and teachers must recognise what is the accepted school morality that they teach and also recognise their own religious or secular morality that oversteps the mark.

5 RE is helping children to be tolerant in a multi-cultural society

This is perhaps the most oft quoted aim of RE. In 1994 the Department for Education and Skills released a circular that enshrined this: 'all those concerned with religious education should seek to ensure that it promotes respect, understanding and tolerance for those who adhere to different faiths' (DES Circular 3/89).

However, if all teachers aim for is a tolerance of others' perspectives then there is little beyond the token recognition of existence. Although tolerance has many positive connotations, to tolerate something or someone is not a laudable aim, it is a step in the right direction but not an end in itself. This involves recognising and celebrating differences. Sometimes, tolerance leads to an uneasy peace in society that can be broken with a single event.

John Hull articulated an approach to RE that could be termed a tolerated vision: 'I am holy, the argument says, and you are holy but the ground between us is unholy ground and we will contaminate each other through harmful mingling of blood if we meet' (Hull, 1991, p. 38). Teece develops this by describing 'the contrasting point of view that recognises that neither you nor I are holy, it is the space between us that constitutes holy ground, holiness being discovered through encounter' (Teece, 1993, p. 8). This goes beyond tolerance and, to borrow from Martin Luther King's vision for society as one group of people is raised, another group is not caused to be made low.

> In a real sense all life is interrelated. The agony of the poor enriches the rich. We are inevitably our brother's keeper because we are our brother's brother. Whatever affects one directly affects all indirectly.
>
> (King, 1967, p. 181)

> Let us be dissatisfied until rat-infested, vermin-filled slums will be a thing of a dark past and every family will have a decent sanitary house in which to live. Let us be dissatisfied until the empty stomachs of Mississippi are filled and the idle industries of Appalachia are revitalized. ... Let us be dissatisfied until our brothers of the Third World of Asia, Africa and Latin America will no longer be the victims of imperialist exploitation, but will be lifted from the long night of poverty, illiteracy and disease.
>
> (King, 2000, pp. 38–39)

Extending King's view of the 'blessed community' that would result, one can relate the view of the experience of the religious and non-religious believers. Cox has argued that:

> It is ... essential to notice that the two elements, the holy outcast and the blessed community, must go together. Without the vision of restored community, the

holiness ascribed to the poor would fall far short of politics and result in a mere
perpetuation of charity and service activities.

(Cox, 1967, p. 133)

This would enable a vision of understanding and respect far beyond a tolerance-based
curriculum.

This is also a curriculum where difference is celebrated as much as commonality. Too
much focus on shared beliefs is a dangerous approach within the RE classroom. A
statement that is intended to placate both Christians and Muslims could be seen to please
neither. The desire to please and accept every voice within Religious Education actually
serves to undermine the learning. It is this type of example that could deter people from
engaging in RE. A number of faiths would find the mingling of their most deeply held
doctrines in a metaphorical melting pot of beliefs alarming. The lowest common
denominator approach to education is characterised by Sivananda, who argues: 'The
fundamentals or essentials of all religions are the same. There is difference only in the
non-essentials' (2004). The Divine Sonship of Jesus Christ would be a central and defining
theme for most Christians, which is in direct contravention to the belief of the oneness of
God within Islam. Neither of these could be seen to be non-essentials. An approach to
RE should not necessitate either mere tolerance, or the syncretisation of faiths so that they
become barely discernable from one another. RE is about recognising similarities and
celebrating and understanding difference.

6 RE is teaching children to accept Christian beliefs and values

The *RE Review* (2013) suggests that 'RE offers distinctive opportunities to promote
pupils' spiritual, moral, social and cultural development. RE lessons should offer a
structured and safe space during curriculum time for reflection, discussion, dialogue and
debate' (p. 15). As such, it has an integral role to play in the discussion of moral values but
it does not, and should not, be about teaching pupils to accept any religious, or non-
religious, worldview's values. However, there are some values that a school, and the
wider society, accepts and promotes that could be compatible with Christian values, but
they could also be compatible with the majority of world religions' worldview. Consider
the Golden Rule, which is often adopted into a school's ethos without reference to its
religious source in the religions of the world:

Christianity: In everything do to others as you would have them do to you.

(Matthew 7:12)

Islam: No one of you is a believer until he desires for his brother that which he desires
for himself.

(An Nawawi, Forty Hadith 13)

Sikhism: Do not harbour hatred against anyone. In each and every heart, God is
contained.

(Guru Arjan Devji, Guru Granth Sahib 259)

Hinduism: This is the sum of duty; do nothing to others which would cause you pain if done to you.

(Mahabarata 13: 114)

Judaism: For the Lord your G–d is G–d of gods, and Lord of lords, a great G–d, mighty, and awesome, who favours no person, and takes no bribe: he executes the judgement of the fatherless and the widow, and loves the stranger, giving him food and raiment. Love therefore the stranger, for you were strangers in the Land of Egypt.

(Deuteronomy 10: 17–21)

Buddhism: it is a very good deed to cast away greed and to cherish a mind of charity. … One should get rid of a selfish mind and replace it with a mind that is earnest to help others.

(The Teaching of the Buddha. Way of Practice II: 9)

In some ways the reaction to this 'aim' of RE brings together the arguments of all of the discussions that have taken place thus far in this chapter. It highlights a teacher's positive neutrality while trying to expand a pupil's experience, understanding and celebration of the world within and outside of their experience.

Suggested aims of RE

It is important for an individual teacher of RE to decide the nature of the aims and purposes of the subject and their teaching for themselves, and the discussion above should help begin that process. It is possible, however, to posit some aims against which a teacher can compare their own or use as a starting point. The following might be suggested:

1   To stimulate interest and enjoyment in Religious Education.
2   To prepare pupils to be informed, respectful members of society who celebrate diversity and strive to understand others.
3   To encourage students to develop knowledge of the beliefs and practices of religions; and informed opinions and an awareness of the implications of religion for the individual, the community and the environment.
4   To give all students equal access to Religious Education and provide enjoyment and success.
5   To develop pupils' own responses to questions about the meaning and purpose of life.

These suggested aims can be compared with aims that can be found in different places of the RE community (see Table 1.1). While maybe the first and fourth are implicit in any teaching of RE and so do not need a focus when outlining 'official' aims, they are integral to the teaching of RE and should be at the centre of everything the RE teacher does.

   While these are very lofty goals for a secondary school child, it is hoped that a child's sense of wonder and respect for others can always be captured through RE. RE should seek for pupils to understand how concepts and attitudes can be related to their own lives as well as the lives of others. RE teachers should aim to provide a basis on which secondary schools can build in achieving these aims.

The legal position of RE

The 1988 Education Reform Act (HMSO, 1989) requires that RE, as a part of the basic curriculum, should be provided for all registered pupils attending a maintained school. The guidance on RE (QCA, 2009) further explores this:

> The curriculum of every maintained school in England must comprise a basic curriculum (religious education RE, sex education and the National Curriculum) and include provision for RE for all registered pupils at the school (including those in the sixth form), except to those withdrawn by their parents (or by students withdrawing themselves if they are aged 18 and over) in accordance with Schedule 19 to the School Standards and Framework Act 1998. For further guidance on the right of withdrawal see Section 9.
>
> (p. 5)

The requirement above does not apply to pupils who are under compulsory school age, although there are many instances of good practice where RE is taught to such pupils. Nor does it apply to a maintained special school (in relation to which separate legislative provision is made). Separate Regulations covering maintained special schools require them to ensure that so far as practicable a pupil receives RE. RE is not part of the National Curriculum. Therefore it is not subject to national statutorily prescribed attainment targets, programmes of study or assessment arrangements (QCA, 2009, p. 5). With no National Curriculum the act stipulates that RE should be taught in accordance with a locally agreed syllabus.

A *Locally Agreed Syllabus* is drawn up by an Agreed Syllabus Conference, which is convened every four years by a SACRE (Standing Advisory Council on Religious Education). In 1988 Local Authorities were required (though they could do so from 1944) to set up a SACRE to oversee RE and Collective Worship in the local authority. There are four committees on a SACRE that constitute its membership:

- Committee A: Representatives of Christian denominations and other religions and their denominations reflecting the principal religious traditions of the area.
- Committee B: Church of England representatives.
- Committee C: Teacher representatives.
- Committee D: LA Representatives (including local councillors).

Some Local Authorities have constitutions that name the principal religions of the area that form part of the SACRE; others accept applications from any religious group and will approve membership of Committee A if it can be shown the religion has a significant local presence. Non-religious groups such as Humanists are often allowed to be a part of SACREs as non-voting members, though this differs among local authorities with some only being allowed as observers, and others as full members.

The work of the SACRE is to:
- Advise the LA on matters related to Collective Worship and RE in schools.
- The SACRE can require the LA to review its Agreed Syllabus.
- Consider applications for determinations (see the discussion below concerning Collective Worship).
- Publish an Annual Report of its work.

Table 1.1 Aims of RE: a comparison

To stimulate interest and enjoyment in Religious Education	To prepare pupils to be informed, respectful members of society who celebrate diversity and strive to understand others	To encourage students to develop knowledge of the beliefs and practices of religions; and informed opinions and an awareness of the implications of religion for the individual, the community and the environment	To give all students equal access to Religious Education and provide enjoyment and success	To develop pupils' own responses to questions about the meaning and purpose of life
Westhill How do I teach RE? (Read et al., 1998, p. 2)	• In RE the role of the teacher is that of educator. • RE will help children to explore a range of religious beliefs and practices and related human experiences. RE has a major contribution to make in helping children to develop a positive and understanding attitude towards diversity in our pluralistic society. RE does not make assumptions about, or preconditions for, the personal commitments of teachers or children.	• RE will help children to explore a range of religious beliefs and practices and related human experiences. • RE has a major contribution to make in helping children to develop a positive and understanding attitude towards diversity in our pluralistic society.	• As in all other subject areas, the teaching of RE must be related to the ages and abilities of the children being taught.	• Children need to develop their own beliefs and values and a consistent pattern of behaviour. • RE has a particularly important contribution to make to the spiritual, moral and social development of children.

To stimulate interest and enjoyment in Religious Education	To prepare pupils to be informed, respectful members of society who celebrate diversity and strive to understand others	To encourage students to develop knowledge of the beliefs and practices of religions; and informed opinions and an awareness of the implications of religion for the individual, the community and the environment	To give all students equal access to Religious Education and provide enjoyment and success	To develop pupils' own responses to questions about the meaning and purpose of life
RE Review (2013), pp. 14–15				
• Religious education contributes dynamically to children's and young people's education in schools by provoking challenging questions about meaning and purpose in life, beliefs about God, ultimate reality, issues of right and wrong and what it means to be human.	• Appreciate and appraise the nature, significance and impact of different ways of life and ways of expressing meaning. • Express with increasing discernment their personal reflections and critical responses to questions and teachings about identity, diversity, meaning and value, including ethical issues. • Enquire into what enables different individuals and communities to live together respectfully for the wellbeing of all. • Teaching therefore should equip pupils with systematic knowledge and understanding of a range of religions and worldviews, enabling them to develop their ideas, values and identities. • It should develop in pupils an aptitude for dialogue so that they can participate positively in our society with its diverse religions and worldviews.	• Describe, explain and analyse beliefs and practices, recognising the diversity that exists within and between communities and amongst individuals. • Appreciate and appraise the nature, significance and impact of different ways of life and ways of expressing meaning. • Explain reasonably their ideas about how beliefs, practices and forms of expression influence individuals and communities. • Find out about and investigate key concepts and questions of belonging, meaning, purpose and truth, responding creatively. • Articulate beliefs, values and commitments clearly in order to explain why they may be important in their own and other people's lives.		• Identify, investigate and respond to questions posed, and responses offered by some of the sources of wisdom found in religions and worldviews. • Express with increasing discernment their personal reflections and critical responses to questions and teachings about identity, diversity, meaning and value, including ethical issues. • Appreciate and appraise varied dimensions of religion or a worldview. • Find out about and investigate key concepts and questions of belonging, meaning, purpose and truth, responding creatively. • Articulate beliefs, values and commitments clearly in order to explain why they may be important in their own and other people's lives. • Teaching therefore should equip pupils with systematic knowledge and understanding of a range of religions and worldviews, enabling them to develop their ideas, values and identities.

To stimulate interest and enjoyment in Religious Education	To prepare pupils to be informed, respectful members of society who celebrate diversity and strive to understand others	To encourage students to develop knowledge of the beliefs and practices of religions; and informed opinions and an awareness of the implications of religion for the individual, the community and the environment	To give all students equal access to Religious Education and provide enjoyment and success	To develop pupils' own responses to questions about the meaning and purpose of life
QCA (National Curriculum for RE, 2007, p. 263)	• RE encourages pupils to develop their sense of identity and belonging. • It enables them to flourish individually within their communities and as citizens in a diverse society and global community. • RE has an important role in preparing pupils for adult life, employment and lifelong learning. • It enables pupils to develop respect for and sensitivity to others, in particular those whose faiths and beliefs are different from their own. • It promotes discernment and enables pupils to combat prejudice.	• It develops pupils' knowledge and understanding of Christianity, other principal religions, other religious traditions, and other worldviews. • It enhances pupils' awareness and understanding of religions and beliefs, teachings, practices and forms of expression, as well as of the influence of religion on individuals, families, communities and cultures.		• RE provokes challenging questions about the ultimate meaning and purpose of life, beliefs about God, the self and the nature of reality, issues of right and wrong and what it means to be human. • It offers opportunities for personal reflection and spiritual development. • RE encourages pupils to learn from different religions, beliefs, values and traditions, while exploring their own beliefs and questions of meaning. • It challenges pupils to reflect on, consider, analyse, interpret and evaluate issues of truth, belief, faith and ethics and to communicate their responses. • RE encourages pupils to develop their sense of identity and belonging.

It can also:

- Give advice on methods of teaching Agreed Syllabus RE including the choice of teaching materials.
- Advise the LA on the provision of training for teachers.
- Monitor inspection reports on RE, Collective Worship and SMSC.
- Consider complaints about the provision and delivery of RE and Collective Worship referred to it by the LA.

The Agreed Syllabus Conference will usually include members from these four committees and a wider group of teachers. An Agreed Syllabus is the legal document from which schools within the Local Authority must teach. It usually outlines content, levels of attainment, suggested skills, suggested concepts and sometimes the expected time allocation. The Agreed Syllabus is the key document in the teaching of RE in local authority schools. The other documents available such as the *RE Review* (2013) and the Non-Statutory National Framework (2004) are useful but are intended to be used by Local Authorities in the construction of their Agreed Syllabus but they remain free to use or reject as much or as little of it as they decide. Schools should not use them to replace the Agreed Syllabus.

The Academy programme, which has led many schools to opt out of local authority control, initially led to some confusion over the place of RE in these schools, and also the role that a SACRE has in relation to them. In being 'freed' from the constraints of the National Curriculum some academies interpreted this to mean that RE was also a part of that freedom. The National Association for Teachers of Religious Education (NATRE) put together a briefing document that outlined the place of RE in academies and Free Schools (NATRE, 2012). This reiterated the legal requirement for all schools to provide RE for all pupils. Academies do not have to follow their locally agreed syllabus; indeed, they are free to follow any agreed syllabus they choose or develop an RE provision that is of the school's design as long as it meets the requirement outlined in law:

> The law requires that local authority RE agreed syllabuses and RE syllabuses used in academies that are not designated with a religious character 'must reflect the fact that the religious traditions in Great Britain are in the main Christian, while taking account of the teaching and practices of the other principal religions represented in Great Britain'.
>
> (*RE Review*, 2013, p. 15)

Voluntary aided schools or Academies with a religious character are required to teach RE as determined by the Governing body.

With regard to the relationship between SACREs and Academies NATRE have outlined:

> A Standing Advisory Council on Religious Education (SACRE) has a statutory remit to advise the Local Authority on Religious Education to be given in accordance with an agreed syllabus and to support the effective provision of collective worship. A SACRE also has within its powers to discuss any matter related to its functions as it sees fit and may therefore include the provision of RE in Academies in its discussions or address such matters as may be referred to it. An Academy or group of academies

can be represented through co-option onto the local SACRE (or indeed any SACRE) if all parties are in agreement.

(NATRE, 2012, pp. 1–2)

The right to withdrawal

Although the act stipulates that RE should be taught to all pupils, parents do have a right to withdraw their child.

> The parent of a pupil at a community, foundation or voluntary school may request that the pupil be excused from all or part of the religious education RE provided. However, much has changed since this right was enshrined in law. In the past the subject was religious instruction rather than religious education as it is now. Religion and belief have become more visible in public life in recent years, making it even more important that all pupils should have an opportunity to engage in RE. Schools should ensure that parents who wish to withdraw their children from RE are aware of the objectives and what is covered in the RE curriculum and that they are given the opportunity to discuss this, if they wish.
>
> (2009, p. 43)

This right to withdrawal is exercised in schools in a variety of ways. A parent can withdraw their child from the whole of RE or specific aspects that they do not want their child to participate in. While not needing to provide any reason for withdrawal, it is beneficial to discuss with parents the nature of their concern. Sometimes it is a misunderstanding of the nature and aims of the subject, often based on their experience as a child. This is another reason why it is so important that a teacher has an understanding of the purpose of their teaching.

Collective worship

All schools should provide a daily act of Collective Worship, which is broadly Christian in character. Within this stipulation of the 1988 Education Act (HMSO, 1989) are two caveats. First, a parent has the right to withdraw their child from any or all acts of Collective Worship. Second, a state school that has a majority of pupils with a different religious background from Christianity can apply for a determination from the SACRE that will allow them to receive an exemption from the 'broadly Christian' stipulation. Although sometimes placed in the hands of the Head of RE in secondary schools it is important to note that these acts of Collective Worship serve a different purpose from RE and should not be considered to be part of the RE provision.

Summary

Within this chapter the following have been explored:

- The discussion about the nature and purpose of RE
- Your own aims in the teaching of RE
- The legal position of RE
- The separate nature of RE and Collective Worship

It is hoped that this chapter has helped the reader to consider their purpose and aims in the teaching of Religious Education. As such, the aims that are constructed should help focus RE teaching and assist teachers and pupils in understanding the value and importance of the beliefs, practices and questions that they engage with in the classroom and beyond.

The legal position of RE is of interest to the RE teacher as it provides the background, and documentation, against which they teach. It also provides information for the RE teacher in arguing for its place in the curriculum in schools where the aims are not sufficient to convince the leadership of its value and importance.

Notes

1 Throughout this book, Religious Education and RE are referred to. This is for ease, and includes Religious Studies, which is used predominantly at Key Stages 4 and 5.
2 To be fair to Michael Gove, when he discusses educated citizens he suggests: 'I don't believe any person is truly educated unless they have learnt self-discipline, self-control, self-reliance, respect for others, how to work in a team, how to defer gratification, how to cope with reverses and the importance of service to others'. However, this exemplification is not in the National Curriculum guidance, and is not implied in any of the documentation.

References

Cox, Harvey (1967) *On Not Leaving It to the Snake*. New York, NY: Macmillan.

Department for Children, Schools and Families (DCSF) (2010) *Religious Education in English Schools: Non-Statutory Guidance 2010*. London: Department for Education.

Department for Education and Skills (DES) (1988) *Education Reform Act 1988: Religious Education and Collective Worship* (circular 3/89). London: HMSO.

Department for Education (DfE) (1994) *RE and Collective Worship* (circular 1/94). London, DfE.

Gibb, Nick (2012) *RE Council AGM Speech*. Available at: www.actforhim.org.uk/noticeboard/Nick_Gibb_RE_Council_AGM_Speech_2012_05_03.pdf (accessed 1 May 2014).

Holt, James D. (2010) 'Beyond the Big Six: Minority Religions in the Secondary RE Classroom'. In Schmack et al. (Eds), *Engaging RE*. Newcastle upon Tyne, UK: Cambridge Scholars (pp. 76–91).

Her Majesty's Stationery Office (HMSO) (1989) *Education Reform Act 1988*. London: HMSO.

Hull, John (1984) *Studies in Religion and Education*. Lewes, UK: Falmer.

Hull, John (1991) *Mishmash: Religious Education in Multicultural Britain – A Study in Metaphor (Birmingham Papers)*. Birmingham, UK: CEM/University of Birmingham.

King, M. L. (1967) *Where Do We Go from Here: Chaos or Community?* New York, NY: Harper & Row.

King, M. L. (2000) 'Honoring Dr. Du Bois, No. 2 1968'. In Esther Cooper Jackson (Ed.), *Freedomways Reader: Prophets in Their Own Country*. Boulder, CO: Westview Press (pp. 31–39).

Lee, Harper (1988 [1960]) *To Kill a Mockingbird*. New York, NY: Warner Books.

Linden, Ian (2012) 'Blender-Free Interfaith Relations' *Huffington Post* 21 November 2012. Available at: www.huffingtonpost.co.uk/ian-linden/interfaith-relations_b_2171456.html (accessed 1 May 2014).

NATRE (2012) *Religious Education (RE) and Collective Worship in Academies and Free Schools Q&A.* Available at: www.natre.org.uk/docstore/DfE_RE%20&%20CW%20in%20Academies%20&%20FS_Q&A_Dec%202012.pdf (accessed 1 May 2014).

OCR (2012) *Religious Studies B (Philosophy and Applied Ethics). General Certificate of Secondary Education. Unit B602: Philosophy 2 (Good and Evil, Revelation, Science). Mark Scheme for June 2012.* Cambridge: OCR.

Ofsted (2010) *Transforming RE.* Manchester, UK: Ofsted.

Ofsted (2013) *Religious education: Realising the potential.* Manchester, UK: Ofsted.

Palmer, Spencer J. (1997) 'Foundations'. In S. J. Palmer, R. Keller, D. S. Choi, and J. Toronto (Eds), *Religions of the World. A Latter-day Saint View.* Provo, UT: BYU (pp. 3–14).

Prothero, Stephen R. (2008) *Religious Literacy: What Every American Needs to Know – And Doesn't.* New York, NY: HarperOne.

Qualifications and Curriculum Authority (QCA) (2000) *Religious Education. Non Statutory Guidance for RE.* London: QCA.

Qualifications and Curriculum Authority (QCA) (2004) *A National Framework for Religious Education.* London: QCA.

Qualifications and Curriculum Authority (QCA) (2007) *The National Curriculum. Statutory Requirements for Key Stages 3 and 4.* London: QCA.

Qualifications and Curriculum Authority (QCA) (2009) *Religious Education in English Schools: Non-statutory Guidance 2009.* London: QCA.

Qualifications and Curriculum Authority (QCA) (2010) *Religious Education in English Schools: Non-statutory Guidance 2010.* London: QCA.

RE Council of England and Wales (2013) *A Review of Religious Education in England.* London: RE Council.

Read, G., Rudge, J., Teece, G., and Howarth, R. B. (1998) *The Westhill Project RE 5-16. How Do I Teach RE* (2nd edn). Cheltenham, UK: Stanley Thornes.

Sivananda, S. (2004, October 17). 'The Unity that Underlies all Religions' from *The Divine Life Society.* Available at: www.dlshq.org/religions/unirel.htm (accessed 1 May 2014).

Teece, G. (1993) *In Defence of Theme Teaching in Religious Education Westhill RE Centre Occasional Papers* November, no. 3. Birmingham, UK: Westhill RE Centre.

Chapter 2

Pedagogies of RE?

Chapter outline

What is a pedagogy?

The main pedagogies of RE:

- A phenomenological, undogmatic, explicit model
- Liberal Christian theological, experiential, implicit models/integrative experiential and phenomenological models
- Human development, instrumental, learning about, learning from models
- An ethnographic, 'interpretive', multifaith model
- A revelation-centred, concept-cracking, Trinitarian Christian Realist model
- A literacy-centred, critical realist model
- A kaleidoscopic approach to RE

What is a pedagogy?

Effectively a pedagogy of RE tries to answer the question of how RE should be taught. This pedagogy will influence how the curriculum, schemes of work and lessons are organised. Michael Grimmitt (2000) outlines this understanding:

> A pedagogy is a theory of teaching and learning encompassing aims, curriculum content and methodology ... or a science of teaching and learning embodying both curriculum and methodology ... to relate the process of teaching to that of learning on the part of the child.
>
> (pp. 16–17)

Before looking at the specific approaches to RE, it is useful to establish the pedagogic background within education as a whole. Stern (2006) notes that there are two main approaches to teaching within which RE finds itself:

1 Behaviourism
2 Constructivism

Behaviourism

Behaviourism argues that all human behaviour can be explained in terms of associations between stimuli, responses and outcomes. Behaviourism places emphasis on external, environmental influences. It holds that organisms are born 'blank slates', that are programmed and conditioned by their experiences. Thus, it holds that any individual differences are a product not of innate or internal factors, but of differing environmental pressures. This is communicated by John Watson, a behavioural psychologist:

> Give me a dozen healthy infants … and my own world to bring them up in and I'll guarantee to take any one at random and train him to become any type of specialist I might select – doctor, lawyer, artist, merchant-chief and, yes, even beggar-man and thief, regardless of his talents, abilities, and race of his ancestors.
>
> (1930, p. 82)

Other behaviourists include Pavlov, Skinner and Thorndike. Crudely applied to education, behaviourism refers to reward and punishment. It will lead the teacher to create the conditions for an effective learning environment and establish high expectations with associated rewards and punishment. Elements of the behaviourist approach evident from researchers such as Bandura and his Social Learning Theory might lead to an emphasis on modelling as an integral practice of teaching. While this is important and effective it may not be as effective at helping pupils acquire complex knowledge or involve qualitative aspects of prior experience. It is constructivism that might be seen to present a more robust theoretical background for the discrete teaching and study of Religious Education.

Constructivism

The second approach in the classroom can be seen to be constructivism. Grimmitt suggests that this is the preferred model

> because the mechanistic basis of the theory underlying instruction (stimulus/ response/ reinforcement) is unable to promote learning which enables pupils to:
>
> • Enter imaginatively and empathetically into the subjective consciousness of religious adherents …
> • make connections between their own feelings, acts and experiences.
>
> (2000, pp. 222–223)

In short, the aims of RE outlined in Chapter 1 cannot be fulfilled without a pedagogy that is underpinned by constructivism.

One of the most important contributors to the cognitive perspective on learning was the Swiss psychologist, Jean Piaget (see Piaget, 1954). Piaget was one of the earliest of a long line of constructivist theorists, whose primary interest was the way in which knowledge and understanding is actively built by the individual; examining how people engage with their environment, linking new concepts and experiences to their existing understandings. In exploring this topic Piaget developed the notion of schemas: mental 'structures' that act as frameworks through which the individual classifies and interprets the world. It is these schemas that allow us, for instance, to distinguish between cats and dogs by looking for key characteristics. On a more sophisticated level, schemas allow a person to interpret and understand knowledge and behaviour in particular roles and contexts.

According to Piaget, as people grow and mature, their schemas become increasingly more complex and intricate, allowing access to more sophisticated understandings and interpretations of the world. Piaget argued that central to this process is a biological urge to maintain equilibrium; a state of balance between internal schema and the external environment. This could be characterised as a person fully understanding what is taking place around them by utilising their existing schemas. If new information is encountered that does not match exactly with existing schemas, a person must consequently adjust and refine these schemas.

A simple example might be a child learning the difference between a cat and a dog:

- The initial schema is formed when seeing a picture of a dog in a book. An adult confirms that the picture is a dog, and the schema of knowledge is formed that a dog has four legs, a tail and two ears.
- The child then encounters what they think is a dog as it has four legs, a tail and two ears. However, in Piagetian terms, disequilibrium occurs when the child experiences new information: the fact that the dog barks and is furry.
- Upon confirmation from an adult, this new information is assimilated into the existing schemas.
- On encountering a furry, four-legged, tailed and two-eared animal, the child thinks it has encountered another dog. Disequilibrium then occurs when the animal meows.
- The contribution of an adult to identify a cat enables the child to accommodate the new animal into their schema, which now distinguishes between a cat and a dog. The child has used their schema of knowledge about a dog to understand what a cat is.

For RE this is an essential part of children's learning: the ability to learn from and make links with prior learning. Two of the aims outlined in Chapter 1 surrounded pupils' engagement with, and attitude towards, RE:

- To stimulate interest and enjoyment in Religious Education.
- To give all students equal access to Religious Education and provide enjoyment and success.

Pupils are able to access, enjoy and see the relevance of RE if it is rooted in their own experience. To a certain extent the study of RE enables pupils to go through the Piagian stages of disequilibrium, assimilation and accommodation. Judith Lowndes (2012) outlined a pyramid that highlighted the incorporation of concepts within the child's own experience into the RE classroom (see figure 2.1).

As the child progresses throughout school they are able to build the conceptual framework they have, and as such the teacher is able to utilise that framework on which to build future learning. While a younger child might need to explore the celebrations they participate in to be able to move on to a discussion of a specific festival, an older pupil would be able to recall both their own experience and the celebration of other religions to build their understanding. As an example, consider the pupil who is familiar with the celebration of Christmas within Christianity and is beginning to learn about the celebration of Wesak in Buddhism. The teacher might begin by trying to elicit some of the elements of the celebration of Christmas, then either have the pupils suggest some activities a Buddhist might perform, or teach in some way the celebration of Wesak. Being able to link it to aspects in their existing schema enables a pupil to accommodate the learning much more effectively. Thus Wesak is not the Buddhist Christmas, but they share common characteristics as well as some fundamental differences (see Figure 2.2).

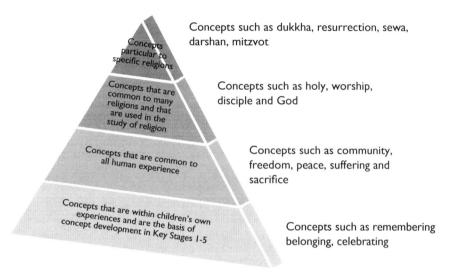

Concepts particular to specific religions — Concepts such as dukkha, resurrection, sewa, darshan, mitzvot

Concepts that are common to many religions and that are used in the study of religion — Concepts such as holy, worship, disciple and God

Concepts that are common to all human experience — Concepts such as community, freedom, peace, suffering and sacrifice

Concepts that are within children's own experiences and are the basis of concept development in Key Stages 1-5 — Concepts such as remembering belonging, celebrating

Figure 2.1 A conceptual pyramid for RE. Adapted from Judith Lowndes (2012)

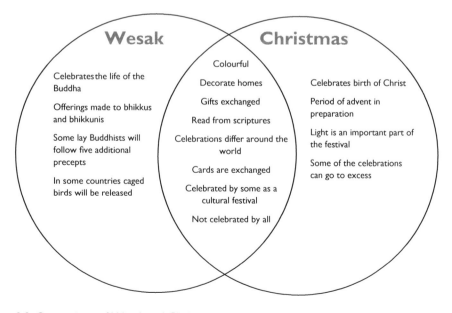

Wesak

Celebrates the life of the Buddha

Offerings made to bhikkus and bhikkunis

Some lay Buddhists will follow five additional precepts

In some countries caged birds will be released

Colourful

Decorate homes

Gifts exchanged

Read from scriptures

Celebrations differ around the world

Cards are exchanged

Celebrated by some as a cultural festival

Not celebrated by all

Christmas

Celebrates birth of Christ

Period of advent in preparation

Light is an important part of the festival

Some of the celebrations can go to excess

Figure 2.2 Comparison of Wesak and Christmas

Mark Peace has developed a four-part pedagogy for teaching that utilises a phase of learning called Discovery. This is a valuable idea, especially in Religious Education.[1] Peace suggests that cognitive models could provide a greater and better basis for the learning process. Although these have had some success in being adopted in classrooms, he sees their adoption as half-baked and 'theoretically ambiguous'. The fact remains, however, that the cognitive model is 'very good at explaining and improving knowledge acquisition and meaning making'. This led Peace to suggest that any pedagogy of learning must utilise an activity at the beginning of the process that gets the pupils to articulate (or discover) what they already know. The four-part pedagogy is as follows: React, Discover, Learn, Reflect (see Figure 2.3).

The aims of the Discovery section are:

- Entirely student-driven activities, of varying length.
- Students respond to stimuli and, in the process, 'discover' subject content for themselves.
- Mobilises existing schemas, but ensures task cannot be completed using just this understanding.
- Usually starts with the 'real world' and then brings in theory.

The intricacies of this approach will be explored in greater detail in Chapter 7, but the utilisation of pupils' prior knowledge is crucial in pupil learning in RE.

For the purpose of effective learning, and also for the engagement of pupils (which go hand in hand) the constructivist approach seems to provide the ideal background for any pedagogy of RE. However, this is not to suggest that the Piagetian approach is the model of constructivism to be adopted. A criticism could be that it is very much a 'lone scientist' approach, whereas other constructivists such as Vygotsky (see Vygotsky, 1962, 1978) place much more emphasis on interaction between learner, environment and other people. Vygotsky argues that social interaction is integral to learning arguing that, left alone, children will develop – but not to their full potential. The gap between actual and potential learning is described as the Zone of Proximal Development (ZPD); it is only through collaboration and a More Knowledgeable Other (MKO) that this gap can be bridged.

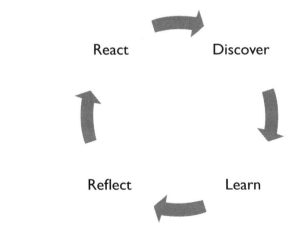

Figure 2.3 Four-part pedagogy

A crucial element in this process is the use of what later became known as 'scaffolding': the way in which the teacher provides students with frameworks and experiences that encourage them to extend their existing schemas and incorporate new skills, competences and understandings. It is important to note that this is more than simply instruction; learning experiences must be presented in such a way as to actively challenge existing mental structures and provide frameworks for the formation of new ones.

One issue raised by Stern (2006) is 'in terms of religious world views, if pupils or their families think that the role of RE is to "reconstruct" pupils' world views' (p. 68). However, its benefits outweigh its possible negatives (though teachers should guard against them).

> For RE, constructivism means getting pupils to talk about the topics and tasks, encouraging purposeful, interesting and creative activities that provide intrinsic motivation. Pupils can work long hours on tasks that really interest them, making incredible discoveries, whilst extrinsic rewards and punishments may have little effect and will never make routine and repetitive work interesting. … Teachers expressing an interest in RE, and demonstrating how important it is as a subject, should help, too. The more that RE can build relationships and conversations within and particularly beyond the school, the more social constructivists will say this is how people learn best.
>
> (Stern, 2006, p. 69)

Although the relationships within an RE classroom are one of the most important contributors to good RE, in the first instance this attention and interest has to be grabbed. While some students, through their own attitudes and efforts, will engage well, there are the disinterested few who for whatever reason need some help to engage. The teacher's enthusiasm may help but some of the behaviourist approaches need to be employed to a conducive environment for learning. Similarly, a piece of work that is done for personal fulfilment is a really great way to learn and engage with RE, but it does not fit in with the assessment framework that schools, parents and often the children demand, therefore clear and comprehensive marking with appropriate rewards need to be used in the current educational climate.

The main pedagogies of RE

With a background of constructivism established as key to learning within any further developments of pedagogy it is possible to explore existing pedagogies of RE. Grimmitt (2000) outlines eight pedagogies of Religious Education (see chapter 2 of his book for an overview). This work *Pedagogies of Religious Education* is a hugely important work that allows proponents of these pedagogies to speak for themselves, outline their views and provide case studies to show their practicality. The pedagogies outlined include:

- A phenomenological, undogmatic, explicit model
- Liberal Christian theological, experiential, implicit models/integrative experiential and phenomenological models
- Human development, instrumental, learning about, learning from models
- An ethnographic, 'interpretive', multifaith model
- A revelation-centred, concept-cracking, Trinitarian Christian Realist model
- A literacy-centred, critical realist model[2].

Building on Grimmitt's work, Blaylock (2004) offered a slightly caricatured version of the pedagogies:

- Unreconstructed phenomenologists
- Interpretives
- Spiritual experientialists
- Humanisers
- Concept crackers
- Postmodern relativist deconstructers and reconstructers.

All of them can be seen, to some extent, to be compatible with constructivist principles. What is missing from this list is a confessional approach to RE – although it holds sway in some parts of the world it should not be a part of Religious Education in England and Wales. Even though in many areas of the world Religious Education is synonymous with Education within a particular religion, this is not the purpose of RE in the United Kingdom. If the aims of RE from Chapter 1 are recalled, it was recognised that RE does not nurture in faith, neither does it aim to provide pupils with all of the facts so that 'they can make their own choice'. Importantly for a discussion of confessionalism within RE it should be noted that non-religious or secular worldviews can also be subject to aspects of this approach. Consider, for example, the writings of Richard Dawkins (for example, 2006), which while erudite and engaging are nonetheless examples of an almost evangelical atheism. Also susceptible to this approach is a cultural relativism or syncretism that is popular in some aspects of society where all religions are seen as the same. As outlined earlier it is crucial to recognise the differences as well as the commonalities between religions and worldviews.

Blaylock tends to agree with the parameters established by Grimmitt. As such, this chapter will explore each of the models outlined by Grimmitt in brief to establish a background against which the pedagogy advocated can be developed.

A phenomenological, undogmatic, explicit model

The phenomenological approach has its roots in the work of Ninian Smart (1969), who argued that religion was an important and valid subject to study. The approach acquired its name because Smart saw it possible to study religion as a phenomenon. Smart's *The Religious Experience of Mankind* outlined six dimensions of religions (he later added a seventh in *The World's Religions* (1989):

- the doctrinal
- the mythological (narrative)
- the ethical
- the ritual
- the experiential
- the social
- the material (aesthetic).

The phenomenological approach sees the study of religion as important in the modern world, as people can understand the various dimensions of the different religions and their impact and importance for the individual believer. In some ways this approach can be seen to be a dispassionate, academic, outsider view of Religious Education. It does, however, systematise the study of religions and lays a very important basis for comparative religious study. Grimmitt argues that 'Broadly speaking if there is a pedagogical principle which should inform the model's pedagogical procedures and strategies it is that: learning and teaching in RE should promote both academic and personal forms of knowledge and understanding' (2000, p. 27). Perhaps its greatest contribution is the demystification of religions other than Christianity, by suggesting that Christianity can be seen among the world religions rather than standing apart.

This pedagogy opens up the various and multi-faceted world of religious experience to the pupils. It begins with the wider practice and beliefs of a religion as a whole and then works its way to the impact that it has on the individual. As such it is perhaps most aligned with a systematic approach to the teaching of RE. A Systems approach adopts a threefold typology:

1　It approaches one system (e.g. Christianity, or another of the world religions). It does not cover everything within the topic but it tries to build up a fairly comprehensive picture of the system.
2　It makes links with shared human experience. This arises out of the subject matter and is not an afterthought or artificial add on. An example might be a discussion of temptations/peer pressure/choices in light of Jesus's temptation.
3　It also then links with children's own concerns and experiences. This approach may make links with a person's own experiences within the faith tradition, or parallel experiences outside of that.

However, it does not necessarily have to follow such an approach. A thematic approach to RE (which will be explored in greater detail in the Human Development model below) is not ruled out in this approach. At a very basic (and misunderstood) level this thematic approach takes topics such as Festivals and discusses them in light of the different faith traditions. While this happens it is not the best example of a thematic approach, rather a theme or question is chosen and explored in light of religions: 'For it is these systems whose beliefs, values and practices serve to interpret, support and challenge human experience and the questions it raises' (Read et al., 1992, p. 41). These can then link with children's own concerns and experiences.

Liberal Christian theological, experiential, implicit models/integrative experiential and phenomenological models

David Hay (2000) argues that 'For committed believers the experiential dimension is by far the most significant aspect of their religion' (p. 72). Religious experience can be seen as the beginning and sustaining influence of a person's religious life. This experiential aspect of religion does not stand in distinction to the other dimensions of religion and, indeed, is grounded in them, but it does provide the most important aspect of religious practice. Perhaps in reaction to the phenomenological approach, where the observable aspects of religion were being studied, Hay and others felt 'that the experiential dimension of religion was being ignored by RE teachers, or at least treated with kid gloves' (2000, p. 73). The argument could be advanced: 'How can pupils understand religion if they cannot empathetically experience religion?'

On one hand, the experiential approach asks children to spend time looking inward to themselves to experience similar questions and the seeking for answers that are at the heart of religion. As such stilling, or guided activities that encourage pupils to reflect on their own identity and the shaping of their own beliefs, can be valuable. A case study published by NATRE for the introduction of the National Curriculum (2007) of a compelling learning experience suggests a fairly simplistic but powerful application of this approach:

> We specifically noted, for example, that while students enjoyed looking at different Hindu celebrations and could understand some simple reasons for them, they didn't really understand the underlying reasons why all people celebrate special events or occasions. Students saw the importance of learning but no empathetic skills were developed and no application for their lives.
>
> In order to help students deepen their understanding of the meaning of celebration, we decided to use a 'stilling' activity that would exercise their imagination and link the key concept of 'practices and ways of life' with questions of 'meaning, purpose and truth' …
>
> Young people were from different or no religious communities, so they were able to exchange views and experiences from their different perspectives. This gave them a better understanding of identity, diversity and belonging as well as different lifestyles. It also reinforced the idea that religious belief helps many people reach an understanding of the meaning and purpose of life.
>
> (Holt, 2008)

A more developed example comes through the work of Sue Phillips and the *Theatre of Learning* (2003) where the practitioner is invited to come 'on a journey with me and my pupils. It is a journey away from a content-led syllabus … into a world of experiential and enactive learning, where we share powerful and meaningful experiences together, which develop both students' and teachers' spirituality' (p. 7). In this way the experiential approach enables the teacher to place the pupils at the centre of their teaching rather than the curriculum. The approach advocated in these files does much to lead the RE teacher back to a focus on the child and their development. The initial activity suggested is 'The Island', in which a lot of the issues surrounding religion are explored through the story of a shipwrecked community. This is carried on into a discussion of the Incarnation in the Christianity publication (Phillips, 2003a). This is an excellent introduction to the concepts of religion, and helps pupils reflect on their experiences and learning at this and future points in their RE experience. The spiritual experiential model can be characterised as being solely concerned with the spiritual aspect of the pupil. However, work by people such as Hay sought to integrate aspects of this approach with phenomenology and the above two examples show how this model can be used to inform further learning.

A second interpretation of the experiential approach can be to have pupils 'experience' some of the practices of religious believers. One example from the *Theatre of Learning* focuses on enhancing pupil understanding of the Eucharist. Two of the instructions from the lesson plan are:

- Raise the music slightly and pass around the loaf of bread asking each pupil to take a piece and eat it and pass it to the next person until the circle is completed.

- After that, fade the music and ask pupils to brainstorm the word 'bread', thinking about what its purpose is for us. Round the loaf of bread they should write all the words they can think of. You could be making a group word collection on the board as they call out the words. The words will all be to do with food and nutrition.

(2003a, p. 76)

Although described as religion-neutral, this is an activity that would need a lot of consideration before being undertaken. Some teachers would be very uncomfortable with an approach to RE that involves pupils in re-enacting ritual, however religion-neutral the activity might seem. Outside of the pedagogical concerns there are also concerns from a religious perspective. The RE teacher could be seen to be taking a ritual that is sacred within the specific context and de-sanctifying it for the education of pupils. It is impossible to experience what a religious believer experiences because it is not practised in the context of belief. As such, teachers need to be very conscious of the reasons why they are doing something, and the aim of the activity. Do the costs outweigh the potential benefits? Relatedly, but not necessarily within the realm of the spiritual experientialist, is the example of dressing a child up in religious clothes, for example the 5Ks. Does this activity de-sanctify the religious symbols of Sikhism and make them mundane?

Human development, instrumental, learning about, learning from models

Within this structure, the aim articulated by the Westhill approach is: 'To help children mature in relation to their own patterns of belief and behaviour *through* exploring religious beliefs and practices and related human experiences' (Read et al., 1992, p. 2). As such, *learning about* and *learning from religion* become central in this approach. The asking of questions based on exploration of beliefs, such as 'What does this have to do with me?' or 'What can I learn from this?' is actually only a slight nod to this approach, and is not what was envisaged where pupils are encouraged to 'Evaluate their understanding of religion in personal terms and evaluate their understanding of self in religious terms (i.e. in terms of the religious beliefs they have learned about)' (Grimmitt, 1987, p. 213).

RE within this model is grounded, centred and completed in the context of shared human experience, through drawing on the experience and inter-relatedness of traditional belief systems and also the beliefs that individuals bring to the classroom. All of these work together 'as a catalyst for [the pupil's] own development' (Rudge, 2000, p. 94). Four underlying pedagogical principles can be outlined:

1   The pupils' personal development is given priority.
2   The teaching and learning must take account of the pupils' own context in the world and their awareness and abilities.
3   Pupils engage in an encounter with religious beliefs and practices, and human experiences that are instrumental to their own development.
4   As pupils encounter religion, this engagement should be designed in such a way as to contribute to their personal development (see Rudge, 2000).

Whereas a systematic approach would draw on one tradition, the shared human experience model would draw on two or more to enable the pupils to develop 'an awareness of issues about life and the ultimate questions they raise' (Rudge, 2000, p. 101). This life-themed approach involves shared concerns and experiences rather than shared topics:

> To take an example, a Key Stage 3 teacher may want to teach the theme of suffering and seek to raise questions with the pupils such as 'What is suffering?', 'Can suffering be a means to an end?', 'How can we cope with suffering?' These questions can be explored from both the pupils' own point of view and from the perspectives of a number of religious traditions. So, for example, in considering the question, 'Has suffering a place?' pupils can consider the teachings of the Buddha. In considering the question, 'Can suffering be a means to an end?' pupils can gain insights into the question by considering what Christians believe about Jesus' suffering, death and resurrection.
>
> (Teece, 1993, p. 10)

An ethnographic, 'interpretive', multifaith model

In simple terms, whereas the phenomenological approach began with the phenomenon of religion and works down to the individual, the ethnographic approach to RE works in reverse. It begins with the practice of the individual and from here strives to construct commonalities, beliefs and practices of religions. The ethnographic approach builds upon the work of Clifford Geertz and contributes to a more varied experience of different religions by exploring the different religious experiences within religions, by exploring the 'insider' voice and experience. Through this approach pupils can come:

> to understand how religious people and religious groups within the same religious tradition interpret and express their understanding of faith in a variety of different ways, [requiring] pupils to become active interpreters of religious meaning making, not just passive observers or recipients of information about a tradition.
>
> (Everington, Jackson, et al., in Grimmitt, 2000, p. 395)

An aspect of religious teaching would never be unaccompanied by an experience or testimony of a believer. It can be seen to be a reaction against the 'chocolate box' approach to religion, where religions are nicely illustrated but are monolithic and one-dimensional in the way they are presented in the classroom. Religions are not neatly packaged; rather they are a collection of diverse beliefs and practices. Blaylock (2004) characterises adherents of this pedagogy as likely to say 'But you know there are no religions – no Christianity just some Christians, no Hinduism just some Hindus' (p. 14). A story that can be used to help understand this approach is that of the 'Blind men and the elephant'. Do teachers of RE explore only one facet of the elephant and as such leave children with an image of a palm leaf (ear) rather than giving them the tools to understand the nature of the whole elephant, or where the ear fits in with the remainder of the beast?

Jackson (2000) outlines the importance of reflexivity in the interpretive approach to RE. He argues that the teacher should encourage three aspects of reflexivity:

- the learner reassessing her or his understanding of her or his own way of life (edification);
- making a constructive critique of the material studied at a distance;
- developing a running critique of the interpretive process.

(p. 134)

As such, it draws all learning back to the pupil, and the pupil's interaction with the insider voice becomes a conversation that leads to understanding. It becomes a dialogic third space between the two parties, which constitutes 'holy ground'. This third space enables a place where a pupil can meet a member of a religion that can transform their understanding of the other, but also their understanding of themselves and their worldview. This chapter applies the third space in this context, and in so doing builds on the work of Jackson and others but recognises it is not evident in descriptions of the pedagogy. The concept of a dialogical third space borrows heavily from the work of Homi Bhabha but diverges from the resultant hybridity models that he suggests such spaces would create. Engagement with a third space as a place of 'radical openness' provides a perfect description of the type of space needed for learning within the RE classroom to be successful. The way that this space can be 'radical' and transformative at the same time is in engaging in a dialogue that is grounded in the pupil's own experience. Returning to the aims of RE outlined in Chapter 1, it is possible to see how they are inextricably linked to the pedagogy a teacher follows or develops.

A revelation-centred, concept-cracking, Trinitarian Christian Realist model

A concept-cracking approach to RE was specifically designed against the background of Christianity and a belief that the teaching of Christianity within state schools had become somewhat superficial and had led pupils to become disengaged and unenthused by the religion and its beliefs and practices. It is in this context that this approach must be understood, while Cooling points out that the approach 'is misunderstood if it is seen to be offering a total package for teaching RE' (2000, p. 165), it is possible to posit that with slight adjustments the approach study could be used as a case study and possibly applied to other religions within a systematic approach.

Rather than exploring a general treatment of beliefs and values, concept-cracking suggests that pupils should be encouraged to explore the concepts that lie at the heart of Christianity, and only through such engagement can pupils hope to come to any degree of understanding the meaning of Christianity for Christians. It sets out with the task of providing a systematic coverage and understanding of the key elements of Christian teaching. In light of the ethnographic approach, which might be used to suggest a plethora of Christianities, Cooling argues that there are definite beliefs and doctrines that lie at the heart of what it means to be a Christian (1996). The atonement of Christ is one such doctrine, and one would imagine the Trinity (though its status as a unifying doctrine will be explored in Chapter 10 on teaching Christianity). If a teacher were to expand this to Islam, for example, the teachings might include Tawhid, prophets, akhirah and so on. It may be possible to think of teachings from all of the other world religions that would fit into the model.

Cooling (2000) breaks down the approach into four steps using the acronym *USER*:

1 *Unpack the concepts*: Teachers should explore the theological concepts that underpin a topic before they teach it. This enables the teacher to be confident in the ideas and teachings being covered.
2 *Select one or two concepts as the focus of the lesson*.
3 *Engage with the pupil's world of experience*: Cooling described this as 'the most important stage in the process' (p. 158). This is where pupils are able to construct a bridge between their own experiences and the concept being developed.
4 *Relate to the religious concept*: The specific religious concept/doctrine is introduced. Pupils should then reflect on what they learn about Christianity and also what they can learn from Christianity.

In this sense, it refocuses the teacher onto the understanding of Christianity, but only secondarily becomes about the pupils' own experiences, as they are informed by the teaching within the classroom. The aim of the approach is to develop a systematic understanding of Christianity and from there enable pupils to learn from it: 'the personal development outcomes of teaching Christianity should result from the development of a systematic understanding of Christianity' (Cooling, 2000, p. 163).

A literacy-centred, critical realist model

The critical realist model sees that RE is about religious literacy, about equipping children in the search for truth. It seeks a cohesive understanding of the relationship between theology and experiential religion. This approach to RE is a reaction against:

> Liberal religious education [which] tends to favour an experiential-expressive model of religion in which religious language is concerned to express spiritual experience rather than describe the way things are in the world. As a result religious doctrines are important not as cognitive truth claims but merely as expressions of religious piety. This is reflected in liberal classrooms, with religious teaching concerned more with the stimulation of the child's capacity for spiritual experience than with issues of realistic religious truth.
>
> (Wright, 2000, p. 72)

Truth claims are subsumed in 'liberal' RE models, which place the child and their spirituality or experience at the centre of all learning. The focus is on the individual rather than questions of truth and an engagement with the external reality that religion seeks to engage. This model could be seen to suggest that other approaches are reducing the religions of the world to an expression of what is held in common; indeed, this paradigm seeks to equip 'pupils to explore conflicting world-views rather than inducting them into a single paradigm' (Wright, 2000, p. 172).

Spirituality remains important within this paradigm but does so as a background against a search for truth. This seems at odds with the aims of RE explored earlier, which suggested that RE is not about presenting pupils with a multitude of options. As such, it could be argued that if there is an objective truth that can be found in this 'search', RE might be moving towards a confessional approach. Andrew Wright (2003) suggests that this characterisation would be erroneous:

> What distinguishes this concern for truth from forms of confessional religious education is that it approaches the question of truth with an open rather than a closed horizon … where confessionalism seeks to transmit one particular answer to the question of ultimate truth, the critical approach is concerned to equip pupils to engage intelligently in the quest for themselves.
>
> (p. 286)

In detailing the pedagogy, Wright provides a three-phase approach within the RE curriculum:

Phase One: The Horizon of the Pupil

   i   basic introduction to the topic
   ii   open exploration of the topic
   iii articulation of initial beliefs.

(Wright, 2000, p. 181)

It is argued that all pupils bring an emerging worldview or theology to the classroom. As such, any discussion of theological concepts or beliefs can take place within the context of the pupils' provisional position.

Phase Two: The Horizons of Religion

   i   presentation of a spectrum of conflicting religious and secular perspectives
   ii   location of pupils' positions within this spectrum.

(Wright, 2000, p. 181)

In this phase, various religious teachings or concepts are explored. These can be from across traditions or within specific traditions. It will then explore the reasons these competing views are held, rather than just being a descriptive narrative.

Phase Three: The Engagement of Horizons

   i   development of critical thinking skills
   ii   conversation across and between horizons
   iii re-articulation of pupils' initial position.

(Wright, 2000, p. 181)

Pupils think critically and theologically about the various positions and 'they embark on the task of discovering meaning within dissonance and ambiguity' (Wright, 2000, p. 183). It then becomes more than a 'pick your preference'; rather, it is a rational and informed exploration of a world of faiths.

Which pedagogy is appropriate to be used?

Although this chapter has argued that a constructivist approach to RE can underpin all of the various approaches to its teaching, the teacher is left with a multitude of pedagogies each with an appeal. It is clear that understanding the aims that a teacher has will have an influence over how they teach, but each of these paradigms explored is compatible, to varying extents, with the aims elucidated in Chapter 1. It could be argued that a pedagogy underpins all teaching, as such it is important for a teacher to find one that underpins their aims and can be used to engage all pupils. If there is to be one pedagogy adopted, this book argues that it should be a 'new' one that could be termed 'the kaleidoscopic approach' to the teaching of Religious Education.

The kaleidoscopic approach

There are elements of each of the pedagogies that are incredibly exciting and could be used to engage all kinds of pupils, and help them experience the type of RE that is aimed for in the initial chapter. It is possible to argue that one of these pedagogies by themselves is not enough and leaves a fairly repetitive approach to RE teaching. By utilising a Kaleidoscopic approach thoroughly grounded in constructivism, the teacher is able to consider what they are trying to achieve, and then find an approach for the particular topic that lends itself to learning in that context. All of them 'can be brilliant, and … can be teamed up in various different eclectic combinations by any teacher' (Blaylock, 2004, p. 13).

Consider an approach to the Resurrection narratives that adopts a critical realist approach. The four accounts found in the Gospels could be seen to have different emphases and even conflicting details. Using the three-phase typology, pupils could explore their initial thoughts about the Resurrection, then move on to the various explanations found in the Gospels and strive to come to a conclusion as to the events of the first Easter for Christians. Alternatively, the topic may be the existence of God where pupils engage with all of the arguments for the existence and non-existence of God and be expected to come to tentative conclusions. This might not be exactly what was intended within the pedagogy but the kaleidoscopic approach is able to focus on developing criticality within a slightly different paradigm.

Within this approach it is possible to explore many different approaches, and so when beginning an introduction to the hajj, pupils may have a guided imagination, which would be based on some of the principles of the experiential model. This makes a bridge with children's own experiences, so is critical to the concept-cracking approach and also the shared human experience model. Other examples could be given from each of the different paradigms, but it is sufficient at this stage to suggest that the teacher examines what they are teaching and be able to call upon the various pedagogies to help them understand how best to approach the topic.

This approach is not without its concerns; in seeking to accept all it could be seen to be diluting what is positive about each one. The approach does not seek to 'accept all'; rather it seeks to place the pupil and their experiences at the heart of the learning process while recognising the validity and distinctiveness of religious belief. Indeed, rather than accepting them all, the kaleidoscopic approach actually rejects them all as individual approaches as they do not provide the mixed and exciting diet that RE seeks to achieve;

similarly, none of them individually recognises the extrinsic and intrinsic nature of truth. It is only when a nuanced combination is explored that all of the strengths of the individual approaches can be harnessed into a complete RE experience. RE can continue without the kaleidoscopic approach, and each of the individual approaches can yield results, but it could be richer with its implementation. All of the individual pedagogies outlined in the chapter build on a body of research and publication; but the body of work is not there to support the kaleidoscopic approach. Although not the subject of a research project, it has been used in many schools to great success as teachers strive to provide an effective RE provision.[3] This book is the first foray into writing to support this approach.

Summary

Within this chapter the following have been explored:

- What is a pedagogy?
- The importance of aims underpinning a pedagogy
- The constructivist nature of RE
- The main pedagogies of RE
- A way forward in utilising aspects of good practice to formulate a new pedagogy.

It is hoped that the chapter has helped the reader to consider their pedagogy in the teaching of Religious Education. As such, the pedagogy that is developed should help produce a cohesive approach to RE that utilises the aims and purposes that were developed in the first chapter.

RE succeeds best when it is linked with pupil experience, and makes a bridge with the content being studied, while maintaining an authenticity in the study of religious belief and practice. It is hoped that teachers will benefit from utilising the approach advocated in this chapter.

Notes

1   The author worked with Mark Peace in a secondary school where this approach was adopted by the Social Science department. Peace is currently Principal lecturer in Education at Manchester Metropolitan University but has never published this material. Copies of the discussion material are in the author's possession.
2   Grimmitt includes a model entitled: 'Constructivist Models of Teaching and Learning in RE'. This has been omitted from the list here as it has been argued that this underpins all learning within RE.
3   The author taught RE in secondary schools for 12 years utilising this approach; was an Advanced Skills Teacher for four years delivering local and national support to schools that implemented the kaleidoscopic approach (though it was without a name at that stage); and, as a University lecturer, encourages his students to implement the principles outlined above.

References

Blaylock, Lat (2004) 'Six Schools of Thought in RE', *Resource*, 27(1), 13–16.
Cooling, Trevor (1994) *A Christian Vision for State Education*. London: SPCK.

Cooling, Trevor (1996) 'Education in the Point of RE – not Religion?: Theological reflections on the SCAA Modle Syllabuses'. In J. Astley, and L. Francis (Eds), *Christianity Theology and RE*. London: SPCK.

Cooling, Trevor (2000) 'The Stapleford Project: Theology as the Basis for Religious Education'. In Grimmitt, Michael (Ed.), *Pedagogies of Religious Education. Case Studies in the Research and Development of Good Pedagogic Practice in RE*. Great Wakering, UK: McCrimmons (pp. 153–169).

Dawkins, R. (2006) *The God Delusion*. London: Transworld.

Department for Education and Skills (DfES) (2004) *Pedagogy and Practice: Teaching and Learning in Secondary Schools*. London: DfES.

Erricker, Clive (2000) *Reconstructing Spiritual and Religious Education*. London and New York: Routledge.

Gearon, L. (2013) *Masterclass in Religious Education. Transforming Teaching and Learning*. London: Bloomsbury.

Grimmitt, Michael (1987) *Religious Education and Human Development*. Great Wakering, UK: McCrimmons.

Grimmitt, Michael (Ed.) (2000) *Pedagogies of Religious Education. Case Studies in the Research and Development of Good Pedagogic Practice in RE*. Great Wakering, UK: McCrimmons.

Hay, David (2000) 'The Religious Experience and Education Project: Experiential Learning in Religious Education'. In Grimmitt, Michael (Ed.) *Pedagogies of Religious Education. Case Studies in the Research and Development of Good Pedagogic Practice in RE*. Great Wakering, UK: McCrimmons (pp. 70–87).

Hay, David and Nye, Rebecca (1998) *The Spirit of the Child*. London: Harper Collins.

Holt, James D. (2008) 'Guided imagination as a basis for understanding the importance of special places' NATRE support materials for implementation of Secondary National Curriculum (2007). Four pages available at: www.natre.org.uk/secondary/casestudy.php?id=8 (accessed 1 May 2014).

Jackson, Robert (1997) *Religious Education: An Interpretive Approach*. London: Hodder.

Jackson, Robert (2000) 'The Warwrick Religious Education Project: The Interpretive Approach to Religious Education'. In Grimmitt, Michael (Ed.), *Pedagogies of Religious Education. Case Studies in the Research and Development of Good Pedagogic Practice in RE*. Great Wakering, UK: McCrimmons (pp. 130–152).

Jackson, Robert (2004) *Rethinking Religious Education and plurality*. Abingdon, UK: Routledge.

Lowndes, Judith (2012) *The Complete Multifaith Resource for Primary Religious Education: Ages 4–7*. Abingdon, UK: Routledge.

Ofsted (2010) *Transforming RE*. London: Ofsted.

Piaget, Jean (1954) *The Construction of Reality in the Child*. New York, NY: Basic Books.

Phillips, Sue (2003) *Theatre of Learning, Experiential RE: Making RE Make Sense*. London: SfE.

Phillips, Sue (2003a) *Teaching Christianity with the Theatre of Learning, Experiential RE*. London: SfE.

Qualifications and Curriculum Authority (QCA) (2007) *The National Curriculum. Statutory Requirements for Key Stages 3 and 4*. London: QCA.

Read, Garth, Rudge, John and Howarth, Roger (1990) *How Do I Teach RE?* Cheltenham, UK: Stanley Thornes.

Rudge, John (2000) 'The Westhill Project: Religious Education as Maturing Pupils' Patterns of Belief and Behaviour'. In Grimmitt, Michael (Ed.), *Pedagogies of Religious Education. Case Studies in the Research and Development of Good Pedagogic Practice in RE*. Great Wakering, UK: McCrimmons (pp. 88–111).

Smart, Ninian (1969) *The Religious Experience of Mankind*. Englewood Cliffs, NJ: Prentice Hall.

Smart, Ninian (1989) *The World's Religions: Old Traditions and Modern Transformations*. Cambridge: Cambridge University Press.

Stern, Julian (2006) *Teaching Religious Education*. London: Continuum.

Teece, Geoff (1993) *In Defence of Theme Teaching in Religious Education*. Birmingham, UK: Westhill RE Centre.

Vygotsky, L. S. (1962) *Thought and Language*. Cambridge, MA: MIT Press.

Vygotsky, L. S. (1978) *Mind in Society: The Development of Higher Psychological Processes*. Cambridge, MA: Harvard University Press.

Watson, John B. (1930) *Behaviorism*. New York, NY: W.W. Norton and Company.

Wright, Andrew (1993) *Religious Education in the Secondary School: Prospects for Religious Literacy*. London: David Fulton.

Wright, Andrew (2000) 'The Spiritual Education project: Cultivating Spiritual and Religious Literacy through a Critical Pedagogy of Religious Education'. In Grimmitt, Michael (Ed.), *Pedagogies of Religious Education. Case Studies in the Research and Development of Good Pedagogic Practice in RE*. Great Wakering, UK: McCrimmons (pp. 170–187).

Wright, A. (2003) 'The Contours of Critical Religious Education: Knowledge, Wisdom, Truth'. *British Journal of Religious Education*, *25*(4), 279–291.

Chapter 3

Spirituality and RE

Chapter outline
What is spirituality?
How do schools, and specifically RE, contribute to spirituality?
Can, and should, spirituality be developed and measured?

There are two reasons for the inclusion of a chapter on spirituality:

1   As outlined in the various pedagogies in the previous chapter spirituality lies at the heart of RE. This includes the spirituality of the pupils and of the religious and non-religious worldviews.
2   As a part of the inspection framework (Ofsted, 2013), Spiritual development must be reported on, and RE contributes significantly to a school's provision.

Spirituality, when engaged with in the RE classroom, provides important learning experiences; however, in a school it can be seen as a vague and amorphous term that needs fully exploring to understand its place within RE and, in a wider sense, the school.

What is spirituality?

In discussing Spiritual Development in a school it is important to understand from the outset what spirituality and spiritual development are. Spirituality has been variously defined. A GCSE module on Spirituality suggested that the following should be included in a definition of the spiritual:

Search for meaning in life
Awareness of aspects of life other than the physical/ material
Feelings of awe, wonder and mystery
The inner world of inspiration and creativity
Awareness of self-identity and self-worth
Recognition of the value of the world and others
Closeness to the Divine.

(AQA, 2002, p. 37)

Ofsted (2013, p. 37) suggest that spiritual development is shown by pupils':

- beliefs, religious or otherwise, which inform their perspective on life and their interest in and respect for different people's feelings and values
- sense of enjoyment and fascination in learning about themselves, others and the world around them, including the intangible
- use of imagination and creativity in their learning
- willingness to reflect on their experiences.

Others have struggled with similar questions. Whatever definition is arrived at it would seem that spirituality is an incredibly personal thing; there are aspects of the above definitions that would be hotly debated by people on all sides of the religious landscape. An article by Erricker (2004) suggested that the spiritual is indefinable for a group; in selecting books on spirituality he chose a selection of books that had developed his own spirituality, rather than being about the topic of spirituality:

> Unlike a recognisable religious tradition that focuses the subject as a discrete discipline to be studied, spirituality is diversely understood and tends to elude definition. ... As for the books that have influenced me, they may not be the most obviously understood under the heading of spirituality, but under very diverse headings.
>
> (Erricker, 2004, p. 14)

It would seem that every author who writes about spirituality has their own slightly different interpretation of what spirituality actually is and how it is to be recognised. Perhaps the most enlightening view of the spiritual is a definition given by Wilfred Cantwell-Smith: spirituality

> like courage, like humility or pride, like love, truth, [and] fear cannot be observed directly. These cannot be investigated 'objectively' – none of them is an object in the world; they are qualities in persons' hearts and minds. They can be suggested, by examples of occasions when, and forms through which, they have found human manifestation. Sensitive observers, being themselves human, can and regularly do move from observing the outward signs towards learning and appreciating the human qualities involved in a particular case – though further occasions may provide new insights.
>
> (1998, p. 12)

Unfortunately Smith is not talking of the spiritual, he is defining his understanding of faith, something he believes has been rejected in favour of a 'quality in our life that they have begun to call "spiritual," or "soul," or other alternatives' (1998, p. 16). Spirituality is only recognisable from outward expressions, but it is impossible to judge the spiritual motivations. Is helping somebody always an expression of spirituality, or can it be purely an expression of humanity? Some would argue that the abilities that humans have to act and reflect on these actions are what make them spiritual. The spiritual needs to be stripped of all of its religious connotations if it is to gain universal acceptance and have applicability in the school.

There are still others, however, who would place the spiritual only in the realm of the religious. They would argue that a person cannot be spiritual without some acknowledgement of the source of the divine within each of us. Spirituality is therefore not real unless associated with a religion:

> When the word 'spirit' is cut loose from a particular tradition it gives up a liveliness and turns into a kind of linguistic Lycra, stretching to accommodate any shape or form. It becomes the property of a New Age style Gnosticism, posing as 'the Holistic Option'. It appears that [the London Millennium] dome theology is going to follow those such as John Hick and Mathew Fox into a humanistic cul-de-sac where all we ever do is talk among ourselves about that which we really cannot talk about. I fear the language of faith will become a kind of spiritual Esperanto which, by trying too hard to belong to everyone, ends up belonging to no-one.
>
> (Gay cit. Copley, 2000, p. 5)

This, however, is to deny the spirit of humankind, and while it can be understood from inside an exclusivist faith, it cannot have a place in a world where all are valued, which also extends to spirituality having a place within the classroom. To find a definition of the spiritual and spiritual development within the educational context, one can go to a variety of places. Ofsted (2004; 2013) and SCAA (School Curriculum and Assessment Authority) (1995) both produced their own interpretation, as have others (see for example Brown and Kadodwala, 1993; Copley, 2000; Erricker and Erricker, 2000; and Wright, 2000). They generally all agree, though in different language, that spirituality within education is to do with a person's understanding of themselves, their relationships with others, the transcendent and, to some degree, the world.

> The first objective is: to promote those qualities and dispositions which affect how people engage with life – how they relate to themselves, others, the world and (for some) with God or Ultimate Being.
>
> (Gent, 2002, p. 6)

This is perhaps most succinctly discussed by Hay and Nye (1998), who base their findings on classroom-based interviews with a number of children. They construct four ideas of consciousness based on the premise that spirituality, including spiritual development, is natural and biological. It cannot be taught because it is 'more about the realities of human relationships than it is about detailed lesson plans' (p. 162). The relational consciousnesses that they develop are:

1   Self-consciousness (I–Self)
2   People consciousness (I–Others)
3   World consciousness (I–World)
4   God consciousness (I–God) (see 1998, Chapter 7).

To make the model acceptable to all and broad enough so as not 'to exclude from its scope the majority of pupils in … schools who do not come from overtly religious backgrounds' (SCAA, 1995, p. P), it might be beneficial to amend I–God to I–Transcendent. This would enable experience outside of the physical to be recognised without reference to God. While the majority of pupils may accept the idea of God, for a significant minority the identification of the transcendent as God may be an obstacle that does not need to be there. Conversely, a pupil's spirituality might be evidenced by a rejection of a belief in God and thus the God consciousness could remain.

It is beneficial to see how using Hay and Nye as a model can also be seen to include the guidance given by Ofsted (2013), SCAA (1995), Westhill College (1998), Kibble (2003) and Hill (1989); a school policy on Spiritual Development could also be explored as an example of spiritual development in practice (see Table 3.1). These particular models have been selected because they seem to represent the mainstream and the successful interpretations of the spiritual in education. Ofsted and SCAA have been included as 'official' declarations, schools have to adhere to Inspection guidelines and so for a school policy to be valid it has to fit into Ofsted's interpretation of the Spiritual. The school itself uses various statements to reflect an understanding of the spiritual for pupils and these have been used as the basis for this framework.

How do schools, and specifically RE, contribute to spirituality?

Having examined a variety of understandings of the spiritual it would seem that all could be contained within the model given by Hay and Nye (with perhaps the exception of Hill, who in his model refers to skills that would be considered more religious than spiritual, e.g. 'to identify and evaluate religious truth claims' (1989, p. 179)). What Hay and Nye do is provide a teacher with the framework within which they can begin their understanding of the spiritual, and from there examine the ways in which they help pupils develop these relational consciousnesses. The policy of the school utilised above fits in very well with all of the understandings presented above and goes further in that it provides the teacher with examples of how these relationships could be developed within the classroom. It is recognised that RE has an integral role to play in the development of spirituality within the school. Linking back to the aims of RE outlined in Chapter 1 it is possible to see how the relational consciousness aspects of spirituality underpin some of these:

- To prepare pupils to be informed, respectful members of society who celebrate diversity and strive to understand others (I–Others).
- To encourage students to develop knowledge of the beliefs and practices of religions; and informed opinions and an awareness of the implications of religion for the individual, the community and the environment (I–Others; I–World).
- To develop pupils' own responses to questions about the meaning and purpose of life (I–Self; I–World; I–God).

Liz Mills completed some research that suggested some ways in which schools could help develop spirituality using the metaphors of windows, mirrors and doors:

> **WINDOWS:** giving children opportunities to become aware of the world in new ways; to **wonder** about life's 'Wows' (things that are amazing) and 'Ows' (things that bring us up short). In this children are learning about life in all its fullness.
> **MIRRORS:** giving children opportunities to reflect on their experiences; to **meditate** on life's big questions and to consider some possible answers. In this they are learning from life by exploring their own insights and perspectives and those of others.

Table 3.1 Definitions of spirituality

	Hay & Nye (1998)	Westhill College (1998)	School Curriculum and Assessment Authority (SCAA)	Ofsted (2013)	Kibble (2003)	School policy	Hill (1989)
I–Self	• Transcending the immediate and the mundane. • Developing particular temperaments and dispositions. • Developing particular sets of character traits and values. • Awareness of being an enduring entity that persists over time and retains a continuity of self-consciousness and self-identity. • Detecting and responding to some of the wonder, mystery and awesomeness of the natural world, social living and personal experience.	• It has to do with the universal search for individual identity. • It is to do with the search for meaning and purpose in life and for values by which to love. • The development of personal beliefs. • An understanding of how beliefs contribute to personal identity. • The belief that one's inner resources provide the ability to rise above everyday experiences. • Asking 'why me?' at times of hardship and suffering.	• Self-knowledge – An awareness of oneself in terms of thoughts, feelings, emotions, responsibilities and experiences; a growing understanding and acceptance of individual identity; the development of self-respect. • Creativity – Expressing innermost thoughts and feelings through, for example, art, music, literature and crafts; exercising the imagination, inspiration, intuition and insight. • A growing awareness of when it is important to control emotions and feelings, and how to learn to use such feelings as a source of growth.	• Beliefs, religious or otherwise, that inform their perspective on life and their interest in and respect for different people's feelings and values. • Sense of enjoyment and fascination in learning about themselves. • Use of imagination and creativity in their learning. • Willingness to reflect on their experiences.	• Using or developing the imagination. • The avenue of challenge. • Pupils ask questions about their own beliefs. • Examining the beliefs and experiences of others in order to encourage a development of their own understanding of themselves and of life.	• Encouraging pupils to consider and discuss their beliefs and those of others. • Promoting understanding of ways that beliefs contribute to individual and group identity. • Being concerned about the search for truth. • Promoting self-understanding. • Encouraging pupils to reflect on their own identity. • Opportunity for problem-solving and discovery. • Presenting the challenge of belief. • Encouraging the enjoyment and excitement of learning. • Requiring pupils to think for themselves. • Developing pupils' capacity to think, to reflect and express themselves on spiritual matters. • Encouraging an openness to being challenged through learning. • Encouraging reflection on questions about religion and the meaning of life. • Heightening the quality of pupils' perceptions.	• Enable students to preserve their self-confidence and self-esteem. • Develop a stable self-concept and personal life goals. • Relation of this subject area to self-development. • Being able to express one's feelings. • The setting apart of moments for private reflection. • To provide opportunities of self-initiated learning, imagination and creative production. • To clarify the necessary role of ultimate beliefs with a view to encouraging students to consider what their own response to this quest will be. • To encourage the setting apart of moments for stillness and reflection on the spiritual aspects of existence.

	Hay & Nye (1998)	Westhill College (1998)	School Curriculum and Assessment Authority (SCAA)	Ofsted (2013)	Kibble (2003)	School policy	Hill (1989)
I—Others		• Detecting and responding to some of the wonder, mystery and awesomeness of the natural world, social living and personal experience. • Recognising, remembering and reliving a select number of significant experiences.	• It has to do with our relationships with other people. • It has to do with our responses to challenging experiences, such as death and suffering. • An appreciation that people have individual and shared beliefs on which they base their lives. • An understanding of how beliefs contribute to personal identity. • Being inspired by human achievement. The belief that one's inner resources provide the ability to rise above everyday experiences. • Recognising and valuing the worth of each individual; developing a sense of community, the ability to build up relationships with others. • The sense of being hurt by injustice or aggression. • A growing awareness of when it is important to control emotions and feelings, and how to learn to use such feelings as a source of growth.	• Beliefs, religious or otherwise, that inform their perspective on life and their interest in and respect for different people's feelings and values. • Sense of enjoyment and fascination in learning about themselves, others and the world around them, including the intangible.	• Working for others in the community. • Examining the beliefs and experiences of others in order to encourage a development of their own understanding of themselves and of life. • Express delight in what is good and wonderful.	• Providing knowledge and opportunities to understand other people. • Exploring the convictions that are central to religious traditions. • Providing opportunities to see from another person's perspective. • Encouraging pupils to consider and discuss their beliefs and those of others. • Presenting the challenge of belief. • Heightening the quality of pupils' perceptions.	• Relation of this subject area to ideas of social responsibility. • To enlarge the capacity of students to empathise with other persons. • To foster those interpersonal and social competencies that enhance learning and the enjoyment of relationships. • To give individual students such responsibilities for other persons. • To help students understand Christianity in its various forms. • To acquaint students with some religious and ideological traditions other than their own. • To enlarge the ability to empathise with the way people who hold different beliefs from themselves see the world. • To foster the capacity to dialogue in a non-threatening way about one's own ultimate beliefs with such people.

Hay & Nye (1998)	Westhill College (1998)	Ofsted (2013)	Kibble (2003)	School policy	Hill (1989)
I–World	• Detecting and responding to some of the wonder, mystery and awesomeness of the natural world, social living and personal experience.	• Creativity – Expressing innermost thoughts and feelings through, for example, art, music, literature and crafts; exercising the imagination, inspiration, intuition and insight. • A sense of awe, wonder and mystery – Being inspired by the natural world, mystery or human achievement. • Feelings and emotions – The sense of being moved by beauty.	• Sense of enjoyment and fascination in learning about themselves, others and the world around them, including the intangible.	• Using or developing the imagination. • The avenue of challenge. • Express delight in what is good and wonderful. • Working for others in the community.	• Developing a sense of awe and wonder. • Promoting awareness of the value of a non-material dimension to life. • Awareness of the mystery that lies at the heart of all being.	• The voluntary expression of feelings of curiosity and wonder. • To encourage the setting apart of moments for stillness and reflection on the spiritual aspects of existence.
I–God	• Transcending the immediate and the mundane. • Awareness of being an enduring entity that persists over time and retains a continuity of self-consciousness and self-identity • Detecting and responding to some of the wonder, mystery and awesomeness of the natural world, social living and personal experience.	• It has to do with the universal search for individual identity. • It has to do with relationships with God. • The development of personal beliefs, including religious beliefs. • A sense of awe, wonder and mystery – Being inspired by mystery. • Experiencing feelings of transcendence – Feelings that may give rise to belief in the existence of a divine being. • Search for meaning and purpose – Asking 'why me?' at times of hardship or suffering; reflecting on the origins and purpose of life; responding to challenging experiences of life. • Creativity – Expressing innermost thoughts and feelings through, for example, art, music, literature and crafts; exercising the imagination, inspiration, intuition and insight.	• Beliefs, religious or otherwise, that inform their perspective on life and their interest in and respect for different people's feelings and values. • Sense of enjoyment and fascination in learning about themselves, others and the world around them, including the intangible. • Use of imagination and creativity in their learning. • Willingness to reflect on their experiences.	• Using or developing the imagination. • The avenue of challenge. • Pupils ask questions about their own beliefs.	• Promoting awareness of the value of a non-material dimension to life. • Awareness of the mystery that lies at the heart of all being. • Encouraging pupils to consider and discuss their beliefs and those of others. • Presenting the challenge of belief. • Exploring the convictions that are central to religious traditions. • Being concerned about the search for truth. • Promoting self-understanding. • Encouraging pupils to reflect on their own identity. • Opportunity for problem-solving and discovery. • Presenting the challenge of belief.	• To make students aware of the universality of the quest of all human beings for a sense of ultimate meaning and purpose, and for deliverance from aspects of the human condition that they find intolerable. • To clarify the necessary role of ultimate beliefs with a view to encouraging students to consider what their own response to this quest will be.

DOORS: giving children opportunities to respond to all of this; to **do** something creative as a means of expressing, applying and further developing their thoughts and convictions. In this they are learning to live by putting into action what they are coming to believe and value.

(Mills, nd)

In light of the relational consciousness explored above, Mills' suggestions seem to be a way to help pupils identify the ways in which spirituality is being explored. These opportunities will perhaps be more apparent and easier within RE, but they should not be limited to just one aspect of the curriculum.

The school outlined in Table 3.1 similarly highlighted different ways of exploring spirituality in the classroom. It outlined spirituality as a way to:

- Encourage children to consider their own values and attitudes.
- Reflect on shared human experience.
- Explore their own and other people's beliefs.
- Provide knowledge and opportunities to understand other people.
- Develop a sense of awe and wonder.
- Promote understanding of how beliefs contribute to identity.
- Promote awareness of the non-physical aspect of life.
- Engage in a search for truth.
- Promote self-understanding.
- Encourage pupils to reflect on their own identity.
- Provide opportunity for problem-solving and discovery.
- Be aware of mystery and questions in all experience and life.
- Present the challenge of belief.
- Encourage the enjoyment and excitement of learning.
- Require pupils to think for themselves.
- Develop pupils' capacity to think, to reflect and express themselves on spiritual matters.
- Explore the convictions that are central to religious traditions.
- Encourage an openness to being challenged through learning.
- Encourage reflection on questions about religion and the meaning of life.
- Provide opportunities to see from another person's perspective.
- Heighten the quality of pupils' perceptions.

As this list is examined, it becomes evident that RE does indeed have an important role to play in the spiritual aspect of the school. These again can be linked to the five aims of RE outlined in Chapter 1 (see Table 3.2), and also the kaleidoscopic pedagogy suggested in Chapter 2.

Table 3.2 The aims of RE and spirituality

1	To stimulate interest and enjoyment in Religious Education.	• Encourage the enjoyment and excitement of learning. • Provide opportunity for problem-solving and discovery.
2	To prepare pupils to be informed, respectful members of society who celebrate diversity and strive to understand others.	• Provide opportunities to see from another person's perspective. • Provide knowledge and opportunities to understand other people.
3	To encourage students to develop knowledge of the beliefs and practices of religions; and informed opinions and an awareness of the implications of religion for the individual, the community and the environment.	• Promote understanding of how beliefs contribute to identity. • Explore the convictions that are central to religious traditions. • Present the challenge of belief. • Reflect on shared human experience. • Explore their own and other people's beliefs.
4	To give all students equal access to Religious Education and provide enjoyment and success.	• Encourage an openness to being challenged through learning.
5	To develop pupils' own responses to questions about the meaning and purpose of life.	• Promote awareness of the non-physical aspect of life. • Engage in a search for truth. • Promote self-understanding. • Develop a sense of awe and wonder. • Heighten the quality of pupils' perceptions. • Encourage reflection on questions about religion and the meaning of life. • Develop pupils' capacity to think, to reflect and express themselves on spiritual matters. • Require pupils to think for themselves. • Being aware of mystery and questions in all experience and life. • Encourage pupils to reflect on their own identity. • Encourage children to consider their own values and attitudes.

There are many opportunities through which RE can help enhance pupils' spiritual development. As this book looks at an approach to, and suggestions for, teaching these 'spiritual experiences' will underpin the various activities suggested.

Can, and should, spirituality be developed and measured?

The spiritual, as understood by all writers, applies to the whole of the curriculum and is a focus for the inspection of a school. It is not just the preserve of Religious Education. SCAA suggested that spirituality can be developed through three areas of school life: 'They are the ethos of the school, all subjects of the curriculum and collective worship' (1995, p. T). Ofsted (1994, p. 9) suggest four (somewhat overlapping with SCAA) areas:

- through the values and attitudes the school identifies, upholds and fosters;
- through the contribution made by the whole curriculum;
- through religious education, acts of collective worship and other assemblies;
- through extra-curricular activity, together with the general ethos and climate of the school.

Spirituality could be the natural part of any effective teacher's approach to education. A school, with its good overall standard of teaching could be seen to meet pupils' spiritual requirements, but its articulation of the provision is perhaps what is focused on. Bill Gent has noted:

> Irrespective of whether schools did in fact adequately provide for pupils' spiritual development or not, I soon became aware of a subtle dynamic taking place.
> Because there is no common vocabulary with which to talk about the spiritual, and uncertainty about what the term connotes, schools were often diffident in speaking about how they promoted pupils' spiritual development. This diffidence – or silence, in some cases – was sometimes taken by Ofsted inspectors as evidence of deficiency: that is, if schools could not talk about how they were promoting pupils' spiritual development, then clearly they were not doing so …
> I increasingly saw a major task as providing schools with the words through which they could understand what 'promoting spiritual development' might mean. Armed with this vocabulary, they could then be far more confident and assertive in articulating and evaluating what they were doing.
>
> (2002, p. 4)

If, therefore, the articulation of spiritual development is part of what is being measured then a school needs to be prepared to outline its contribution, but whether spirituality can be developed and how this can be measured is an intriguing discussion. If the relational consciousness model is accepted the question arises as to how it can be developed and measured, and whether it is the school's responsibility to do this. By the language they employ, Ofsted suggest that people can be developed spiritually, hence there must be some yard stick against which this could be measured. James Fowler suggested a theory of faith development that was able to be generalised to the world as a whole. His approach is summarised below in Table 3.3 (the framework is taken from Fowler, 1981, cited in Sutcliffe (Ed.) 2001, pp. 143–151).

Table 3.3 Stages of faith development

Stage	Name	Key characteristics (quotes from Fowler, 1981)	Age
Pre	Infancy and undifferentiated Faith	The seeds of trust, courage, hope and love are fused in an undifferentiated way and contend with sensed threats of abandonment, inconsistencies and deprivations in an infant's environment. The emergent strength of faith in this stage is the fund of basic trust and the relational experience of mutuality with the one(s) providing primary love and care.	0–4
1	Intuitive- projective	The child can be powerfully and permanently influenced by examples, moods, actions and stories of primally related adults. The imaginative processes underlying fantasy are unrestrained and uninhibited by logical thought. Imagination in this stage is extremely productive of long-lasting images and feelings that later, more stable and self-reflective valuing and thinking will have to order and sort out. The gift or emergent strength of this stage is the birth of imagination, the ability to unify and grasp the experience-world in powerful images and as presented in stories that register the child's intuitive understandings and feelings towards the ultimate conditions of existence.	3/4–7/8
2	Mythical-literal	Is the stage in which the person begins to take on for him- or herself the stories, beliefs and observances that symbolise belonging to his or her community. Beliefs are appropriated with literal interpretations, as are moral rules and attitudes. Symbols are taken as one dimensional and literal in meaning. In this stage the rise of concrete operations leads to the curbing and ordering of the previous stage's imaginative composing of the world. The new capacity or strength in this stage is the rise of narrative and the emergence of story, drama and myth as ways of finding and giving coherence to experience.	6/7–11/12 and some adults
3	Synthetic-conventional	A person's experience of the world now extends beyond the family. A number of spheres demand attention: family, school or work, peers, street society and media, and perhaps religion. Faith must provide a coherent orientation in the midst of that more complex and diverse range of involvements. Faith must synthesise values and information; it must provide a basis for identity and outlook. A person has an 'ideology', a more or less consistent clustering of values and beliefs, but he or she has not objectified it for examination and in a sense is unaware of having it. The emergent capacity of this stage is the forming of personal myth, the myth of one's own becoming in identity and faith, incorporating one's past and anticipated future in an image of ultimate environment unified by characteristics of personality.	11/12–17/18 and some adults

Stage	Name	Key characteristics (quotes from Fowler, 1981)	Age
4	Individuative-reflective	The person must begin to take seriously the burden of responsibility for his or her own commitments, lifestyle, beliefs and attitudes. The person must face certain unavoidable tensions: individuality versus being defined by a group or group membership, subjectivity and the power of one's strongly felt but unexamined feelings versus objectivity and the requirement of critical reflection; self-fulfilment or self-actualisation as a primary concern versus service to and being for others; the question of being committed to the relative versus struggle with the possibility of an absolute. Typically translates symbols into conceptual meanings. This is a 'demythologising' stage. Its ascendant strength has to do with the capacity for critical reflection on identity (self) and outlook (ideology).	17/18 and/or 30s–40s
5	Conjunctive	This stage develops a 'second naivete' in which symbolic power is reunited with conceptual meanings. Here there must also be a new reclaiming and reworking of one's past. There must be an opening to the voices of one's deeper self. Importantly, this involves a critical recognition of one's social unconscious – the myths, ideal images and prejudices built deeply into the self-system by virtue of one's nurture within a particular social class, religious tradition, ethnic group or the like. What the previous stage struggled to clarify in terms of the boundaries of self and outlook, this stage now makes porous and permeable. The new strength lies in the rise of the ironic imagination – a capacity to see and be in one's or one's group's most powerful meanings while simultaneously recognising that they are relative, partial and inevitably distorting apprehensions of transcendent reality.	Rare before 30
6	Universalising	Becomes a disciplined, activist incarnation – a making real and tangible – of the imperatives of absolute love and justice of which Stage 5 has partial apprehensions. The self engages in spending and being spent for the transformation of present reality in the direction of a transcendent actuality. Persons exhibit qualities that shake our usual criteria of normalcy. Their heedlessness to self-preservation and the vividness of their taste and feel for transcendent moral and religious actuality give their actions and words an extraordinary and often unpredictable quality. Their devotion to universalising compassion. Their enlarged visions of universal community. Their leadership initiatives often involve strategies of non-violent suffering and ultimate respect for being. They have become incarnators and actualisers of the spirit of an inclusive and fulfilled human community.	Rare ever

While spiritual development within a school might be somewhat transferable to Fowler's outline, the language and characteristics he uses are not pertinent to a 'secular' educational situation as they are based very much on faith. Such a framework also gives rise to the question of whether it is a teacher's role to place a child in a level in such a way that they might place them in relation to an end of key stage statement.

> Many people, especially those who have left their teenage years, identify with what Fowler says regarding the ways that they relate the religious tradition into which they are born. Others, however, who are born into families which are not part of a worshipping community are sometimes less satisfied with the account.
>
> (Westhill, nd, p. 7)

SCAA suggested a means of measuring development that seems to echo some of Fowler's structure:

> The notion that pupils will develop spiritually raises the expectation that this is an area in which pupils can make progress. Whilst not advocating a model of linear progression, the steps to spiritual development might include:
>
> • recognising the existence of others as independent from oneself;
> • becoming aware of and reflecting on experience;
> • questioning and exploring the meaning of experience;
> • understanding and evaluating a range of possible responses and interpretations;
> • developing personal views and insights;
> • applying the insights gained with increasing degrees of perception to one's own life.
>
> (1995, p. Q)

While accepting these statements as evidence of a 'spiritual person' the lineal development of spirituality could be argued against; similarly, the appropriateness or feasibility of measuring this development should be questioned. Others have also sought to identify an 'end product' (see for example Newby, 1996, and Beck, 1999). If one were to accept any definition while giving something to aim for, rather than merely groping in the dark and hoping to achieve what the school thinks best, it would make things even more complicated.

> The aim … is to give pupils some vision of what is important in life – or better, the equipment to find their own vision – the ability to see the wonder of the world, the value of other people and their viewpoints, the excitement of discovery, the joy of creation, the fun of working, the need to serve, and perhaps the disposition to honour truth, desire goodness, and delight in beauty.
>
> (Raynor, 1998, p. 14)

A teacher's role in spiritual development is paramount. A danger associated with this is that the spiritual development available would only be a reflection of the teacher's spirituality rather than an individual pupil's. As laudable as this 'end product' would be, who would be in place to assess it? Surely it would need to be someone on 'higher ground', and most of the human race will still be striving to achieve these ideals.

Lever (2003) experimented with Wright's typography of the spiritual (based on four horizons: Christianity, universal religiosity, liberal humanism and post-modernism) in assessing spiritual development. He used 'Learning from Religion' assessment levels in forming opinions and conclusions. Lever's results suggest many problems with adopting one view of the spiritual, and also in trying to assess it: 'The first thing that became apparent is that very few pupils were completely or even mainly of one category. ... Assessment should be integral to the process, and may not always be as clearly defined as the system may expect (pp. 8, 10).

While Lever feels it is possible to collectively assess spiritual development on the basis of assessment levels, his arguments seem unconvincing and inconclusive. Spiritual development is only assessed as far as it is synonymous with attainment targets, and it does not cover all of the areas discussed in a definition of the spiritual. Moran suggests concern for the idea of development, for the area of spiritual development it can be argued that:

> The close association of growth and development needs careful scrutiny if one is to talk of moral development, religious development, and human development. The image of growth is limited in manoeuvrability and variety. Yet for discussing morality, religion, or life as a whole we need rich, flexible, multi-dimensional imagery. A general use of the word development requires a meaning that includes growth but also can connote other kinds of movement. One of the first dictionary meanings of growth is 'increase by natural development.' Logically, that implies there are other kinds of development besides growth.
>
> (1983, p. 3)

In using Moran's explanation of the language of development, one realises the possibilities of the word. However, its understanding in common usage renders it a barrier to understanding (this common understanding is evidenced in Ofsted's interpretation (see 1994, pp. 6–7; also 2013).

If spirituality cannot be measured objectively then it seems as though the role of the spiritual in a school and within RE is to provide opportunities whereby the spiritual can be fostered in the life of an individual. It is not the role of the school to measure or establish criteria for development. It can only hope to enable pupils to grow and flourish as is evidenced by an Ofsted observation of a Year 9 Geography lesson: 'Such approaches cause students to examine their feelings and engage spiritually with the subject matter. The learning that results becomes, therefore, more a part of them as they feel for the knowledge they acquire' (Morton, 2002, p. 15). And further in the analysis of the school as a whole:

> The aim is to harness the energy and curiosity of young people. It seeks to ensure that learning goes beyond knowledge and understanding to the impact that the acquisition can have on the way students perceive their own lives in a global community. Such approaches respond to the college's commitment to experiment, make use of failures and celebrate successes. The college is striving for this view of learning and personal development, intertwined across subjects and pastoral structures, to pulse through the veins of daily practice. An important feature underpinning this view of learning is that students have opportunities to reflect on their known lives and their relationships with each other and the adults in the school.
>
> (Morton, 2002, p. 16)

Rather than on spiritual development, it would perhaps be better to inspect schools on how well they give opportunities in which the spiritual can flourish. This would reflect the reality of practice within schools and RE lessons, and also remove a lot of the worry from the constructing of policy documents. Surely it is more important to have the experience than to analyse and measure it? Classrooms thus become a place of mutual fellowship and participation, where the relationships are preeminent as pupils strive to develop their spirituality, however they understand that. The personal nature of all experience would be respected and pupils would be free to ask and explore questions as they learn how to discover and research. In essence, the classroom and the school become a microcosm of life as a whole as pupils struggle with their personal identity and spirituality.

Summary

Within this chapter the following have been explored:

- The nature of spirituality.
- The underpinning nature of spirituality for the school and RE.
- The possibility that schools should provide opportunities for spiritual flourishment rather than a measuring stick for spiritual development.

It is hoped that the chapter has helped the reader to consider the nature of spirituality and how it plays a role in the life of a school, its pupils and specifically in the teaching of RE. Spirituality underpins RE but should not be the beginning and end of everything that takes place, rather it should help the teacher understand that RE and spirituality are both about relationships. As such, RE has a crucial role in providing children with opportunities for spiritual flourishment. This chapter may also help the teacher utilise the spiritual in a way that is not daunting or indeed confusing.

References

AQA (2002) *GCSE Religious Studies Specification B*. Manchester, UK: AQA.

Beck, J. (1999) 'Spiritual and Moral Development and Religious Education'. In A. Thatcher (Ed.), *Spirituality and the Curriculum*. London: Cassell (pp. 153–180).

Brown, A. and Kadodwala, D. (1993) 'Spiritual Development and the School Curriculum'. In Erricker, C. (Ed), *Teaching World Religions*. London: Heinemann (pp. 33–34).

Cantwell-Smith, W. (1998) *Patterns of Faith Around the World*. Oxford: Oneworld.

Carr, D. (1996) 'Rival Conceptions of Spiritual Education', *Journal of Philosophy of Education*, *30*(2), 159–178.

Copley, T. (2000) *Spiritual Development in the State School*. Exeter, UK: University of Exeter.

Erricker, C. (2004) 'Spirituality on the Bookshelf', *Resource*, *26*(2), 14–16.

Erricker, C. and Erricker, J. (2000) *Reconstructing Religious, Spiritual and Moral Education*. London: Routledge.

Fowler, James W. (1981) *Stages of Faith*. New York, NY: Harper & Row.

Gent, B. (2002) 'Spiritual Development and School Life: Finding the Words', *Resource*, *24*(2), 4–7.

Hay, David and Nye, Rebecca (1998) *The Spirit of the Child*. London: Harper Collins.

Hill, B. (1989) 'Spiritual Development in the Education Reform Act: A Source of Acrimony, Apathy or Accord?', *British Journal of Education Studies*, *37*(2), 169–182.

Kibble, D. (2003) 'Sailing between Ofsted, Scylla and Charybdis: A Yorkshire School Gives New Meaning to Spiritual Development', *International Journal of Children's Spirituality*, 8(1), 32–41.

Lever, G. (2003) *Thinking, Emotional Literacy and Spiritual Development*. Oxford: Farmington Trust.

Mills, Liz (nd) *Spiritual Development: The Doughnut and the Hole*. Available at: www.crackingre.co.uk/htdocs/crackingre/secure/teachSupp/donut.html (accessed 1 May 2014).

Moran, G. (1983) *Religious Education Development*. Minneapolis, MN: Winston Press.

Morton, D. (2002) *Inspection Report. Egerton Park Arts College*. Manchester, UK: Ofsted.

Newby, M. (1996) 'Towards a Secular Concept of Spiritual Maturity'. In R. Best (Ed.), *Education, Spirituality and the Whole Child*. London: Cassell (pp. 93–107).

Ofsted (1994) *Spiritual, Moral, Social and Cultural Development. An Ofsted Discussion Paper*. Manchester, UK: Ofsted.

Ofsted (2013) *Religious Education: Realising the Potential*. Manchester, UK: Ofsted.

QCA (2000) *Religious Education and Collective Worship*. London: QCA.

Raynor, D. (1998) 'Spiritual Development in Religious Education'. In P. Lievers, S. Bennett and J. Grove, *Handbook for RE in Key Stage 3*. Solihull, UK: Solihull MBC (pp. 12–27).

School Curriculum and Assessment Authority (SCAA) (1995) *Spiritual and Moral Development. SCAA Discussion Papers No.3*. London: SCAA.

Sutcliffe, J. (Ed.) (2001) *Tuesday's Child. A Reader for Christian Educators*. Birmingham, UK: Christian Education.

Westhill RE Centre (nd) *Distance Learning in RE Study Guide and Workbook. Religious Education and Spiritual Development*. Birmingham, UK: University of Birmingham.

PART II

Planning in Religious Education

Chapter 4

Assessment and RE

Chapter outline

The importance of assessment

The focus on concepts, attitudes, skills and knowledge in assessment

What is the process of assessment?

Stepping stones for progress at Key Stages 3, 4 and 5

Assessment as central to the learning and teaching process including:

- Planning the learning outcomes
- Planning for differentiation
- Planning the tasks for pupils
- Planning the questions to be asked

The importance of assessment

There is sometimes trepidation and fear with which some RE teachers approach the issue of assessment. The question arises as to what is being assessed and against what the product should be judged. Some people suggest that RE is not a subject that can be assessed. However, this is not really up for discussion. Agreed syllabuses and exam specifications require assessment. In the words of one headteacher: 'R.E. teachers should stop moaning about assessment and just get on with it'.

Assessment is the process by which teachers measure the progress of students, and should be an integral part of the process of learning and teaching. This chapter comes before the chapter on planning because it is crucial for the teacher of RE to utilise assessment at every stage of the learning process, and recognise that it is not a bolt-on that occurs after the planning has taken place or, in extreme cases, after the teaching has occurred. As RE teachers consider the aims and purpose that they have for their students they will be better able to recognise what it is they are trying to assess, and what it is that they cannot; indeed, there are some aspects of the subject that are best left unencumbered from the demands of formal assessment. This attitude to not all things being assessed is reflected in a satirised version of the Sermon on the Mount.

Then Jesus took his disciples up the mountain and gathered them around. He taught them saying:

Blessed are the poor in spirit for theirs is the kingdom of God.
Blessed are the meek.
Blessed are they that mourn.
Blessed are the merciful.
Blessed are they who thirst for justice.
Blessed are you when you are persecuted.
Blessed are you when you suffer.
Be glad and rejoice for your reward is great in Heaven.

And Simon Peter said, 'wilt we be having a test on this?'
And Phillip said, 'I don't have any paper.'
And Bartholomew said, 'Does it matter about my spelling?'
And Mark said, 'Do we have to hand this in?'
And John said, 'The other disciples didn't have to learn this.'
And Matthew said, 'Can I go to the toilet?'

Then one of the Pharisees who was present asked to see Jesus' lesson plan and enquired of Jesus, 'Where are your learning and assessment objectives?'
Another asked, 'What range of teaching strategies did you draw from, and do you have differentiated provision?'
A third Pharisee asked to see a cross-section of work.
And Jesus wept.

(source unknown)

However, assessment is central to teaching and learning, and just as teachers should be clear about the purposes of RE they should similarly be clear about the purposes of assessment. The Teaching and Learning Research programme has summarised the main purposes of assessment into three broad categories:

1   The use of assessment to help build pupils' understanding, within day-to-day lessons.
2   The use of assessment to provide information on pupils' achievements to those on the outside of the pupil teacher relationship: to parents (on the basis of in-class judgments by teachers, and test and examination results), and to further and higher education institutions and employers (through test and examination results).
3   The use of assessment data to hold individuals and institutions to account, including through the publication of results which encourage outsiders to make a judgment on the quality of those being held to account.

(Mansell, James and the Assessment Reform Group, 2009, p. 8)

It could be argued that these categories decrease in day-to-day importance, but the reality is that in schools all three of these purposes are important and should form part of the teacher's focus on assessment, though always maintaining the integrity of the subject and the aims behind it. In *Realising the Potential*, Ofsted (2013) recognises the danger that an over-emphasis on category 3 can bring to RE at Key Stage 3 and 4 (Key Stage 5 might also be included):

> This approach frequently leads pupils to a superficial and often distorted understanding of religion. In the schools visited, work related to investigating religions and beliefs was often too easy. One pupil expressed a common view: 'We don't really need to understand the fundamental beliefs and practices of a religion in order to take this exam; we just have to repeat what the religion teaches about various issues'.
>
> (p. 17)

The demands of the examination/assessment had become the purpose and aim of RE rather than the deepening of knowledge and understanding to meet the teacher's aims. This highlights an interesting dichotomy: on one hand, teachers are expected to prepare pupils to sit an examination; this does and will continue to form the end result of a student's education at ages 16 and 18. On the other hand, the demands of the examination can lead to a superficial treatment of topics that is unlikely to fulfil the needs of RE. Indeed, Ofsted further highlighted that 'Most of the GCSE teaching seen failed to secure the core aim of the examination specifications: that is, to enable pupils "to adopt an enquiring, critical and reflective approach to the study of religion"' (2013, p. 5). This dichotomy is unnecessary and the balance between these two seemingly competing demands will be explored further in Chapters 8 and 9, which explore teaching at Key Stage 4 and Key Stage 5 respectively.

To enable assessment to take place it is important to note that there are two main types: *summative* and *formative*.

- *Summative* assessment takes place at the end of a piece of learning and is often the terminal or final assessment of learning. GCSE and A-level examinations would be examples of summative assessment; other examples may include end-of-unit/year exams (though whether they are purely summative is debatable).
- *Formative* assessment takes place throughout the learning process, it helps students and teachers understand where they are and how they can make progress. Formative assessment is on-going; as such, while an end-of-year exam may be seen to be summative it can become formative if the learning measured in the exam is used to inform future learning and teaching.

For RE to be effective the major proportion of assessment undertaken should be formative; indeed John Rudge has argued that 'It is only formative assessment which benefits the pupils directly in their learning' (2000, p. 109). As an example, it is impossible for a teacher to be able to plan effectively for a lesson if they do not know the learning and progress that has already been made by pupils. Without this knowledge it is possible for the lesson to be inappropriately pitched and no progress to be made. This links back to the constructivist nature of RE teaching where a pupil's prior knowledge, experiences and abilities are used as a basis on which to build future learning.

This raises the question as to what progress looks like in RE. Against what measure are pupils making progress? It is possible to go into some schools and see the same type of task being repeated again and again with everybody thinking that progress is being made. Consider the student who, in Year 7, writes a narrative about the life of the Buddha, and then in Year 9 completes the same task about the life of the Prophet Muhammad (pbuh). Is progress being made? Certainly knowledge is being increased, but making progress is not solely about knowing more facts and events; the RE teacher is not preparing students for a pub quiz, rather it is about using this knowledge to show progress in students' understanding of concepts, skills and attitudes (see Read et al., 1998).

Concepts

Concepts are the main focal point of any educational programme. They are essentially ideas that help people to make sense of their experiences of a great variety of things, objects, information, events and occurrences. They help people to interpret these experiences (Rudge, 1991, p. 23).

Within RE concepts help the student to interpret the experiences of others within a particular tradition. They also provide opportunities to deal with wider issues and relate them to the religious tradition and also to a pupil's own life experience. In Chapter 2 the centrality of concepts as building bridges between pupil experience and pupil learning was explored. The pyramid that was adapted from Lowndes' (2012) work (see Figure 2.1) illustrates how students make conceptual progress:

- Stage 1: Concepts that are within the children's own experience.
- Stage 2: Concepts common to all human experience.
- Stage 3: Concepts common among different religions.
- Stage 4: Concepts particular to a specific religion.

Utilising the concept-cracking view that students should explore the central and most important concepts of a religion, it is important that progress and opportunity to explore the different stages are given. In every topic there can be found concepts at each level of the pyramid. If the Life of Jesus is taken as an example, the following concepts can be suggested (Table 4.1):

In this example, it may seem that the topic is inundated with concepts while having no evident underlying concept development. On closer examination, the general concepts of *authority, forgiveness, the treatment of others* and *commitment,* and the specific concept of *Son of God,* seem to be returned to again and again. Pupils should be able to use the life and teachings of Jesus to recognise the Christian view of him as the Son of God, but also the impact of his life on Christians and non-Christians with regard to the issues of forgiveness, the treatment of others and commitment. At certain points students could be asked to reflect on the centrality of these concepts to the Christian faith, how these concepts affect Christians today, and also their own attitudes towards these concepts. On occasion, however, it may be necessary for the teacher to be explicit in the development of these concepts.

A further example might be found in a unit of work exploring aspects of Hindu dharma:

Table 4.1 The conceptual stages and exemplar concepts in the Life of Jesus

Stage	Concepts
1	Belonging; Celebration; Right and wrong.
2	Authority; Evil; Justice; Fairness; Temptation; Forgiveness.
3	Life After Death; Initiation; Sacrifice.
4	Nativity; Incarnation; Son of God; Baptism; Holy Ghost; God the Father; Parable; Miracle; Messiah; Blasphemy; Atonement; Resurrection.

Table 4.2 The conceptual stages and exemplar concepts in Hinduism

Stage	Concepts
1	Symbolism; Remembrance; Senses; Rules; Festival; Celebration; Remember.
2	Nature; Way of Life; Morals; Guidance.
3	Scripture; Worship; Shrine; Offering; Prayer; God; Life after death.
4	Dharma; Ahisma; Brahman; Puja; Atman; Samsara; Reincarnation; Karma; Caste.

What the teacher should be aware of is that as the pupil progresses within RE the first three stages become somewhat conflated. Life after death as a concept that is shared by different religions may become within the pupil's own 'experience' as an aspect of prior learning. Thus, it becomes possible to utilise concepts from other aspects of the RE experience to help a pupil make progress. Utilising concepts also helps learning within RE to go beyond the superficial description of practices, but to explore the concepts that underlie beliefs and practices, 'For example, they can focus on Hindu ideas about reincarnation, not what happens at a Hindu burial. It's clearer. Focused on what really matters' (Wedell, 2009, p. 9). Further, John Rudge suggests that concepts take the pupils beyond knowledge to understanding:

> For example, in studying the five Pillars of Islam, it is important that pupils grasp both the context of the practices within Islam and their meaning for Muslims. To do so, they need to relate the practice of the five pillars to the concept of *ibadah*, or service (to Allah). They begin to show understanding of the five pillars when they can explain how the practice of giving zakah, for example, reflects the principle of ibadah.
>
> (2000, p. 112)

When a pupil has explored the nature of authority within the context of the life of Jesus, they can then bring that learning and experience to bear when exploring the concept of authority and its meaning within the Jewish experience of the Torah.

The use of conceptual development as a grounding for the teaching of RE is not limited to a particular approach. Indeed, if the curriculum is designed with concepts at the heart then the teacher is free to use either a systematic or thematic approach. The learning becomes less an accumulation of facts and more a journey to explore what lies at the heart of religions and religious experience. Enabling the pupils to make links and draw on prior experience is a constructivist approach to learning.

Attitudes

In some ways the development of attitudes is inherently tied up with the development of concepts: 'We see the development of attitudes as having as much importance as the development of concepts in RE. The two go together' (Rudge, 1991, p. 29).

However there should be attitudes outside of the concepts that RE seeks to develop. Referring back to the aims of RE developed in Chapter 1, two of them cover attitudes that might be developed:

- To prepare pupils to be informed, respectful members of society who celebrate diversity and strive to understand others.
- To encourage students to develop knowledge of the beliefs and practices of religions; and informed opinions and an awareness of the implications of religion for the individual, the community and the environment.

These attitudes should be covered within all areas of RE and are crucial to successful learning; however, it is evident that not all attitudes can or ought to be assessed in RE. RE provides opportunities for reflection and development of the individual. Linking back to the exploration of spiritual development in Chapter 3, it is possible to suggest that preparing pupils to be 'respectful members of society who celebrate diversity and strive to understand others' is an area that should be given opportunity to flourish, but is not necessarily assessable. However, the development of attitudes is key within the RE classroom.

Skills

In identifying skills to be developed throughout RE it is important to note that the skills are not necessarily specific to the subject, but that there might be skills that are enhanced through the study of RE. The utilisation of a wide range of skills in the learning of RE enables pupils to find tasks exciting and work together (See Ofsted, 2013, p. 25). Within Ofsted's *Realising the Potential* and the RE Council's *RE Review*, it is possible to highlight some of the skills that can be found within RE:

- enquiry
- ask pertinent and challenging questions
- to gather, interpret and analyse information
- to draw conclusions and evaluate issues using good reasoning
- argument
- expressing their own opinions.

(Ofsted, 2013, pp. 9 and 31).

- investigating religions and worldviews through varied experiences, approaches and disciplines
- reflecting on and expressing their own ideas and the ideas of others with increasing creativity and clarity
- becoming increasingly able to respond to religions and worldviews in an informed, rational and insightful way
- critical and personal evaluation

- find out about
- investigate
- respond creatively
- enquiry
- articulate beliefs, values and commitments clearly.

(RE Council of England and Wales, 2013, pp. 13, 15 and 60)

This list is not exhaustive but it gives an indication of the variety of skills that could be utilised within the teaching and learning of RE. Indeed, the RE Council articulates one of the curriculum aims of RE to be: 'Gain and deploy the skills needed to engage seriously with religions and worldviews' (2013, p. 15). These skills are necessary to enable the pupils to show progress within RE and to meet some of the aims and purposes of RE. Skills are therefore central to the assessment of RE, as through deploying the skills pupils are able to show progress, and the correct choice of teaching method and the associated skills employed by the learner enable the conceptual framework explored earlier to be developed and enhanced.

Two 'real-life' examples can be used to show how the choice of skills to be employed, coupled with the concepts and aim of learning, can produce progress or no progress in RE.

The topic is Muslim prayer. After an introduction to prayer by the teacher the class are asked to design their own prayer mat based on the initial discussion. To some extent the skill being employed is to respond creatively. However, few aspects of any other skills are being employed. Through this task a pupil may be able to articulate a very low level skill of recognising some different symbols.

(RE Council of England and Wales, 2013, p. 66)

For the majority of secondary school pupils, as a stand-alone task, this is not a stretching or skilful piece of RE.

The topic is Muslim prayer. Groups of four are given a variety of resources including a prayer mat, a video clip showing prayer, a summary of prayer from two Muslim children. The pupils should then respond creatively through a letter which clearly explains the process of prayer, the meaning of the various actions (including the importance of submission to God) and the reasons why they think Muslims might pray and the effect it has on their lives. This employs a very small scale enquiry approach where pupils gather, interpret and analyse information; investigate religions and worldviews through varied experiences; find out about; and articulate beliefs, values and commitments clearly. A focus on skills enables pupils to become more engaged and part of the learning process which enables them to explain how and why individuals and communities express the meanings of their beliefs and values.

(RE Council of England and Wales, 2013, p. 66)

Skills and their associated outworkings thus become important in enabling pupils to progress within RE.

What is the process of assessment?

As is evident from the discussion of concepts, skills and attitudes it is impossible to talk about assessment without talking about planning. An awareness of assessment at every stage of the planning and teaching of RE is important to enable progress to be made by pupils in the learning. One of the key principles of Assessment for Learning is the centrality of assessment to planning:

> *Assessment for learning should be part of effective planning of teaching and learning.* A teacher's planning should provide opportunities for both learner and teacher to obtain and use information about progress towards learning goals. It also has to be flexible to respond to initial and emerging ideas and skills. Planning should include strategies to ensure that learners understand the goals they are pursuing and the criteria that will be applied in assessing their work. How learners will receive feedback, how they will take part in assessing their learning and how they will be helped to make further progress should also be planned.
>
> (Assessment Reform Group, 2002, p. 2)

Planning becomes about more than the accumulation of knowledge, but about progress in knowledge, skills, attitudes and concepts. These are specifically planned for and the learning journey of the pupils is evident throughout long-term, medium-term and short-term planning (these will be explored in detail in Chapter 5). The underlying principles of assessment should underpin all the planning and teaching that takes place within RE; the Assessment Reform Group suggested ten such principles. Assessment for Learning:

1   is part of effective planning
2   focuses on how students learn
3   is central to classroom practice
4   is a key professional skill
5   is sensitive and constructive
6   fosters motivation
7   promotes understanding of goals and criteria
8   helps learners know how to improve
9   develops the capacity for self-assessment
10   recognises all educational achievement.

Space does not allow for an in-depth treatment of each of these principles, but some of them will be touched upon in exploring the process of assessment within RE. However, before beginning a discussion of the integration of assessment into planning, it is important to know the criteria and standards against which pupils are to be assessed.

Stepping stones to progress at Key Stage 3

The 2014 National Curriculum moved the assessment of Key Stage 3 away from levels of attainment; indeed, at its implementation, the Department for Education (DfE) outlined that 'Assessment levels have now been removed and will not be replaced. Schools have the freedom to develop their own means of assessing pupils' progress towards end of key stage expectations' (2014, p. 3). At the time of writing, it is unclear what schools will do to replace levels, but it is possible to suggest ways forward, and the opportunities that will be provided by the move away from levels. In the short term, Agreed Syllabi will continue to have levels as their standard of progression and assessment but, as indicated by the *RE Review* (RE Council of England and Wales, 2013), there may well be a move towards the utilisation of an end of Key Stage statement approach to the measurement of progress. This will bring RE into line with all the National Curriculum subjects, and as such will probably be the way forward within the assessment of RE (even though it was also what was in place 20 years ago).

The National Association of Headteachers (NAHT), responding to the changes in the assessment requirements of the whole curriculum, suggested that 'level descriptors and National Curriculum levels, whatever their other faults, had given the profession a common tool to communicate with each other and with stakeholders' (2014, p. 13). In utilising assessment as a tool for progression it is this that will be missing, as such a common tool to measure progress should be adopted within the RE syllabus. In constructing these measures of progress it is not necessary to dismiss all that has come before; a lot of work had gone into the design and use of the Attainment Target levels in RE. In the sense that these are fit for purpose, and reflect progression in RE it is possible to suggest that these levels continue to be used, without the numbers being attached. With the two 'old' attainment targets being *learning about* and *learning from* religion, 'I can' levels of progression can be suggested (see Tables 4.3 and 4.4).

Although the level numbers remain, in this example it is for ease to show progression; their usefulness as a shorthand of reporting what a pupil can do has now become redundant, and this is a change that is not necessarily for the worse. Consider, for example, the pupil who is given a level 7 for a piece of work on the life of the Prophet Muhammad. The only feedback they receive is that they are working at a level 7. The number has become a lazy shorthand for reporting to the pupil what they have achieved, and in this real example it actually indicated that the child had worked hard and produced a very detailed piece of work, rather than reflecting any RE skills at level 7. In the move away from levels it becomes incumbent on the teacher in giving feedback to articulate the skills and knowledge developed, and then to use the next descriptor to suggest ways of improvement. Feedback, then, might look something similar to the following.

> Well done. In your piece of work you have explored the life of Muhammad well. You have retold the story of Muhammad (pbuh). You included all of the major events. You also describe why Muhammad (pbuh) is important for Muslims, mentioning the Night of power and why this is important, and also other reasons, for example 'because he is the founder of Islam and set an example for people to follow'. You also suggest how one of these might make someone behave differently.
>
> *Target:* You could suggest how the life and example of the Prophet might make someone behave differently including examples, e.g. 'if someone lived the teachings of Muhammad (pbuh) they would ... '

Table 4.3 AT1 'I can' levels

Level 1	Level 2	Level 3	Level 4	Level 5	Level 6	Level 7	Level 8	EP
• I can tell an outline of a religious story. • I can identify places, people and things that are religious.	• I can retell a religious story. • I can identify some religious beliefs, teachings and actions. • I know some things are shared by more than one religion. • I can suggest what religious symbols mean, or that religious stories and actions have a meaning.	• I can describe some religious beliefs and teachings, and their importance. • I can describe how some beliefs and teachings are found and reflected in festivals and actions. • I can make links between beliefs and teachings and the way religion is expressed.	• I can describe the key beliefs and teachings in religions. • I can link beliefs and teachings with each other. • I can make comparisons between religions. • I can show an understanding of what belonging to religion involves. • I understand that religious beliefs, ideas and feelings can be expressed in different ways. • I can give meanings to some symbols, stories and language. • I can use technical religious words.	• I can explain how some beliefs, teachings and features of religious life are shared by different religions. • I can explain how beliefs, teachings and features of religious life make a difference to the lives of individuals and communities. • I can show how individuals and communities use different ways to express their religion.	• I can use my own knowledge to explain the beliefs and teachings of religion. • I can use my own knowledge to explain what it means to belong to a faith community. • I can use my own knowledge to explain how beliefs and ideas can be shown in a variety of ways in different contexts and groupings. • I can use correct technical religious words.	• I can relate religious teachings, practices and lifestyles to their historical and cultural contexts. • I can relate religious influences on individuals, communities and society to their historical and cultural contexts. • I can relate the many different ways in which religion is expressed using evidence and examples. • I can relate that religion is expressed in texts, metaphor and symbolism using evidence and examples.	• I can analyse the influence of religious beliefs and teachings on individuals, communities and society. • I can account for the influence of religious beliefs and teachings on individuals, communities and society. • I can analyse and account for different views of religious practices and lifestyles. • I can analyse and account for different views of religious expression. • I can use appropriate evidence and examples in all of these.	• I can distinguish and actively explore different interpretations of the nature of religious belief and teaching. • I can give a balanced analysis of religions' sources, validity and significance and of their importance for believers of practices and lifestyles and of the issues raised by diversity in a plural society. • I can give a balanced analysis of the meaning of language in religion in the light of philosophical questions about its status and function.

Table 4.4 AT2 'I can' levels

	Level 1	Level 2	Level 3	Level 4	Level 5	Level 6	Level 7	Level 8	EP
A**T****2**	• I can share my own experiences and feelings. • I can say what I think is interesting and important. • I can say what I think is interesting and important in religions.	• I can be sensitive to others' experiences and feelings. • I can be sensitive to people's beliefs and opinions on right and wrong. • I realise that some questions which cause people to wonder are difficult to answer.	• I can compare some of my own ideas and experiences with others. • I can identify what influences my life. • I can make links between people's beliefs, values and the things they do and are committed to. • I can make links between my own beliefs, values and the things I do and am committed to.	• I ask questions and suggest answers from my own and others' experiences of important people from religion. • I ask questions and suggest answers from my own and others' experiences about puzzling aspects of life and moral and religious issues. • I make reference in those to the teachings of religions. • I show an understanding of why certain things are held to be right or wrong.	• I can explain my response to questions of identity and experience, meaning and purpose. • I can explain my response to other peoples' values and commitments.	• I can clearly explain the experience of inspirational people. • I can relate the experiences of inspirational people to my own and others' lives. • I can clearly explain religious views on questions of meaning and purpose, and on contemporary moral issues. • I can relate these religious views to my own and others' views.	• I can evaluate religious and other views on human identity and experience. • I can evaluate religious and other views on questions of meaning and purpose. • I can evaluate religious and other views on values and commitments. • I use appropriate evidence and examples to support all of these.	• I can give an informed and well argued account of my own views, values and commitments regarding identity and experience in the light of different religious and other views and feelings. • I can give an informed and well argued account of my own views, values and commitments regarding questions of meaning and purpose and contemporary moral issues in the light of different religious and other views and feelings.	• I can place all religious and non-religious views within a comprehensive religious and philosophical context. • I can make well informed and reasoned judgements about religions' significance.

It will still be important for the teacher to be aware of the expectation for the particular Key Stage, so that the expected reporting of working towards/at/above the average for a child in their year group could be reported as required by the school. In this model, there are specific examples of good practice in Agreed Syllabi where the levels are tied in with the End of Key Stage Statements (see, for example, Cheshire East, 2013). The average pupil entering secondary school could be seen to be working at a level 4; on leaving Year 9, the pupil will be at levels 5 and 6. Having this knowledge of levels or stepping stones of progress will help a teacher plan for their class and individual pupils.

The second possibility is to rely purely on the End of Key Stage Statements to help the teacher to plan to help their pupils and classes make progress. An example of this is provided by the *RE Review* (RE Council of England and Wales, 2013) where only End of Key Stage Statements are produced. By themselves, these statements have serious shortcomings in being able to be used to inform and measure progress. Unlike the levels that are staged with small increments and go beyond what is expected at Key Stage 3, the End of Key Stage Statements have large gaps between them and, in the *RE Review* at least, stop at Key Stage 3 leaving no room for progression beyond the average pupil at the end of Year 9. The reasoning behind this must be that Key Stage 4 moves onto GCSE and this is fine for pupils in Key Stage 4, however, the able pupil at Key Stage 3 must have somewhere to go beyond the average descriptor or they will be left treading water and losing interest for long periods of their Key Stage 3 experience.

To enable the end of Key Stage Statements to work, they must be broken down into stepping stones of progress, not dissimilar to the way levels have been used. The *RE Review* moved away from what can be seen as the artificial separation of *learning about* and *learning from* religion, rather it suggested that these be combined and articulated together into three aims against which progress can be measured and developed. These three aims were referred to earlier, but a restatement of them is important:

A. Know about and understand a range of religions and worldviews, so that they can:

- describe, explain and analyse beliefs and practices, recognising the diversity which exists within and between communities and amongst individuals;
- identify, investigate and respond to questions posed, and responses offered by some of the sources of wisdom found in religions and worldviews;
- appreciate and appraise the nature, significance and impact of different ways of life and ways of expressing meaning.

B. Express ideas and insights about the nature, significance and impact of religions and worldviews, so that they can:

- explain reasonably their ideas about how beliefs, practices and forms of expression influence individuals and communities;
- express with increasing discernment their personal reflections and critical responses to questions and teachings about identity, diversity, meaning and value, including ethical issues;
- appreciate and appraise varied dimensions of religion or a worldview.

C. Gain and deploy the skills needed to engage seriously with religions and worldviews, so that they can:

- find out about and investigate key concepts and questions of belonging, meaning, purpose and truth, responding creatively;
- enquire into what enables different individuals and communities to live together respectfully for the wellbeing of all;
- articulate beliefs, values and commitments clearly in order to explain why they may be important in their own and other people's lives.

(RE Council of England and Wales, 2013, pp. 14–15)

The combination of the two attainment targets should help a more cohesive and less fragmented approach to RE to be developed; learning from will be a natural part of learning about. Utilising the aims and their associated End of Key Stage Statements it is possible to suggest stepping stones of progress between the Key Stages.

Similar work has been suggested by *RE Today* (2014) where 'eight steps up' in RE are suggested (pp. 42–45). The advantage of *RE Today*'s work is that it utilises the three aims but builds in progression beyond that of an average Key Stage 3 pupil. However, it might be possible to suggest that in designing their own stepping stones of progression teachers or local authorities could utilise elements of the GCSE requirements to enable pupils to make progress (see below).

Stepping stones to progress at Key Stage 4

GCSEs in England are in a state of flux as a transition is made to new specifications and a new grading system. This will entail a new language of assessment to be learned by teachers, but should not drastically alter the day-to-day assessment that they undertake in helping their pupils make progress. Teachers and schools may be judged on grades 5–9, rather than A*–C, but the underlying principles of assessment using grade descriptors and their associated levels of attainment in examination mark schemes will continue. As such, the stepping stones in assessment will remain much the same. However, the use of grade descriptors in helping pupils make progress within their RE skills at GCSE has not been as widespread as the use of examination mark schemes to measure progress. While the use of exam questions to prepare pupils for exams, and also to measure progress are important, they are not, and should not be, the only yardstick against which GCSE pupils should be measured. Ofsted have suggested 'Teaching in many of the GCSE lessons observed placed too much emphasis on ways of passing the examination rather than focusing on extending pupils' learning about religion and belief' (2013, p. 17). It is suggested that one reason for this is the time allocated to RE, however, it could also be suggested that teachers can help pupils make progress by enabling opportunities to extend pupils' learning especially in terms of depth, which will enable them to be prepared for the examination, but also:

1   To stimulate interest and enjoyment in Religious Education.
2   To prepare pupils to be informed, respectful members of society who celebrate diversity and strive to understand others.

Table 4.5 Stepping stones of progress KS1–KS3 A: Know about and understand (see RE Council, 2013)

A: Know about and understand

	Key Stage 1			Key Stage 2			Key Stage 3		
Describe, explain and analyse beliefs, and practices, recognising the diversity that exists within and between communities	**Recall and name** different beliefs and practices	**Find out meanings** behind beliefs and practices		**Describe** features of the religions and worldviews	**Reflect** on features of the religions and worldviews	**Make connections** between different features of the religions and worldviews	**Explain** ways that the history and culture of religions and worldviews influence individuals and communities	**Appraise (discuss and argue)** reasons why some people support and others question the influences of religions and worldviews on individuals and communities	**Interpret and analyse** the influence of religions and worldviews on individuals and communities
Identify, investigate and respond to questions posed by, and responses offered by, some of the sources of wisdom found in religions and worldviews	**Retell** some religious and moral stories	**Explore and discuss** sacred writings and sources of wisdom and recognise the communities from which they come	**Suggest meanings** to some religious and moral stories	**Describe links** between stories and other aspects of the communities they are investigating	**Respond** thoughtfully to a range of sources of wisdom and to beliefs and teachings	**Understand** links between stories and other aspects of the communities they are investigating maybe by offering opinions	**Explain** the range of beliefs, teachings and sources of wisdom and authority	**Explain and argue** why religions and worldviews might be seen as coherent systems or ways of seeing the world	**Interpret and analyse** the coherence of religions and worldviews and the way that they are practised
Appreciate and appraise the nature, significance and impact of different ways of life and ways of expressing meaning	**Recognise** some different symbols and actions which express a community's way of life	**Recognise similarities** between communities		**Describe** a range of beliefs, symbols and actions		**Understand** different ways of life and ways of expressing meaning	**Explain how** individuals and communities express the meanings of their beliefs and values in many different forms and ways of living	**Explain why** individuals and communities express the meanings of their beliefs and values in many different forms and ways of living	**Enquire critically** into the variety, differences and relationships that exist within and between beliefs, values and ways of living

Table 4.6 Stepping stones of progress KS1–KS3 B: Express and communicate (see RE Council, 2013)

B: Express and communicate

	Key Stage 1	Key Stage 2	Key Stage 3	
Explain reasonably their ideas about how beliefs, practices and forms of expression influence individuals and communities	**Ask and respond to questions** about what communities do, and why / **Identify** what difference belonging to a community might make to individuals	**Describe** varied examples of religions and worldviews / **Explain, with reasons,** the meanings of religions and worldviews to individuals and communities	**Explain** the religions and worldviews that they encounter clearly, reasonably and coherently / **Explain, with reasons,** the significance of religions and worldviews to individuals and communities	**Evaluate** religions and worldviews drawing on a range of introductory level approaches recognised in the study of religion or theology / **Interpret** a wide range of ways in which commitment and identity are expressed
Express with increasing discernment their personal reflections and critical responses to questions and teachings about identity, diversity, meaning and value	**Observe and recount** different ways of expressing identity and belonging / **Respond sensitively** for themselves	**Suggest why** belonging to a community may be valuable, in their own lives / **Suggest why** belonging to a community may be valuable for the diverse communities being studied	**Understand** the challenges of commitment to a community of faith or belief / **Explain** a wide range of ways in which commitment and identity are expressed	**Evaluate and analyse** controversies about commitment to religions and worldviews / Account for the impact of diversity within and between communities
Appreciate and appraise varied dimensions of religion	**Recognise some similarities** between different religions and worldviews / **Respond sensitively** to some similarities between different religions and worldviews	**Describe** different dimensions of religion / **Explore and describe similarities and differences** between different religions and worldviews	**Understand similarities and differences** between different religions and worldviews / **Explain** responses to the question: what is religion?	**Evaluate** the question: what is religion? / **Analyse** the nature of religion using the main disciplines by which religion is studied

Table 4.7 Stepping stones of progress KS1–KS3 C: Gain and deploy skills (see RE Council, 2013)

C: Gain and deploy skills

Key Stage 1	Key Stage 2	Key Stage 3
Find out about and investigate key concepts and questions of belonging, meaning, purpose and truth, responding creatively **Explore** questions about belonging, meaning and truth	**Express** their own ideas and opinions in response using words, music, art or poetry **Discuss and present** their own and others' views on challenging questions about belonging, meaning, purpose and truth	**Apply ideas** of their own thoughtfully in different forms including (e.g.) reasoning, music, art and poetry **Explore** some of the ultimate questions that are raised by human life in ways that are well-informed **Give reasoned personal responses** to ultimate questions **Express insights** that draw on a wide range of examples including the arts, media and philosophy
Enquire into what enables different communities to live together respectfully for the wellbeing of all **Respond** with ideas to examples of co-operation between people who are different	**Describe** ways in which diverse communities can live together for the wellbeing of all **Respond thoughtfully** to ideas about community, values and respect	**Understand and apply** ideas about ways in which diverse communities can live together for the wellbeing of all **Examine and explain** issues about community cohesion and respect for all in the light of different perspectives from varied religions and worldviews **Evaluate** issues about community cohesion and respect for all in the light of different perspectives from varied religions and worldviews **Analyse and interpret** issues about community cohesion and respect for all in the light of different perspectives from varied religions and worldviews
Articulate beliefs, values and commitments clearly in order to explain reasons why they may be important in their own and other people's lives **Find out** about questions of right and wrong	Begin to **express** their ideas and opinions about questions of right and wrong in response **Discuss and apply** their own and others' ideas about ethical questions, including ideas about what is right and wrong and what is just and fair	**Express** their own ideas clearly in response to ethical questions, including ideas about what is right and wrong and what is just and fair **Apply** their own and others' ideas about ethical questions, including ideas about what is right and wrong and what is just and fair **Explore and explain** significant moral and ethical questions posed by being human in ways that are well-informed **Express** insights into significant moral and ethical questions posed by being human in ways that are well-informed and which invite personal response **Use reasoning to respond** to significant moral and ethical questions that may draw on a range of examples from real life, fiction or other forms of media

3   To encourage students to develop knowledge of the beliefs and practices of religions; and informed opinions and an awareness of the implications of religion for the individual, the community and the environment.
4   To give all students equal access to Religious Education and provide enjoyment and success.
5   To develop pupils' own responses to questions about the meaning and purpose of life.

One way this could be done is to focus on the content, skills and knowledge (and attitudes) that form the basis of GCSE specifications rather than an over-emphasis on the final exam; to allow pupils to have learning experiences that are not necessarily assessed by exam question, but whose progress is measured. The tools available for this assessment are the grade descriptors, which can similarly be turned into stepping stones.

These are subject to change as new requirements are given to the examination boards to produce specifications. The process would be the same whatever the content of the grade descriptors. This in no way takes away the need to focus on preparation for the exam by using practice exam questions, but it does make them supported and strengthened by excellent assessment that takes account of the needs and strengths of different pupils. Pupils are able to be assessed through different media and products and are given the opportunity to see their progression in RE in a way that is not formulaic or disheartening. Thus, assessment:

• focuses on how students learn;
• is sensitive and constructive;
• fosters motivation;
• helps learners know how to improve;
• develops the capacity for self-assessment;
• recognises all educational achievement.

Further exploration of how this can be integrated into teaching and learning can be found later in this chapter and in Chapter 5.

Stepping stones to progress at Key Stage 5

In a similar way to Key Stage 4 assessment, it is possible to argue that A-Level teaching is focused around preparing pupils for public examinations. This is right and proper, but should not be to the detriment of the pupils or at the expense of the richness and depth of Religious Studies. One element of the four-part pedagogy outlined in Chapter 2 is the importance of reflecting and reacting. Reflecting indicates where a pupil is after the learning input; the reaction stage involves the necessity of booster or extension readings. This enables those who need support to have structured reading and activities to be put in place, while those who have 'got it' are able to expand their experience and learning by exploring concepts and knowledge in greater depth. Assessment of all kinds, not just exam practice, enables pupils of all abilities to be stretched and have their achievement recognised. The teacher of Key Stage 5 will utilise examination mark schemes, but also grade descriptors that show pupils how to make progress.

Again, these are subject to change as new requirements are given to the examination boards to produce specifications.

Table 4.8 Stepping stones of progress KS4 (based on grade descriptors in Edexcel, 2012)

In describing, explaining and analysing, using knowledge and understanding I …	demonstrate basic knowledge and understanding of religion	demonstrate a sound knowledge and understanding of religion	demonstrate detailed knowledge and thorough understanding of religion
	describe, with some reasons, the significance and impact of beliefs, teachings, sources, practices, ways of life and forms of expressing meaning	describe and explain the significance and impact of beliefs, teachings, sources, practices, ways of life and forms of expressing meaning	describe, explain and analyse the significance and impact of beliefs, teachings, sources, practices, ways of life and forms of expressing meaning
	show some awareness of the meaning and importance of the religion(s) and/or beliefs studied	show awareness of the meaning and importance of the beliefs and practices of the religion(s) and/or beliefs studied	interpret, draw out and explain the meaning and importance of the beliefs and practices of the religion(s) and/or beliefs studied
	sometimes recognise and make simple connections between religion and people's lives	can describe the impact of beliefs and practices on the lives of believers	assess the impact of beliefs and practices on the lives of believers
		recognise how differences in belief lead to differences of religious response	explain, where appropriate, how differences in belief lead to differences of religious response
	communicate ideas using everyday language	communicate ideas using specialist vocabulary appropriately	understand and use accurately and appropriately a range of specialist vocabulary
In using evidence and reasoned argument to express and evaluate personal responses, informed insights and differing viewpoints I …	offer an opinion about the issues studied	use argument in my responses	use reasoned argument
	present reasons to support an opinion	use relevant evidence to express and evaluate different responses to issues studied.	use a range of evidence to respond to religious beliefs, moral issues and ultimate questions recognising the complexity of issues
	refer to different points of view		demonstrate informed insight in evaluating different points of view
	show some understanding of the complexity of the issues by describing different points of view	refer to different points of view	
	make judgements about these issues	make judgements about these issues	reach evidenced judgements about these beliefs, issues and questions

Table 4.9 Stepping stones of progress KS5 (based on grade descriptors in Edexcel, 2013)

In selecting and demonstrating knowledge and evidence I ...			
select limited but relevant material	present information that is mostly relevant to the task and material accurate	select accurate and relevant material	address the question specifically and select relevant material
show basic understanding of relevant features or key ideas often using generalisations	deploy limited knowledge, some of which is accurate	explain clearly relevant features or key ideas	deploy comprehensive and mostly accurate knowledge, expressed lucidly
support this with occasional examples and/or sources of evidence	make occasional reference to examples and sources of evidence	support this using examples and/or sources of evidence	support this using examples and sources of evidence
show limited accurate use of technical language and terminology	show limited accurate or consistent use of technical terms	use accurately a range of technical language and terminology	use a range of technical language and terminology accurately and consistently competently explain appropriate examples and/or relevant sources/scholars
demonstrate little understanding of the key ideas	demonstrate basic understanding of key ideas	show evidence of being familiar with issues raised by relevant scholars, or a variety of views, where appropriate	
In critically evaluating and justifying a point of view I ...			
demonstrate little organisation and/or limited coherence	demonstrate some organisation/ coherence to the argument being made	construct a coherent and well-organised argument	construct a coherent and well-organised evaluative argument
offer simplistic examples to support a personal point of view	utilise limited examples/ sources of evidence	support the argument by examples and/or sources of evidence	demonstrate an informed viewpoint and evidence of own thinking
offer mainly descriptive answers with little argument, justification or evaluation	demonstrate few personal insights, or little convincing argument or justification of a point of view with minimal evaluation	identify strengths and weaknesses of the argument	show understanding, different arguments and views
use language and expression that lacks precision	use accurate expression	use accurate and fluent expression	use proficient, fluent and accurate language

Assessment is central to the learning and teaching process

Assessment is used at every step of the learning and teaching process. The next chapter will explore the various steps of planning, but at this point it is possible to highlight where the discussion so far in this chapter can be used to frame the planning process. It could be suggested that the four main areas where a knowledge of the assessment requirements and procedures can be most beneficial in building the RE learning experience are:

- Planning the learning outcomes.
- Planning for differentiation.
- Planning the tasks for pupils.
- Planning the questions to be asked.

Planning the learning outcomes

How does a teacher know if their lesson/unit of work is pitched appropriately? How do they know that what they are asking of the pupils is helping them to make progress? The answer lies in the use of the various stepping stones (or their equivalent) that have been explored above. If the class is at a particular stage in the learning journey then it is possible to suggest aspects of the different stepping stones to help them make progress. It is here that RE as more than the accumulation of knowledge becomes central to planning, learning and teaching. Consider the Year 7 class who are completing a unit of work on the Founders of the world's religions.[1] In this series of lessons the pupils are asked to retell the story of the Buddha, Muhammad, Jesus, Abraham and Guru Nanak; it might be assumed that progress is made because more knowledge is accumulated, but it is imperative that pupils are challenged to develop skills and concepts within RE. This work could be pitched at a Key Stage 1 level if all pupils are asked to do is retell the stories:

> the most common contributor to low standards in RE is 'low expectations' seen in written tasks which 'lack challenge' [and] a regular diet of completing sentences, pointless drawing or illustration and short 'comprehension' answers to questions in a text book or work-sheet.
>
> (Wintersgill, 2000, p. 2)

In contrast to this, appropriate progress and challenge are enabled when stepping stone language is employed. Using the life of Abraham as an example it is possible to suggest the possible progression that might take place:

The learning outcomes would become framed around where the pupils are and enable them to make progress. For a Year 7 lesson the outcomes might be framed as:

- Pupils will be able to *describe* events from the life of Abraham and their importance for Jews.
- Pupils will be able to link aspects of the life of Abraham with the Jewish belief in the Almighty.
- Pupils will be able to show how the life of Abraham makes a difference to the life of a Jewish person today.

This type of process would be repeated at Key Stage 4 and Key Stage 5 utilising their stepping stones.

Table 4.10 'I can' levels for the life of Abraham

I can retell a religious story.
I can suggest meanings in religious stories.
I can be sensitive to others' experiences and feelings.

I can *describe* some religious beliefs and their importance.
I can understand how some beliefs are shown in people's behaviour.
I can make links between people's values and commitments.

I can describe key beliefs and teachings and link them with other parts of Judaism.
I can give meanings for some stories using religious words.
I can suggest answers to questions based on the experiences of important people.

I can show how important beliefs make a difference to the lives of individuals and communities.
I can make an informed response to other people's values and commitments.

I can explain the principal beliefs and teachings using technical language.
I can explain the experience of inspirational people and relate it to others' lives.

Planning for differentiation

Differentiation is a challenging skill for teachers and sometimes the system in other areas of the curriculum does not allow for proper differentiation to take place. Consider the old 'SATs' system in the primary school where pupils were able to sit an examination that tested them up to a level 5. Towards the end of the SATs system it was possible for a Year 6 pupil to achieve a level 6. However high those levels may have been considered it still placed a cap on pupil progress and achievement. Sometimes this takes place in RE when a task is designed to assess certain Key Stage 3 skills and knowledge, where pupils are not able to access the lower or upper levels of achievement. If assessment of RE is to be accessible to all, and celebrate the achievement of all, then it is necessary to utilise stepping stones to ensure that all pupils are catered for.

In the sample lesson above about the life of Abraham (see Table 4.10) there needs to be opportunity if there is a pupil who is working at a Key Stage 1 level to attempt to retell the story. In this way differentiation is able to meet the needs of this pupil. At the other end of the spectrum, if a child is meeting the upper levels of Key Stage 3 expectations, there needs to be a place for them to go to show progression. It is for this reason that the *RE Review* does not go far enough in stopping the End of Key Stage Statements at Key Stage 3; it is therefore necessary to utilise the 'old' 8-level scale or the GCSE stepping stones to enable a child to make progress. Without this differentiation for the more able in RE, it would be akin to the maths pupil who on mastering two sheets of addition to 10 is given a sheet of the same kind of sums to do again, rather than being helped to take a step up, resulting in a reduction in challenge and motivation.

Planning the tasks for pupils

When a teacher knows the expectations of the pupils they have in the class focusing on the stepping stones, they are able to plan tasks that enable them to assess pupil progress. If a teacher knows that they will be teaching the life of Abraham, and is aware of the assessment requirements before the task is planned they are able to meet the needs of pupils. This is a far better way than designing a task and then seeing how it can be assessed; this method utilises assessment as a bolt-on to the learning and teaching process rather than being central to it.

Different schools will have different assessment requirements. In an ideal world what is being suggested in this chapter is that rather than end-of-unit/year exams (except in terms of external examinations) the assessment of pupils should take place throughout their school experience. While all lessons and work will be appropriately pitched, there will be specific pieces of work that are designed for detailed feedback to enable pupils to evidence progression. These 'assessment tasks' at all Key Stages should be varied in requirement, not just in terms of expectation, but also presentation. This allows pupils to work to their strengths and show their learning in a way that takes account of their needs. This can be directed by the teacher in utilising a mixed diet of submission, or can be led by pupil choice. This enables an assessment profile to be built up across the year and enables all to succeed.

If a school requires end-of-unit/year exams, in terms of Key Stage 4 and 5 these provide opportunities for pupils to practise for examinations by sitting exam-style papers, but this should only be one tool that is used in building up a pupil's assessment profile. In terms of Key Stage 3, it is possible to structure an examination that builds on the principles outlined in this chapter. It is difficult to see how a percentage in a factual recall exam could be linked to progress in anything except pub quiz knowledge. An examination based on stepping stones can become a valuable tool in the learning and teaching process. Consider the following 'examination' question about the temptations of Jesus (the presentation would be much more pupil friendly).

1   In the story of the temptations of Jesus, who tempted Jesus?
2   What do Christians believe is the devil's role in the world?
3   Below are two pictures of the devil (Picture A is of a demonic being; Picture B is of a person taken from the image of Satan in *The Miracle Maker*). Christians believe that the devil is a real being, someone that causes evil and suffering.
　　A   Explain why you feel that thinking of the devil in picture A will help Christians resist any temptation.
　　B   Explain why you feel that thinking of the devil in picture B will help Christians resist any temptation.
　　C   Are there any reasons why pictures A or B will not be a help to Christians when thinking about the devil?
4   List five things that a person might be tempted by in the world today.
5   What can a Christian learn from how Jesus reacted to the temptations, when they try to resist temptations?
6   Christians believe that rather than a horned devil sitting on your shoulder, the devil works through your thoughts and sometimes what other people say to you. How will a Christian try to resist temptation?
7   Write down one thing that you might be tempted to do wrong.
8   What would you do to stop yourself doing this thing?
9   Do you think a Christian would approve of the things you would do? Explain your answer.

For this question there is a mark scheme that does not assess all of their answers but focuses on pupils' abilities rather than their knowledge.

What was really pleasing about this exam was the reaction of the pupils to its style. The exam became a teaching tool in itself.

> I think the exam was beneficial to me because it made me realise how he felt and why people behave as they do.
>
> (Lee)

> I thought the exam was also teaching us what Jesus was really like and what he accomplished. So I think the test was a good idea because now I know stuff I didn't know before.
>
> (Dean)

> After doing the exam I know more about Jesus and what he thought of people.
>
> (Gary)

> … it has put the Christian religion into perspective.
>
> (Ben)

Table 4.11 Mark scheme for The Temptations of Jesus

Level statement	Criteria
Can reflect upon key questions.	Correctly identifies the devil as the source of temptations or lists some temptations faced by people.
Can demonstrate an awareness of explanations given by religions about evil and suffering. Show an ability to reflect on these and offer their own responses.	Identifies correctly the role of the devil in the world, and how the idea of a devil helps people resist temptation (this can be limited to a general statement or one of the pictures). They will also offer some ways in which temptation can be resisted, either for a Christian or for themselves.
Can demonstrate a knowledge of the explanations given by religions about evil and suffering. Show an ability to analyse these and offer their own responses.	Identifies correctly the role of the devil in the world, and how the idea of a devil helps people resist temptation (this should be related to the pictures). They will also offer ways in which temptation can be resisted by Christians and themselves. For Q9 there will be a simple statement of 'they would' or 'they wouldn't'.
Can demonstrate knowledge and understanding of the responses to key questions offered by major religions. Can analyse and compare these and offer their own considered and supported responses.	Identifies correctly the role of the devil in the world, and how the idea of a devil helps people resist temptation (this should be related to the pictures). The reasons why the pictures may not help a Christian will also be discussed. They will also offer ways in which temptation can be resisted by Christians and themselves. In answering Q9 there should be some reflection on how they are or are not related.
Can demonstrate understanding of the responses to key questions offered by different religions. Can evaluate these responses and relate to their own views with supporting evidence.	As previous but in answering Q9 there will be a direct relation (or not) between their own and Christian responses.

Planning the questions to be asked

Questioning is an integral skill for all teachers; it is, however, a skill that needs to be developed. In assessing pupil learning and progress, it is not just the formal questions that are asked in written work that are important but the questions that form the basis of planning and the questions that are asked in the classroom. In assessing pupil progress within lessons there are various tools that can be used to enhance their effectiveness.

Design the questions to be asked prior to the lesson

By utilising the stepping stones outlined above, various levels of questions can be designed to take account of the different abilities within the class. If skills and thought are required rather than, or in addition to, factual answers then it is easier to measure progress. It can be as simple as 'Why do you think Abraham is important to Jewish people today?' If there are pupils who are working at varying levels then the teacher is able to design questions to check their progress as a form of differentiation.

Use targeted questions

While 'hands up' may be appropriate at certain points, the use of targeted questions enables the teacher to check understanding and progress much more effectively, while increasing motivation and attention. With 'hands up' it is possible for pupils to leave it to the other pupils that they know will answer, and therefore hide in the corner. Similarly, in trying to involve other pupils it is possible to demotivate the eager by ignoring their attempts to contribute. There are potential pitfalls to be aware of in using targeted questions, such as putting pupils on the spot, which makes them uncomfortable. This can be overcome through: the use of 'I wonder' questions, which ask pupils to speculate; the choice of specific questions appropriate to ability; the use of 'think, pair share' where all pupils through discussion are able to have answers ready that they have discussed with a partner. The benefits far outweigh the potential pitfalls.

Allow pupils time to think

Teachers, on average, wait 0.9 seconds for an answer to a question (see Rowe, 1974 and Borich, 1996). The concept of 'wait time' is explored by Mary Budd Rowe (1974). Her work analysed the audio recordings of numerous high school Biology lessons (Hurd and Rowe, 1966). Rowe noted that most of the lessons were characterised by fast paced interactions between the teacher and their pupils. She noted that occasionally the pace seemed to be slower, yet the quality and quantity of pupil response was of a higher standard. The thinking time on the slower recordings was between three and five seconds. Rowe suggested that the improved quality of pupil response was linked to a greater wait time between the question and response. This hypothesis was the catalyst for a multitude of studies into the nature and effects of wait time in the classroom. Further research confirmed this; the number of inferences that showed evidence of reasoned arguments also significantly increased when the wait time was not curtailed at one second (Atwood and Rogers, 1973). In addition to this an increase in wait time can raise the number of questions asked by pupils in a lesson. Rowe (1986) found that, as a general rule, pupils ask questions in lessons somewhat infrequently and that such questions are normally to clarify instructions. Research using the extended wait time produced results to the contrary. Students were shown to ask insightful questions that demonstrated a logical process of cognition and higher level thinking (Honea, 1981).

Stahl (1994) explained the reasons why wait time is of such vital importance: 'Information processing involves multiple cognitive tasks that take time. Students must have uninterrupted periods of time to process information; reflect on what has been said, observed or done; and consider their personal response to it' (p. 23).

In 2004, guidance designed to enhance teaching and learning pedagogy within secondary schools was published by the Department for Education (DfE, 2004). The guidelines outlined the benefits of effective questioning: recall, linking new ideas to existing knowledge and enabling students to become independent in the way they think. It went on to explain that certain skills and techniques must be employed in order to ensure that questions have the desired effect. Adequate wait time of at least three seconds is clearly outlined as an essential technique to employ.

It has also been recognised that wait time is a way to raise pupil achievement, especially when questions demand a higher order of thinking, and that regular exposure to questions posed in such a way increases the achievement levels in written cognitive tasks (Muijs and Reynolds, 2001; Wragg and Brown, 2001). Allowing pupils to think about a response may be slightly uncomfortable but it enables more thoughtful answers to be given. In addition, a pupil could ask a friend.

Build explanations through a series of questions

Although the teacher is the fount of all knowledge, it is important within the classroom to utilise pupils in developing answers and explanations. This is an important skill and can seem to be counter intuitive to the teacher's impulse to provide answers. In building an understanding of the life of the Buddha it is possible to begin with some fairly simple questions, but by asking other pupils to add to answers, suggest symbolism or lessons to be learned from specific events, a complete explanation is developed that focuses pupils and shows them what they have learned rather than what the teacher knows.

Q. The Buddha saw a sick man, why do you think this was such a shock for him?

A. He had never seen anyone suffering before.

Q. What other types of suffering did he see?

A. A dead man and an old man.

Q. What did these people teach the Buddha?

A. That suffering exists for everyone.

Q. What Buddhist teaching does this link with?

A. The Four Noble Truths.

Q. If he discovered the first noble truth, why do you think he left the palace?

A. To try to find a way to overcome suffering.

Q. Why do you think that might be important?

This may seem slightly artificial, and to some extent it is, but it is much more effective in a classroom situation where when it is done well it enhances the learning and progress of pupils.

Encourage pupils to ask questions

This is at the heart of the enquiry approach to RE, but it also enables teachers to measure the starting point of pupils and places pupils at the centre of their own learning. This could be as simple as the teacher asking:

What would you like to ask the Buddha about when he saw the four sights?

Or

What would you like to ask a Buddhist about the four sights?

Another type of questioning might be to use a murti of Ganesh as a stimulus and have the class ask questions about the statue. If pupils are asking questions about why he has an elephant's head it suggests a different starting point from if they are exploring the symbolism of the goad and the single tusk. When pupils ask their own questions they tend to be more focused when trying to discover the answers.

There are many other skills to master in questioning, but they are not just to be used to check factual knowledge; rather, used effectively, they can be used as a part of the assessment process in establishing a baseline and then measuring progress.

Summary

Within this chapter the following have been explored:

- The importance of assessment
- The focus on concepts, attitudes, skills and knowledge in assessment
- The process of assessment
- Stepping Stones for progress at Key Stages 3, 4 and 5
- Assessment as central to the learning and teaching process, including:
  - planning the learning outcomes
  - planning for differentiation
  - planning the tasks for pupils
  - planning the questions to be asked.

It is hoped that this chapter has helped the reader to consider the nature of assessment within the secondary school, and also its centrality to the entire process of learning and teaching. Without a knowledge of where the pupils are beginning and what they are trying to achieve, it is impossible to help them make progress. Too many people feel that progress is measured by knowledge; if teachers of RE are to prepare their pupils for more than a pub quiz, or to pass public examinations, it is imperative that they focus on knowledge, concepts, skills and attitudes to enable them to meet the aims of good RE. Assessment thus becomes the beginning, middle and end of the learning process underpinning everything else that takes place.

Note

1   This is not to suggest that this is an appropriate unit of work, rather that it utilises a real-life example.

References

Assessment Reform Group (2002) Assessment for Learning: 10 Principles. Research-based

Atwood, R. and Rogers, V. (1973) An Investigation of the Relationship Among Question Level, Response Level and Lapse Time. *School of Science and Mathematics*, 73, 591–594.

principles to guide classroom practice. Available at: http://assessmentreformgroup.files.wordpress.com/2012/01/10principles_english.pdf (accessed 1 May 2014).

Borich, G. D. (1996) *Effective Teaching Methods*. Columbus, OH: Prentice Hall.

Cheshire East (2013) *Engaging, Encounter, Reasoned Response. Agreed Syllabus for Religious Education for use in Cheshire East Schools*. Cheshire, UK: Cheshire East Council.

Department for Education (DfE) (2004) *Pedagogy and Practice: Teaching and Learning in Secondary Schools* Unit 7: Questioning. London: DfE.

Department for Education (DfE) (2014) *National Curriculum and Assessment from September 2014: Information for Schools*. London: DfE. Available at: https://www.gov.uk/government/uploads/system/uploads/attachment_data/file/300743/NC_assessment_accountability_quals_factsheet_Mar_2014__010414_.pdf (accessed 1 May 2014).

Edexcel (2012) *Specification. Edexcel GCSE Religious Studies*. London: Pearson.

Edexcel (2013) *Specification GCSE Religious Studies*. London: Pearson.

Honea, J. (1981) An Investigation of the Influence of Wait Time on Student Attitudes Toward Selected Social Studies Topics. *Dissertation Abstracts International*, 41(9) 3598-A.

Hurd, P. and Rowe, M., B. (1966) A Study of Small Group Dynamics in the Bscs Laboratory Block Program. *Journal of Research of Science Teaching*, 4(2) 67–73.

Lake, J. (1973) The Influence of Wait Time on the Verbal Dimensions of Student Inquiry Behavior. *Dissertations Abstracts International, 34*, 6476-A.

Mansell, W., James, M. and the Assessment Reform Group (2009) *Assessment in Schools. Fit for Purpose? A Commentary by the Teaching and Learning Research Programme*. London: Economic and Social Research Council, Teaching and Learning Research Programme.

Muijs, D. and Reynolds, D. (2001) *Effective Teaching: Evidence and Practice*. London: Paul Chapman.

National Association of Head Teachers (NAHT) (2014) *Report of the NAHT Commission on Assessment*. Haywards Heath, UK: NAHT

Ofsted (2013) *Religious Education: Realising the Potential*. Manchester, UK: Ofsted.

RE Council of England and Wales (2013) *A Review of Religious Education in England*. London: RE Council.

RE Today (2014) 'A New Way of Assessng with Eight Steps'. In *RE Today* (Spring 2014), pp. 42–45.

Read, G., Rudge, J., Teece, G., and Howarth R. B. (1998) *The Westhill Project RE 5-16. How Do I Teach RE* (2nd edn). Cheltenham, UK: Stanley Thornes.

Rowe, M. B. (1974) Reflection on Wait Time: Some Methodological Questions. *Journal of Research in Science Teaching*, 11(3), 263–279.

Rowe, M. B. (1986) Wait Time: Slowing Down May be a Way of Speeding Up. *Journal of Teacher Education*, 37 (January–February), 43–50.

Rudge, John (1991) *Assessing, Recording and Reporting R.E.* Birmingham, UK: Westhill College.

Rudge, John (2000) 'Assessment in Religious Education'. In A. Wright and A. M. Brandom (Eds), *Learning to Teach Religious Education in the Secondary School. A Companion to School Experience*. London and New York: Routledge (pp. 107–121).

Stahl, Robert (1994) *'Think-Time' and 'Wait-Time' Skillfully in the Classroom.* Bloomington, IN: ERIC Clearinghouse for Social Studies/Social Science Education.

Tobin, K. (1980) The Role of Wait Time in Higher Cognitive Learning. *Review of Educational Research*, 57, 69–95.

Wedell, Katherine (2009) *The Living Difference Evaluation Project Report. How far does the Hampshire Agreed Syllabus 'Living Difference' facilitate effective teaching and successful learning in RE? An exploratory study.* Available at: http://democracy.portsmouth.gov.uk/Data/Standing%20Advisory%20Council%20 for%20Religious%20Education%20(SACRE)/20090325/Agenda/sacre20090325r04.pdf (accessed 1 May 2014).

Wintersgill, B. (2000) Task-setting in Religious Education at Key Stage 3: A Comparison with History and English. *REsource: The Journal of the Professional Council for Religious Education*, 22(3), 10–17.

Wragg, E. C. and Brown, G. (2001) *Questioning in the Secondary School*. London and New York: Routledge.

Chapter 5

Planning and RE

The importance of planning

The old adage, if a person fails to prepare they are preparing to fail, is nowhere more applicable than within teaching. Planning is the bedrock of effective learning and teaching. Ofsted (2010) have noted that this is particularly true within RE where effective learning is a result of 'planning where learning was sequenced in such a way as to help pupils develop their critical skills systematically' (p. 22); and a major factor

> in successful innovation included detailed planning linked to rigorous self-evaluation; clear systems, timescales and criteria for evaluating impact that drew on detailed data and information from a wide range of stakeholders [and] carefully designed professional development programmes for staff to implement the new approaches.
>
> (p. 31)

This makes it evident that effective planning is not just about the individual lesson, but the curriculum as a whole and the approaches to learning taken. Significantly, Ofsted (2013) highlighted ineffective RE as often lacking coherence in planning and suggested that all schools 'improve lesson planning so that teaching has a clear and straightforward focus on what pupils need to learn and engages their interest' (p. 7). In designing the overall RE curriculum it is also important to utilise a coherent approach that is not subject to a teacher's whims or interests, but rather focuses on the underlying purpose of RE and the learning which will achieve that purpose. As such, a 'spiral' curriculum, which returns to the important purposes and the various concepts, will help pupils see the links between what they are learning, what they have learnt and their own experiences.

There are various facets to planning. Bassett, Bowler and Newton suggest that:

> In order to achieve an effectively planned lesson, a number of factors must be considered. These include pupil prior learning, the ways that pupils learn, the requirements of the curriculum, appropriate methods of teaching to suit the needs of all learners and resources. In addition to these points, lesson evaluation informs the planning process.
>
> (2013, p. 99)

The purpose of this chapter is to tie the various elements of RE teaching already explored in previous chapters, and build upon them to explore how effective lessons and curricula can be planned.

Stages of planning

There are various stages involved in planning:

*   Long term
*   Medium term
*   Short term.

Each of these stages is crucial to go through to ensure a coherent and effective RE curriculum within the school.

Long-term planning

Long-term planning begins with the Agreed Syllabus, or the examination specification, which outlines the content to be addressed. Some Agreed Syllabi (for example Hampshire, Portsmouth and Southampton Councils, 2011) include detailed approaches and methods for the teaching of RE, and Ofsted have suggested this is good practice:

> Some recent agreed syllabuses and their accompanying guidance provided examples of good practice in using enquiry, but these were not sufficiently widespread and it was taking time for them to have an impact. While some new syllabuses aspired towards an enquiry-based approach, they lacked the necessary detail and guidance. Some examples of planning that accompanied agreed syllabuses were poor, often compounding teachers' confusion about RE.
>
> (2013, p. 13)

However, this is not crucial to effective planning if the teacher/department has sufficient vision for the subject to ensure a progressive and cohesive curriculum. Indeed, it could be said that too prescriptive an approach by Agreed Syllabi might limit innovation within RE. What is important, however, is that RE teachers have access to others to help develop their vision for RE. As Academies may select their own approach to RE, linking with other schools will provide opportunities for robust RE.

The Agreed Syllabus/Exam Specification will usually provide a list of content to be covered within a particular Key Stage; it is then in the hands of the teacher to navigate any aspects of choice and how the content is to be organised. The syllabus might require the teaching of Christianity and two other world religions, in which case the RE department should consider the religions that are represented within the school and the local community to determine the breadth of study undertaken. On the other hand the syllabus might require the teaching of all six major world religions at Key Stage 3 (Oldham, 2014), which might translate into a curriculum overview that looks similar to Table 5.1:

Table 5.1 Key stage 3 curriculum plan (systematic)

Year 7	Year 8	Year 9
	Autumn term	
Judaism	Islam	Buddhism
	Spring term	
Christianity	Islam	Sikhism
	Summer term	
Christianity	Hinduism	Secular worldview

Alternatively, the use of themes or areas of enquiry might be utilised to organise the curriculum. The following table utilises Oldham's Agreed Syllabus Programme of Study Requirements (2014):

Table 5.2 Key Stage 3 curriculum plan (thematic)

Year 7	Year 8	Year 9
	Autumn term	
Beliefs and concepts	Expressions of spirituality	Rights and responsibilities
	Spring term	
Beliefs and concepts	Expressions of spirituality	Religion and science Global issues
	Summer term	
Authority	Ethics and relationships	Interfaith dialogue

This type of planning could be termed 'extreme' long-term planning as it lacks any type of detail and provides little beyond the framework against which the curriculum will be built. There is, however, some degree of judgement and justification that has been used for the organisation of the curriculum at this early stage. For example, it could be argued that beliefs and concepts in religions underpin all other expressions of religious belief and spirituality; as such, it is imperative to lay this grounding in Year 7; or that more time is given to Islam because of the communities in and around Oldham.

The development of these frameworks into long-term plans might look something akin to Table 5.3. It should be noted that for the purpose of this book this is a slightly caricatured and simplistic view of the curriculum, as some elements lend themselves to a systematic exploration, while others would be better explored thematically:

Table 5.3 Year 7 long-term planning

Year 7
Autumn term (12 lessons)
Judaism • Beliefs and concepts: G-d, truth, the world, human life, and life after death • Authority: different sources of authority and how they inform Jewish people's lives • Expressions of spirituality • Ethics and relationships • Religion and science • Rights and responsibilities • Global issues
Spring term (12 lessons)
Christianity • Beliefs and concepts: God, truth, the world, human life, and life after death • Authority: different sources of authority and how they inform Christians' lives • Expressions of spirituality
Summer term (11 lessons)
Christianity • Ethics and relationships • Religion and science • Rights and responsibilities • Global issues

Moving on from this stage of planning, it is possible to begin to suggest topics and concepts for each lesson. In exploring the beliefs that are central to Christianity, and following on from a small unit of work on the nature of belief and God in different religious and non-religious worldviews, the possible breakdown of lessons in a focus on the 'Life of Jesus' might be explored. It was felt that a study of the Life of Jesus independent of other things would be more beneficial and coherent. For example, the Nativity story is studied at this point as the beginning (?) of Jesus's life.

As the basis of all belief for Christians, the life of Jesus and its importance is the pre-eminent topic in any study of Christianity.

> In our general introduction to the study of Christianity as a world religion the rather formidable complexity and diversity of the religion was stressed and illustrated. Without in any way underestimating the significance of this complexity, we can also recognise that the one unifying factor among this diversity is the figure of Jesus.
>
> (Read, Rudge and Howarth, 1986, pp. 5–7)

The person of Jesus has been selected because from him all other Christian belief and practice spring. If pupils are to understand Christian belief and why Christians behave the way they do, then an understanding of the life of Jesus and its importance is imperative. In this unit, however, it goes far beyond a history lesson – it is the Christ of faith that is studied as he impacts on the Jesus of history. Why is his life important today and what impact does it have on Christians? Therefore learning objectives for the unit should begin to be formulated as they will inform the next stage of planning (see Chapter 4). For a unit around the life of Jesus in Year 7 these might include being able to:

• Communicate confidently a sound knowledge of the life of Jesus.

- Recognise the significance of Jesus and his life within the Christian tradition.
- Understand the impact of the life of Jesus and his teachings on the life of a Christian.
- Recognise and discuss the importance of the suffering and death of Christ.
- Understand the impact of the life of Jesus and his teachings on the life of a non-Christian.

With these constructed it is possible to outline different topics from the Life of Jesus:

Table 5.4 Christianity unit of work plan

Lesson	Topic
Lessons 1 and 2	Nativity*
Lesson 3	Baptism
Lesson 4	Temptations
Lesson 5	Parables
Lesson 6	Sermon on the Mount*
Lesson 7	Miracles
Lesson 8	What did people think about Jesus?*
Lesson 9	The Last Supper
Lesson 10	The last week of Jesus's life
Lesson 11	Why is the death of Jesus important to Christians?*
Lesson 12	The Resurrection

Note: *Denotes a topic chosen for assessment.

Underlying this selection of topics is the important focus on concept development. The three general concepts chosen as the drivers for the unit of work are Forgiveness, Treatment of others and Commitment. These would lead into the central conceptual themes of Christianity of atonement, agape and discipleship. The various concepts could be explicitly developed in the various topics outlined below.

Table 5.5 Concept development in Life of Jesus unit of work

Focus within unit	Forgiveness	Treatment of others	Commitment
Nativity	✔	✔	✔
Baptism	✔		✔
Temptation	✔	✔	✔
Parables	✔	✔	✔
Sermon on the Mount	✔	✔	✔
Miracles	✔	✔	✔
Last Supper	✔	✔	✔
What did people think?	✔	✔	✔
Last week of Jesus's life	✔	✔	✔
Resurrection	✔	✔	

Medium-term planning

At this stage thought should be given to the learning activities that will form the bulk of each lesson. An awareness of which topics will be formally assessed will also help shape the various activities that will contribute to the formative assessment procedures and tasks. Consideration should be given to the general ability of the students, and objectives refined accordingly so that the unit is appropriately focused and allows all pupils to make progress. In beginning to construct the various approaches to teaching and learning in each lesson, the teacher is able to ensure that there is conceptual development rather than just going from one topic to the next, and that different activities are used so that there is not an over reliance on a particular approach. It is possible to break down the various lessons to see a balance:

Table 5.6 Learning activities in Life of Jesus unit of work

Title	Main activity	Learning activity
Nativity	Children's storybook about Nativity and Christmas	Investigation, Art, Literacy, Creativity, Enquiry, Empathy, Analysis
Baptism	Diary entry from witness's perspective	Empathy, Expression, Art
Temptations	Series of questions based on *The Miracle Maker* extract	Watching, Offering conclusions, Analysis, Art
Parables	Reflective activity on The Good Samaritan and *Another Day in Paradise*. Social action project	Listening to music, Reading, Empathy, Thinking, Analysis, Team work
Sermon on the Mount	Card sort and implications for individual Christians	Card sort, Enquiry, Analysis
Miracles	Drama activity	Reading, Drama, Analysis, Reasoning
Last Supper	Analysis of artwork and scripture	Art, Analysis
What did people think?	Exploration of the two sides of Jesus – from the perspective of disciples and his 'enemies'	Enquiry, Analysis
The Last Week of Jesus's Life	*The Lamb of God* video, newspaper account from different viewpoints	Watching, Note taking, newspaper, Empathy
How do you feel …?	Utilisation of the various perspectives on Jesus's death	Empathy
Resurrection	What happened on the first Easter morning? Comparison of the various Biblical accounts	Enquiry
Throughout		Brainstorm and discussion

It is important that the activities chosen are both varied and engaging; various points to consider will be developed further in Chapter 7.

What a medium-term plan looks like depends on the school and the amount of detail that is put into it. Two examples are given below. The first (Table 5.7) is a sketching out of the general progress that the teacher hopes the pupils will make and various topics and concepts to be covered. Table 5.8 is far more detailed and is designed for use by non-specialists. These are not set in stone and should be under constant adaptation – teachers must not be afraid to change their approach if things are not working.

Table 5.7 Medium-term plan exemplar

Lesson no.	LEARNING OBJECTIVES (to be refined in Lesson Plan) Pupils should:	POSSIBLE TEACHING ACTIVITIES Teachers should plan to:	LEARNING OUTCOMES AND ASSESSMENT OPPORTUNITIES Pupils should demonstrate that they can:	POINTS TO NOTE (e.g.: key points, 'difficult' topics, health & safety, spiritual, moral, social and cultural elements, literacy, numeracy, EAL ICT)
1	• Learn to understand what types of belief there are and where they are on the spectrum • Aim to have a knowledge and understanding of the kind of God that Christians worship	• Help pupils understand key words • Write a job spec for the Christian God	• Know and use the key words: omniscient, omnipotent, omnibenevolent, omnipresent • Explain the Christian concept of God and why he can be seen as an object of worship	• Spiritual • Literacy – key words
2	• Aim to have a knowledge of the key points of the design argument for the existence of God.Learn to understand how the natural world assists people in believing in God	• Examine pieces of art/poetry/photography that convey a 'sense of wonder' • Organise small groups of pupils to discuss them and also talk about any moments when they have experienced a feeling of awe when surrounded by nature • Include analysis of scripture	• Explain the design argument for the existence of God in detail. Use evidence to support their description of the argument. Outline the strengths of the argument	• Spirituality • Enquiry
3				

Table 5.8 Scheme of work exemplar

Key issue or question	Concepts/ key words	Possible teaching strategies	Assessment	Resources	Duration
What are three important teachings of Guru Nanak and why are they important to Sikhs? Look at the three important teachings, how would you apply them to your life? Objectives: Communicate confidently a sound knowledge of the life of Guru Nanak. Recognise the significance of Guru Nanak and his life within the Sikh tradition.	Guru Sikh Learner Teacher Master God Founder Example God Equality Teaching Obituary	As a starter, ask pupils to write two sentences to change the world. Collect and share these to compile ten sentences to change the world from the whole class. Pupils should then be introduced to the life of Guru Nanak. They will try to examine the symbolism of a passage that teaches about the role and importance of Nanak. They will then watch animated world faiths and take notes about the different sections of the life of Guru Nanak. Pupils should prepare an obituary for Guru Nanak. In this should be described the events of his life. After this, pupils should attempt the following two questions: What are three important teachings of Guru Nanak and why are they important to Sikhs? Look at the three important teachings, how would you apply them to your life?	Life of Guru Nanak and his importance	Nanak teacher sheet; Nanak pupil sheet; Animated world faiths video; Obituary blank	Two lessons
What beliefs about God can we find in the stories of the ten Gurus? How do your beliefs about God compare or contrast with the Sikh beliefs about God? Objectives: Understand the impact of teachings of the ten Gurus on the life of a Sikh. Have a knowledge and understanding of the Sikh belief in God and his place and involvement in Sikh history and the lives of Sikhs today.	Guru Successor God Unity	Pupils should be briefly introduced to the lives of the nine successors to Guru Nanak. Using the internet (www.sikhs.org/10gurus.htm) pupils should find one teaching about God by each of the Gurus. They should then summarise the teachings of Sikhism about God in one paragraph. Pupils should reflect on these beliefs based on their own views.	AT2	Ten Gurus sheet Ten Gurus chart	One to two lessons

Note: *Denotes a topic chosen for assessment.

The medium-term plan is often called a Scheme of Work; in contrast to the short-term planning it may not explore issues such as differentiation. Medium-term planning is more of a road map, which is built upon by short-term planning.

Short-term Planning

The short-term planning, or lesson plan, is the bespoke document for the individual class and pupils therein. While the medium-term plan may provide the ideas and the general ideas, lesson planning is the document and the process by which the teacher is able to help pupils progress, and is focused around their needs. Ofsted (2013) noted that sometimes an undue burden is placed on teachers by the demands of planning:

> Many teachers used a generic form for lesson planning. While seeking consistency is understandable, many of the plans seen required teachers to refer to a large number of cross-curricular and whole-school issues. Because teachers were more anxious to complete the plan than concentrate on securing high-quality RE learning, the focus on RE was often sacrificed. One lesson plan seen, for example, required teachers to provide information on: reading and literacy strategies, including key words and literacy objectives; numeracy skills; links to pupils' spiritual, moral, social and cultural development; higher-order Bloom's questions; and progress indicators.
>
> (2013, p. 11)

In response to this, the process of lesson planning will focus on the core process of planning for learning and teaching while recognising that other requirements may be placed on teachers.

What is the pupils' prior learning?

Lesson planning begins with the question: 'What is the pupils' prior learning?' This question refers to the progress the class, and individual pupils, have made with regard to concepts, attitudes, skills and knowledge prior to this lesson. Asking this question will help provide a pitch and starting point for the lesson. If the pupils are at a certain level of understanding then the pitch of the lesson should be at that level and seek to help pupils progress from that point (see Chapter 4). It is also about knowledge; where did the pupils get up to in the previous lesson and what did they understand? As well as being based on individual class data, the answers to the question of prior learning begin with the teacher's evaluation of individual and class learning from the previous lesson. In this way, progression is shown not just within lessons but across lessons, which is crucial to effective RE. Including concepts and skills as a focus, in addition to knowledge, enables progress to be shown even if a new topic is explored. Planning must always start from the assessment of the learning in the previous lesson.

What progress do I want the pupils to have made by the end of the lesson?

From this point, the teacher is able to move on to the question: 'What progress do I want the pupils to have made by the end of the lesson?' This is when learning objectives and outcomes specific to the lesson are designed. Bassett et al. outline what is meant by these terms: 'Learning objectives link to the observable outcomes of the lesson, i.e. to what pupils are expected to be able to do. Specifying the expected learning outcomes for the lesson will help you clarify your learning objectives' (2013, p. 107).

These learning outcomes should be accessible to the pupils within the class, though some may be accessible to the pupils at the lower or upper ends of the ability range in the classroom. Utilising the stepping stones outlined in Chapter 4 will help the teacher set appropriate learning outcomes. Clear learning outcomes will enable the teacher to assess and evaluate the lesson effectively. In many schools the teacher will also be expected to share these with the pupils at the beginning of the lesson, and to review them at the end of the lesson. These must therefore be absolutely clear not only to the teacher, but also to the pupils. In some school contexts you will find them expressed as WALT (we are learning to), and tasks will be expressed in terms of WILF (what I'm looking for.) This language can be seen to enable pupils to take 'ownership' of their learning. In some lesson plans, assessment opportunities are put by the side of learning outcomes (see Table 5.9) to remind the teacher that it is these against which pupils are making progress.

Table 5.9 Assessment of learning outcomes

Learning outcomes:	Assessment opportunities:
What learners should be able to demonstrate during/by the end of the lesson	*What evidence will be gathered to confirm progress against the learning outcomes?*
1	
2	
3	

What learning activities should be used to help pupils make progress against the learning outcomes?

The learning outcomes will be composed of elements of knowledge, skills, concepts and attitudes (not necessarily at the same time) and it is against these that learning and teaching activities must be developed to enable the pupils to make progress.

The most common structure to a lesson is that of a starter, main activity and plenary. This enables a learning journey to be undertaken. In essence, the starter establishes a baseline of what pupils understand, a teaching input takes place and then the plenary assesses the progress that is made, and signposts that progress to pupils, observers and teachers alike. There is much in this process that lends itself to help pupils make and recognise progress. The starter is key to beginning learning as soon as pupils enter the classroom; some schools utilise a 'bell task', which pupils are engaged with on entry before all are settled for the main starter. However, to rigidly adhere to this process is to miss the importance of stages of learning. It is possible to 'chunk' lessons: in essence to utilise different learning activities for short periods of time to keep the pupils focused and the pace of the lesson moving. The teacher should be constantly aware of the progress that pupils are making in order to cut short or extend the periods of time available for particular activities. As such, mini plenaries throughout the lesson are often needed, to check progress before moving on. These might be evidenced in a lesson plan to maintain the focus on progress:

Table 5.10 Lesson plan activity grid

Learner Activity: What are the learners doing? What is strategy for learning? What is the differentiation for the activity (enable/extend)?	Teacher activity: Including class management, organisation, teaching points and questions	Learning outcomes addressed:	Assessment opportunities: Assessment of learning; How will evidence be recorded?

Returning to the four-stage process of learning outlined in Chapter 2, in beginning anew it is important for learning to go through the Discovery phase. This phase enables pupils to recognise their prior learning and make bridges to their own experiences. One example of this Discovery approach is exemplified through the beginning of an exploration of the Design argument at Key Stage 5. A series of pictures is shown to the pupils and they are to outline how the picture could be used to show evidence for the existence of God.

Table 5.11 Design argument Discovery task

Object	How it could be used as evidence
Planet	
Baby	
Grove of trees	
Eye	
Pocket watch	
Seascape	
Storm	

The expectation would be that pupils will have explored Paley's watch before, and be able to make logical arguments for the others surrounding beauty, the carbon cycle, working together, God's power and other elements of design within their own experience. Over a series of activities/lessons pupils would explore the design argument in depth, referring back to their own 'simplistic' arguments. This same activity would be used as a plenary to the learning (not necessarily in the same lesson):

Table 5.12 Design argument review task

Object	How it could be used as evidence	Aspect of design
Planet		
Baby		
Grove of trees		
Eye		
Pocket watch		
Seascape		
Storm		

The pupils would then be expected to utilise language such as the aesthetic argument, the anthropic principle, and so on, to show their progress.

Specific examples of effective learning and teaching activities will be explored in Chapter 7, but at this point it is sufficient to suggest that the activities undertaken should be focused on pupil progress and enabling the pupils to be central to the learning process. At this stage of planning it is also important for the teacher to ask themselves:

- What is the learning environment for this lesson?
- What resources are available and needed?

How can progress be made by all pupils?

Central to learning and teaching is the belief that all pupils can make progress in RE. The teacher should ensure that the lesson is accessible to all. The class is likely to include some pupils from groups who are classified as being at risk of underachieving, special educational needs pupils, gifted and talented pupils, or new arrivals. Planning must take account of the diversity of needs to be found in the classroom. Even in an apparently homogenous group, there will be those who are relatively more, or less able, or who have particular physical needs (e.g. visual or hearing impairment) that may affect their learning. The teacher may also need to consider the range of learning styles represented in the class, and to ensure that the activities reflect their needs. The whole area of inclusion and RE will be explored in Chapter 6, but at this point it is important to recognise within planning what steps will be taken to differentiate, and also to assess, the progress that has been made by all pupils. It is for this reason that assessment for learning includes activities such as questioning, mini whiteboards, red and green cards, answering of questions in books, snowballing, and so on to ensure that all pupils are able to evidence their progress. In measuring this progress it is important to review some of the principles of assessment outlined in Chapter 4.

What progress has been made by pupils?

The lesson does not end when the bell goes; rather, effective teachers take the opportunity to evaluate their lessons and the progress made by pupils. Early in a teacher's career it is important that this evaluation is done formally and written down. More experienced teachers may find that this process becomes a natural part of the learning and teaching process and may do it informally. Usually the questions that should be asked by the teacher include:

- Were the learning outcomes achieved?
- If not, how is this to be addressed?
- Were there any particular individuals/groups who made good/poor progress?
- What pupil (individual and/or group) learning targets could be set for next lesson?
- How successful was the learning and teaching approach?
- What was the impact of teaching on pupil learning?
- What changes are needed for future sessions?
- Were learners working appropriately?

As a whole, answers to these questions will inform the starting point and approaches of the next lesson. It is possible at this point in planning that the teacher could focus on individuals' progress. The pupils chosen to focus on in the next lesson could be drawn from the assessment of the previous lesson. The teacher may wish to ensure that pupil x participates in discussion, that pupil y completes more work than last time or that pupil z extends her ability to use religious terminology appropriately. It should be possible to track between mark books/lists and lesson plans to see why particular pupils are being 'targeted' on particular occasions, and the progress that is being made. It should also be evident from your 'target-setting' in comments on the pupils' work. 'Targeting' in this way also aids assessment. By taking a pupil from the 'top', 'middle' and 'bottom' ability ranges, the teacher can sample the understanding of the class by targeted questioning, and use this to inform future planning. These targeted pupils can be rotated each week.

There are other elements to lesson planning, but these are the areas that will best ensure that pupils are making progress within and across lessons:
In the midst of all of this, however, it is important to recognise that:

> The lesson plan is a plan, not a straitjacket, for learning. When they are beginning their career most teachers do follow their lesson plans closely, but in time they learn to develop the skill and confidence to adapt that which is taught in response to pupil reactions. This may mean moving the lesson in a different direction from the anticipated in response to issues that arise in the classroom. A good rule of thumb for the beginning teacher is to stick to the lesson plan as closely as possible, but be aware that there is no need to panic if you find yourself deviating from it.
>
> (Backus, 2000, p. 67)

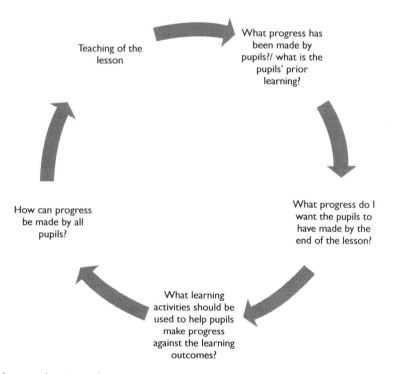

Figure 5.1 Lesson-planning cycle

Planning is supposed to support rather than hinder effective learning and teaching in RE.

Summary

This chapter has explored the importance of planning and the process of planning. It has taken a step-by-step approach to the process of planning, beginning with the Agreed Syllabus/Specification through the curriculum framework in a school, to the medium-term plans and then to lesson planning itself. Just as assessment should be regarded as a professional skill, it is imperative that planning is seen to be such. It is integral to effective learning and teaching and helps to ensure that pupils are able to make progress. This chapter should be used in conjunction with Chapter 4 on assessment; the two go hand in hand. Reference should also be made to the following two chapters on inclusion and RE and the effective teaching of RE. These all go together to ensure that RE is excellent and that pupils make progress.

References

Backus, Jo (2000) 'Developing Programmes of Study' in A. Wright and A. M. Brandom (Eds), *Learning to Teach Religious Education in the Secondary School. A Companion to School Experience.* London: Routledge (pp. 49–70).

Bassett, Sophy, Bowler, Mark and Newton, Angela (2013) 'Schemes of work, units of work and lesson planning'. In S. Capel, M. Leask and T. Turner (Eds.) *Learning to Teach in the Secondary School: A Companion to School Experience* (6th edn). Abingdon, UK: Routledge (pp. 99–111).

Hampshire, Portsmouth and Southampton Councils (2011) *Living Difference Revised: the Agreed Syllabus for Hampshire, Portsmouth and Southampton.* Winchester, UK: Hampshire County Council.

Ofsted (2010) *Transforming RE.* Manchester, UK: Ofsted.

Ofsted (2013) *Religious Education: Realising the Potential.* Manchester, UK: Ofsted.

Oldham (2014) *Thinking, Enquiry, Creativity, Response. Oldham Religious Education Syllabus 2014–2019.* Oldham, UK: Oldham Council.

RE Council of England and Wales (2013) *A Review of Religious Education in England.* London: RE Council.

Read, Garth, Rudge, John and Howarth, Roger (1986) *The Westhill Project RE5-16. Teacher's Manual.* London: Mary Glasgow Publications.

Chapter 6

Inclusion and RE

The importance of inclusion

Inclusion in schools, and in particular in RE, is multi-faceted. Ofsted (2000, p. 4) outlined those groups of people who might find themselves excluded in the education system and therefore part of the schools' efforts at inclusion:

- girls and boys;
- minority ethnic and faith groups, Travellers, asylum seekers and refugees;
- pupils who need support to learn English as an additional language (EAL);
- pupils with special educational needs, gifted and talented pupils;
- children 'looked after' by the local authority;
- other children, such as sick children, young carers, those children from families under stress, pregnant school girls and teenage mothers, and
- any pupils who are at risk of disaffection and exclusion.

The inclusion agenda is therefore very broad in scope, and the question could be asked as to why inclusion is so important. Perhaps because it is indicative of the possibility that everybody is from a group that can be marginalised, stereotyped and excluded. Most, if not all, people are a minority in some way, shape or form.

It takes a teacher to look beyond the bare facts of a child's record or circumstances and focus on the individual. Individuals are able to break out of the bonds of what was expected by someone in a particular social situation because of expectations that never place any cap on their success or ambition. A contrasting experience is one highlighted by Malcolm X in his autobiography:

> I happened to be alone in the classroom with Mr Ostrowski, my English teacher. He was a tall, rather reddish white man and he had a thick moustache. I had gotten some of my best marks under him, and he had always made me feel that he liked me. I know that he probably meant well in what he happened to advise me that day. I doubt that he meant any harm. It was just in his nature as an American white man. He told me, 'Malcolm, you ought to be thinking about a career. Have you been giving it thought?' The truth is, I hadn't. I had never figured out why I told him, 'Well, yes, sir, I've been thinking I'd like to be a lawyer' …
>
> Mr Ostrowski looked surprised, I remember, and leaned back in his chair and clasped his hands behind his head. He kind of half-smiled and said, 'Malcolm, one of life's first needs is for us to be realistic. Don't misunderstand me, now. We all here like you, you know that. But you've got to be realistic about being a n***er. A lawyer – that's no realistic goal for a n***er. You need to think about something you can be. You're good with your hands – making things. Everybody admires your carpentry shop work. Why don't you plan on carpentry? People like you as a person – you'd get all kind of work.
>
> (Malcolm X, 1968, pp. 117–118)

Interestingly, Mr Ostrowski did not adopt that mind-set with all of his pupils:

> What made it really begin to disturb me was Mr Ostrowski's advice to others in my class –all of them white. Most of them had told him they were planning to become farmers. But those who wanted to strike out on their own, to try something new, he had encouraged. Some, mostly girls, wanted to be teachers. A few wanted other professions, such as one boy who wanted to become a county agent; another, a veterinarian; and one girl wanted to be a nurse. They all reported that Mr Ostrowski had encouraged what they had wanted.
>
> (Malcolm X, 1968, p. 118)

Teachers should ask themselves the question: 'Do we sometimes unconsciously place barriers in the way of our pupils' achievement and development?' It may not be said in the same way and with such stark bluntness but it may be implicit through actions and expectations. It can be suggested that there are two areas where teachers and schools can have an impact in their dealings with children from minority backgrounds (whatever that minority might be):

1 Achievement.
2 A feeling that they belong, can contribute to, and are a part of the school and the wider society.

The experiences and backgrounds of individual groups may differ, but the barriers they encounter can be overcome in a number of ways that can be applied to all and help all pupils make progress and feel a valuable part of the education system. While focusing on the cultural aspects of inclusion, it is possible to suggest that all people who find themselves on the margins of society and schools may withdraw themselves from that particular environment as not meeting their needs.

Inclusion and achievement

Some of the underachievement can be related to socioeconomic circumstances, but not all. It has been argued that 'continuing underachievement endangers social cohesion and leaves personal and economic potential unrealised' (DfES, 2003, p. 4). It is not just the individual that is affected by the underachievement, but society as a whole. If an 'inclusive' society where everybody is respected and valued for who they are and where every person has the opportunity to reach their potential is to be realised then various things need to be put into place to help everybody have such opportunities. The DfES (2003, pp. 4–5) identified various characteristics of schools that successfully raise the achievement of all pupils; the ones that apply to individual RE teachers include:

* *High expectations*: Every pupil is expected and encouraged to achieve their potential by teachers and parents. These expectations are underpinned by the practical use of data to monitor the achievement of particular groups of pupils to pinpoint and tackle underperformance.
* *Effective teaching and learning*: Lessons are planned and delivered as effectively as possible, with support provided for bilingual pupils, and teachers are able to reflect the cultures and identities of the communities represented in the school in their lessons (this will be explored in Chapter 7).
* *Ethos of respect, with a clear approach to racism and bad behaviour*: There is a strong ethos and culture of mutual respect where pupils are able to have their voices heard. There are clear and consistent approaches to bad behaviour, bullying and tackling racism across the whole school with a focus on prevention (this will underpin all of RE).
* *Parental involvement*: Parents and the wider community are positively encouraged to play a full part in the life and development of the school.

The argument of Chapter 4 established the necessity of ensuring all tasks and lessons are appropriately pitched with high expectations of progress to be made by pupils. Within RE, tasks should be linked to assessment criteria by which teachers and pupils would be clear about what was being assessed. Tasks would be focused and valuable, and high expectations would be established. Beyond the establishment of tasks for the class as a whole, it is important to establish realistic and high expectations for those with special educational needs and those who are considered to be gifted and talented within RE. There is a variety of ways that differentiation can be undertaken to enable these individual children to make progress and to be challenged significantly.

High expectations: special educational needs

Within all secondary schools there is a range of abilities to be found; some of these children have been identified as having special educational needs (SEN), needs that the teacher should be aware of and differentiate work and tasks accordingly to help the pupil make progress. This sounds rather straightforward, but is, in fact, one of the most difficult tasks that a teacher of RE will undertake in day-to-day teaching. The question is how to provide work that is challenging without being patronising to pupils who may already feel different. There are many suggestions that could be made about the variety of tools a teacher could use; some are more useful than others. Differentiation for these pupils needs to be focused on RE rather than, as sometimes happens, their literacy skills or keeping the pupils occupied and quiet.

Much current good SEN practice works well at the level of improving basic skills of reading and writing. This is an important instrumental aim of RE and a way in which RE might contribute to the general aims of education. The general aim of literacy cannot, however, be an intrinsic aim of RE and it is certainly not a basis for compulsory RE for students with special educational needs, particularly those with general learning difficulties. If RE had nothing more to offer than practising to read and write, surely these students would be better on intensive literacy courses with specialist teachers (Orchard, 2001, p. 4).

There are, however, elements of SEN practice that lack challenge and test comprehension. The use of cloze exercises is fairly common, but they have to be designed very carefully if they are not to be comprehension activities at best, or guessing games at worst. These may be activities that concentrate the pupil but are dubious in the RE educational value. Sentence starters may be much more effective, or a card sort, matching exercise or a labelling of particular objects. These would enable pupils to 'identify places, people and things that are religious' (old level 1) rather than be involved in a literacy skill activity.

Good RE differentiation focuses on skills and concepts and progression within these. QCA (2001, p. 6) suggested ways in which RE is crucial to pupils with SEN:

In particular, RE offers pupils with learning difficulties opportunities to:

* develop their self-confidence and awareness
* understand the world they live in as individuals and as members of groups
* bring their own experiences and understanding of life into the classroom
* develop positive attitudes towards others, respecting their beliefs and experience
* reflect on and consider their own values and those of others
* deal with issues that form the basis for personal choices and behaviour.

In response to these opportunities, pupils can make progress in RE:

* by moving from a personal to a wider perspective
* by increasing their knowledge of religious beliefs, practices and experiences
* through developing understanding of the meaning of stories, symbols, events and pictures
* through developing and communicating their individual responses to a range of views.

It is evident that these opportunities are taken from the 'lower levels' of the then attainment levels. This suggests the importance of utilising the stepping stones when designing tasks for SEN pupils. If the class is working at a level 5 but 'Anne' is working at level 2, the way to differentiate the work is by providing learning outcomes that enable Anne to access level 2 and 3. However, sometimes Anne's literacy may be low, but her verbal RE ability is much higher; at this point thought must be given to the information that she is given and what she is asked to do with that information to show progress. This might include:

- The utilisation of images to illustrate points rather than an over reliance on text.
- Key words being highlighted.
- Sequencing activities.
- True or false tasks.
- Thinking skills activities.

Some teachers had the opinion that thinking skills activities were best designed for the more able, and they are incredibly useful for that group of pupils; but they are equally accessible for all pupils, including those with SEN. Vivienne Baumfield (2002) offered a number of different ways that thinking skills could be implemented within RE. The following activities have their inspiration from Baumfield's work but show how they can be applied in many different circumstances.

Fortune lines

One of the key features of RE is the use of stories (see Chapter 7); but a retelling of stories while perhaps being accessible to all does not necessarily engage pupils with the story, and may not leave a lasting understanding or help them understand the concepts therein. The use of a fortune line is an alternative that should engage all pupils. Baumfield suggests that they allow 'the pupil to make connection between the beliefs and teaching of religion and the possible experiences and emotions of the founders and followers' (2002, p. 42). The following example utilises the events of the Last Week of Jesus's life.

INSTRUCTIONS

- Choose twelve events from the events of the last week of Jesus's life.

Table 6.1 Blank events of the last week of Jesus's life for a fortune line

	Event
A	
B	
C	
D	
E	
F	
G	
H	
I	
J	
K	
L	

- You will be given a copy of a fortune line graph similar to below:

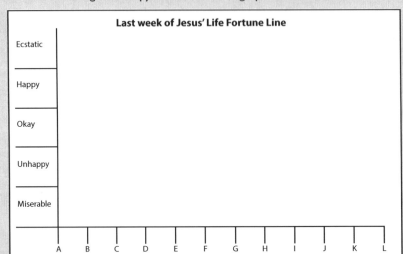

Figure 6.1 Fortune line of the Last Week of Jesus's Life

- Plot how you think Jesus would have felt at each of these points (this should be a line diagram).
- Using a different coloured pen plot how you think Peter would have felt at each of these points.

REFLECTION

- Why did you choose these events?
- Are there any better words to describe how Peter and Jesus might have felt? Write them down next to the statements.
- For each of the twelve events explain why you think Jesus and Peter might have felt this way.
- Did anyone in the class disagree with you? Why do you think this is?
- Why do you think Jesus and Peter would have felt differently about the same events? Explain your answer using examples.

An alternative version provides the events for the pupils; the descriptions could be illustrated to help those who are less confident readers.

INSTRUCTIONS

You will be given a copy of a fortune line for the Last Week of Jesus's life, similar to below.

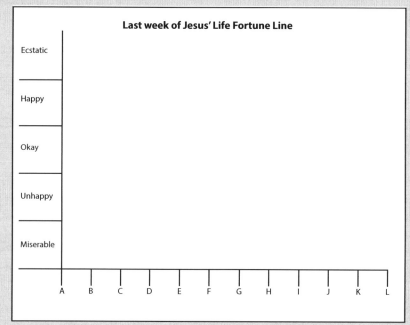

Figure 6.2 Fortune line of the Last Week of Jesus's Life (2)

• For each of the events of the Last Week of Jesus's life, plot how you think Jesus would have felt at each of these points (this should be a line diagram).

• Using a different coloured pen plot how you think Peter would have felt at each of these points.

LIST OF EVENTS

A   Everyone travels to Jerusalem to celebrate the Passover. People tore off the branches of trees to lay at Jesus's feet.

B   Jesus shares the Passover meal with his disciples. He shares the bread and wine.

C   He announces that one of his disciples will betray him.

D   Peter says that he will die for Jesus.

E   Jesus says that Peter will deny knowing him.

F   Jesus prays in the Garden of Gethsemane.

G   The disciples fall asleep.

H   Jesus is arrested.

I   Jesus is condemned to death.

J   Peter denies knowing Jesus.

K   Jesus is crucified.
L   Jesus is risen.

REFLECTION

- Are there any better words to describe how Peter and Jesus might have felt? Write them down next to the statements.
- For each of the twelve events explain why you think Jesus and Peter might have felt this way.
- Did anyone in the class disagree with you? Why do you think this is?
- Why do you think Jesus and Peter would have felt differently about the same events? Explain your answer using examples.

In both of these examples, pupils engage with the story but the activities can be seen to be at least an old level 4 where pupils 'ask questions and suggest answers from their own and others' experiences of important people from religion'.

Similar and different

A similar and different activity is good as a starter or plenary to a topic (see Figure 6.3). It enables pupils to begin to make links between religious beliefs, practices and people. These can be completed on various themes and topics. For example, the festivals of light (Christmas, Diwali and Hanukah) can be compared, or at Key Stage 5 the Leibnizian, Thomist and Kalam Cosmological arguments can be explored. It is an ideal way to check understanding.

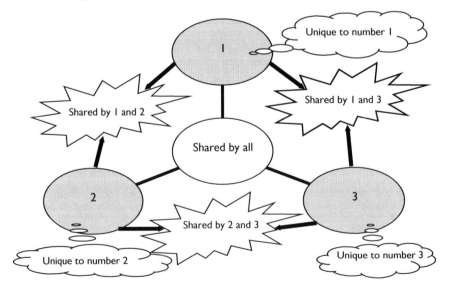

Figure 6.3 Similar and different template

Case study I

A special school that utilises a skills-based curriculum in RE:

Table 6.2 Skills-based approach in a special school

Skill	Definition	Example

Investigate	• asking relevant questions.
	• knowing how to use different sources as a way of gathering information.
	• knowing what constitutes evidence for understanding religion(s).
		• Y10 prepared questions about the Jewish religion to ask the Rabbi:
		  who is the most important Jewish leader in history?
		  how many years have gone in the Jewish calendar, and what year is it now?

Interpret	• the ability to draw meaning from artefacts, works of art, poetry and symbolism. • the ability to interpret religious language. • the ability to suggest meaning of religious texts.	• interpreting: the meaning of the Buddhist shrine by exploring the objects.
Reflect	• the ability to reflect on feelings, relationships, experience, ultimate questions, beliefs and practices.	• reflecting: Buddhist assembly where pupils shared objects, feelings and art.
Empathise	• the ability to consider the thoughts, feelings, experiences, attitudes, beliefs and values of others. • developing the power of imagination to identify feelings such as love, wonder, forgiveness and sorrow. • the ability to see the world through the eyes of others, and to see issues from their point of view.	• using a doll to facilitate role play about the death of a child in the story of the Buddha and Krisha Gotami. A child held the doll and said: 'She's dead. I'll have to let her go'.
Analyse	• distinguishing between belief, opinion and fact. • distinguishing the features of different religions.	• identifying differences and similarities in holy books.
Synthesise	• linking together significant features of religion together in a coherent pattern. • connecting different aspects of life into a meaningful whole.	• linking features of celebration on Festival days – eating and partying.

Skill	Definition	Example
Express	• the ability to explain concepts, rituals and practices. • the ability to identify and articulate matters of deep concern and to respond to religious issues through a variety of means.	• expressing own prayer ritual to class.
Apply	• making the association between religions and individual, community, national and international life. • identifying key religious values and their interplay with secular ones.	• applying harvest beliefs to the community.
Evaluate	• the ability to debate issues of religious significance with reference to evidence and argument. • weighing up the respective claims of self-interest, consideration for others, religious teaching and individual conscience.	• finding and ranking the ten Commandments, personal response.

These and other thinking skills activities will engage, enthuse and help pupils of all abilities make progress if they are used appropriately, and assessment is seen to go beyond traditional written methods. Consider the Key Stage 4 lesson about abortion laws in the UK. It is possible that pupils are asked to complete a series of questions that show their understanding of what the law says. It is possible to differentiate this activity by chunking the amount of text and having questions immediately below the text where the answer can be found. For all pupils, whether SEN or not, this is a comprehension activity. The better activity engages pupils in a discussion about the changes they would make to the abortion laws. They are still engaging with the material but in a way that requires them to develop arguments utilising supporting evidence.

It is therefore evident that in differentiating for SEN pupils, it is possible to create lessons and resources that will benefit and engage all. This is very evident when QCA's guidance from 2001 (p. 8) is read:

Staff can make RE more accessible by focusing on the senses. They can improve access by:

- using sensory materials and resources through sight, touch, sound, taste or smell, for example, music, tactile artefacts, plants in a sensory garden
- giving pupils first-hand experiences, for example, visitors to school, visits to religious buildings, involvement in festivals
- organising a range of activities to give personal experiences, for example, dance, drama, visits to a range of environments
- helping pupils to understand and appreciate their world and its diversity.

Staff can also improve access by:

- using a range of resources, for example, interactive/sensory stimuli, information and communication technology (ICT), to increase pupils' knowledge of religions and the elements in them
- using specialist aids and equipment
- providing support from adults or other pupils when necessary, while allowing pupils the space, time and freedom to develop skills for themselves
- adapting tasks or environments and providing alternative activities where necessary, for example, tactile story books, puppets, role play, presenting work as a painting instead of writing
- being aware of the pace at which pupils work and of the physical and mental effort required
- balancing consistency and challenge, according to individual needs.

It is important to return to the idea that differentiation can focus around skills and concepts. This is evident in the example of two special schools. While recognising that the special schools teach pupils with severe SEN, it is possible to learn from their experiences as the pupils therein are able to make progress within RE.

Case study 2

Case study 2 is described by Ofsted (2012). In this a school explores 'a new form of creative RE for children with special needs that valued their powerful life experiences rather than a traditional deficit model based on their limited literacy' (p. 2). The curriculum topics are arranged around five keys:

- *Key 1: Connection – what links can be made with pupils' own lives?* The story of Diwali begins with the idea that sometimes we go away but it is good to be back home. We establish the link between pupils' experiences of respite care, their daily journeys home, and the story of Rama returning from exile.
- *Key 2: Knowledge – what is at the burning core of the faith?* By cutting out peripheral information, and going straight to the core, we teach what is central and powerful.
- *Key 3: Senses – what sensory elements are in the religion?* It is important to include sensory experiences that are linked to RE.
- *Key 4: Symbols – what are the symbols that are the most accessible?*
- *Key 5: Values – what are the values in the religion that speak to us?* This Key makes values central. So, for example, a unit on the life of the Buddha might use a Jataka story to focus on the importance of patience. This links with pupils needing to wait for help with their work, or waiting for the school transport to arrive.

(adapted and edited from Ofsted, 2012)

This second example could be seen to draw on the idea of conceptual development and the pyramid outlined in Chapter 2 (Figure 2.1).

- *Stage 1*: Concepts that are within the children's own experience.
- *Stage 2*: Concepts common to all human experience.
- *Stage 3*: Concepts common among different religions.
- *Stage 4*: Concepts particular to a specific religion.

What can be seen from both of these examples is that both approaches would be successful in any classroom. Indeed, in the next chapter on effective learning and teaching in RE, some of the approaches outlined here form a central part for every learner.

Differentiation for pupils with SEN is not a bolt on to the RE experience, rather it can be central to the classroom experience. The tools that will help SEN pupils learn will help all pupils; it should be ensured however that there are opportunities to make progress at an appropriate and challenging level. Although differentiation has been discussed extensively here it is impossible to explore all of the different suggested methods; the focus should be on the appropriate progress, pitch and experiences and then moving on from there to designing activities for pupils.

High expectations: gifted and talented pupils

It is necessary for the teacher to ask questions of themselves about whether asking able pupils to complete relatively low-level tasks is of benefit. For example, an old level 2/3 skill is to retell a religious story, yet the practice of doing this continues well into the secondary school. Pupils need to know the story and if asked will probably want to complete the storyboard, but do teachers meet the needs of the more able as they are failed to be stretched to the extent of their ability? Lat Blaylock has discussed what giftedness might look like in RE:

> Giftedness in RE might be distinguished from high attainment scoring in other subjects. For example, the child who is gifted with regard to RE might show particular skills of insight, application and discernment, making sense and drawing meaning from religious symbols, metaphors and sacred writing at a high level.
>
> (2001, pp. 14–15)

It might be argued that a gifted child in RE is one working naturally beyond the expectations of their year group. There is a difference between able and gifted, but for the sake of this discussion the two could be treated in a similar way. Mirroring differentiation for pupils with SEN, the stepping stones of progress within RE should be used to stretch the more able. There are many ways of constructing higher level tasks, but they work best when rooted in the work pupils have been completing, so that they are not separate from the rest of the class. What should never happen is that pupils are asked to complete work of a similar level as extension work. Pupils can easily become bored and it is at this point they have the potential to become disengaged and potentially disruptive.

Potential activities will utilise engaging tasks to help pupils make progress. This may involve helping pupils make progress against the higher levels in the stepping stones, but it might also include utilising skills and activities that could be seen to be more suited to the key stage above where the pupil is. For Key Stage 5 pupils this might include utilising what might be considered 'university' level reading. At every stage of RE there is also the opportunity to have pupils engage in extension reading to more fully explore topics, arguments and the application of religious beliefs and practices. An example at Key Stage 3 might be the utilisation of fantasy literature. For example pupils might explore the writings of JRR Tolkien and CS Lewis who were Christians and close friends. They shared ideas and some beliefs. Both wrote Creation Myths – Tolkien's can be found in *The Silmarillion* and Lewis's in *The Magician's Nephew*. Both of these have music as the creative force, but both share Christian undertones. The task could be to read each of these excerpts and highlight the sections that have echoes of Christianity. For example in *The Silmarillion* Melkor introduces discordant notes into the perfect creation – this would be reminiscent of Satan. Another example might be the analysis of chapter 9 of *The Rise of Nine* by Pittacus Lore as an accurate reflection of the various avatars of Lord Vishnu. Other activities might include the reading of specific articles on topics or concepts. These could extend knowledge or help pupils apply the knowledge, skills and concepts they have explored in class. One example came on 3 May 2006 when *The Independent* published an article entitled 'Is Pope poised to sanction condoms? Vatican's rethink on ban signals historic move to cut the spread of Aids'. This article could have been used to extend pupils' thinking about attitudes to contraception and the religious beliefs that underpin them. Questions that could be used as a focus for progress and challenge include:

1   Make a list of the beliefs that underpin the Roman Catholic Church's teaching on contraception.
2   Make a list of the arguments for and against the sanctioning of the use of condoms in Roman Catholicism.
3   Based on the evidence you have collected do you think the Roman Catholic Church *will* sanction the use of condoms?
4   Based on the evidence you have collected do you think the Roman Catholic Church *should* sanction the use of condoms?
5   Why could there be a difference between your answers to 2 and 3?

At Key Stage 5 there are various events and articles that could be used to stimulate thought and argument. In the field of philosophy and ethics there are philosophy series that could stimulate thought and discussion. One example is the volume *Ender's Game and Philosophy: Genocide is Child's Play* (Wittkower and Rush, 2013), in which various topics that could stimulate extension work and the application of learning include:

•   'What would Saint Thomas Aquinas do?' – this chapter being an analysis of double effect in the novel, and by extension the film.
•   'Weaponized Virtue' – this chapter begins a discussion of Aristotle's Virtue Ethics.

These types of writings are not limited to discussion of philosophy and ethics, as was shown earlier in discussion of Vishnu in *The Rise of Nine*, so an analysis of the Christian belief of agape could be explored through the role of amity and abnegation in the *Divergent* trilogy written by Veronica Roth. Indeed, there are many articles that link popular culture with aspects of religion. 'How far is Aslan a reflection of Christian beliefs about Jesus?' can be accessed at many different levels from Year 7 all the way up to PhD. The role of popular culture will be explored in greater detail in the next chapter.

A different type of activity for the gifted and talented might include them engaging in research and comparing it with what has been taught and explored in class. Below is an activity based on the Ten Commandments.

Ten Commandments activity

These commandments have been said to underpin most people's moral codes and the laws of the land.

TASKS

1   Which laws of the UK are underpinned by the Ten Commandments? Explain your answer.
2   Why do you think these commandments have become law in the UK?

> 3   Design a questionnaire designed to investigate a person's moral code and the impact of the Ten Commandments on it.
> 4   From what they have said, do they think the Ten Commandments have had an impact on their morals?
> 5   Does their moral code seem at odds with this conclusion? Why do you think this is?
> 6   Do you agree that the Ten Commandments underpin most people's moral codes and the laws of the land? Explain your answer.

This task is designed to assess whether pupils are working at Level 8 of the RE Attainment Levels. The particular statements that have relevance for this task are:

* I can analyse the influence of religious beliefs and teachings on individuals, communities and society.
* I can account for the influence of religious beliefs and teachings on individuals, communities and society.
* I can use appropriate evidence and examples in all of these.

A further extension technique might be found in the use of thinking skills. In addition to the ones outlined earlier, 'Mysteries' and 'Fact or Opinion' will be explored briefly here.

Mysteries

A mystery presents pupils with a number of statements that outline a particular scenario.

HOW WILL ANGUS VOTE?

A Bill to repeal the ban on hunting has come before Parliament. Angus is an MP who has been given a free vote (this means that no matter what his party says he can vote how he wants). Examine the evidence below and then come to a conclusion about how Angus will vote.

* Angus is 34 years old.
* Angus is a lay Methodist preacher.
* He believes he should be a good steward as it teaches in the Bible.
* His Mum and Dad are farmers in the Lake District.
* He is a Labour MP.
* He is a vegetarian.
* He boycotts products created by Huntingdon Life Sciences.
* He is very close to his parents.
* His wife's parents run stables in Surrey.
* His constituency contains a lot of people who participate in hunts.
* He went on one hunt when he was 14.

You are not to decide for him. Rather, weigh up all the evidence and decide how he will vote.

His vote will be ....

The reasons I think this are ....

This task is designed to assess whether pupils are working at higher levels. The particular statements that have relevance for this task are:

- I can analyse the influence of religious beliefs and teachings on individuals, communities and society.
- I can account for the influence of religious beliefs and teachings on individuals, communities and society.
- I can use appropriate evidence and examples in all of these.

WILL JESUS BE PUT TO DEATH?

Read the following evidence.

- Jesus healed a man on the Sabbath.
- His followers believe him to be the Messiah, the Son of God.
- He healed a paralysed man by saying that his sins were forgiven.
- He associates with tax collectors and unclean women.
- He has said that Pharisees are hypocrites.
- His mother and father are called Mary and Joseph.
- He entered Jerusalem and people were laying palm leaves at his feet, saying 'Hosanna to the Son of David' (meaning the King of the Jews).
- He did great miracles such as feeding 5,000 people with five loaves and two fishes.
- He says that the religious leaders are corrupt and do things for glory rather than trying to please God.
- He threw the tables over in the Temple telling everyone they were dirtying his father's house.
- He drank water with a Samaritan.

Question

Will Jesus be put to death?

Why?

These activities enable pupils to think beyond that which is expected by normal class activities. They enable discussion and the justification of a viewpoint.

Fact or Opinion

People sometimes say that there are no right or wrong answers when doing thinking skills activities. This is misleading. The key is to emphasise what constitutes good judgement when faced with ambiguous or complex situations. The conclusions may be uncertain and subject to interpretation but the processes of good thinking in RE can be demonstrated.

(Baumfield, 2002, p. 33)

A 'Fact or Opinion' activity involves pupils classifying statements and justifying their choices.

THE QUR'AN – FACT OR OPINION

Below are twelve statements about the Qur'an. In pairs you should decide if they are Fact or Opinion. Write down 'Fact' or 'Opinion' next to each statement. When you have completed this, explain your reasons for choosing to label them as 'Fact' or 'Opinion'.

1   The Qur'an was revealed to Muhammad by the Angel Jibra'il.
2   The Qur'an is made up of 114 suras.
3   The Qur'an has had a huge impact on my life. It has made me believe that there is no god but Allah, and Muhammad is his prophet.
4   The Qur'an was just made up by Muhammad and his friends.
5   Muhammad received the message of the Qur'an while on Mount Hira.
6   Muhammad's friends wrote the Qur'an down after he died.
7   Muslims believe that the Qur'an contains the words of Allah.
8   The message of the Qur'an affects people's lives.
9   Translating the Qur'an out of the original Arabic makes it lose its message.
10   The Qur'an should be treated with respect.
11   The Qur'an proves that Allah exists and that Muhammad is his prophet.
12   People can think what they want about the Qur'an, it's just a book.

- How did you decide something was a fact?
- What made something an opinion?
- Which statements did you find the easiest and the hardest to decide about?
- Would Muslims agree or disagree with your findings? Explain your answer.
- Why do we have to deal with a lot of opinion in RE?

As with the differentiated activities outlined for use with SEN pupils, it is possible to see how the utilisation of such techniques might benefit all pupils, but care should be taken to ensure that all pupils are challenged at a level that is appropriate to them.

Inclusion and integration

A feeling that they belong, can contribute to, and are a part of the school and the wider society

Pupils who find themselves isolated and perhaps as a result of this isolation the victims of bullying, whether racist or not, are at risk of creating greater social problems:

> children who feel ostracised at school are at greater risk of joining gangs or engaging in maladaptive behaviour. Students who feel pain or threat, particularly over something out of their direct control, often come to experience frustration and resentment towards the social groups they blame for their feelings.
>
> (Davies, 2008, p. 42)

The early life of Malcolm X is an extreme example of this; victimisation by the 'white' authorities led him to tar everyone with the same brush and this is, to some extent, what happens for people in school who are ostracised – they react against the group that they see as responsible, leading to the disintegration of society.

Teachers, and in particular RE teachers, have a crucial role to play in the prevention of ostracism. This will mainly be done in the classroom, through the discussions that take place and the attitudes that are shown and are allowed to flourish. This does not mean ignoring any divergent opinions or attitudes that arise, but confronting them. In effect, teachers become 'border crossers: able to listen critically to the voices of their students as well as able to critique the language in which histories of conflict was expressed' (Davies, 2008, p. 93). Shutting a child down, or sweeping their comments under the carpet, does little but retain the status quo or exacerbate the situation. A multiculturalism underscored by cultural relativism may result in a society of shared values, expressed in specific cultural forms. But this leads to a certain fragility of social interaction related to a fear of upsetting others and so the unwillingness to talk about, say, gender issues, will give rise to 'walls of silence'.

There needs to be an open and frank discussion about issues. Engaging in discussion will require extra work on the part of RE teachers, to learn about the various cultures, religions and ethnicities that make up the school. Part of this can be done through research, but the vast majority will be done through interaction with the pupils, their parents and perhaps the wider communities.

Two such examples from a secondary school teacher evidence how pupils from a variety of minority backgrounds can feel as though their culture, religion or ethnicity was valued and accepted:

In the second school I worked in there was a large Muslim population. For a number of years the school had allowed an annual Iftaar meal. This allowed Muslims to practise their religion communally and as a part of the larger school community. However, it also had the potential for there to a be an 'us' and 'them' mentality. The Iftaar meal was opened up for any to attend, although there were small numbers of non-Muslims who attended, there was a large number of staff. The pupils were enthused to see their religious customs supported by teachers. In turn teachers were able to interact with Muslims beyond the classroom, and learn a little bit more about the faith of pupils.

As a child my only interaction with Jehovah's Witnesses was a girl who didn't come into assemblies. As a teacher I first encountered Sarah when she came to visit me to complain about a colleague who was her RE teacher. Whenever she raised any question he would treat her dismissively. An example was her disagreeing with him when he taught that Christians believe Jesus was crucified on a cross – Jehovah's Witnesses believe he was crucified on a tree. Rather than treating her concern openly, he dismissed it as an irrelevance. The next year, I had the opportunity to teach Sarah, and learn more about her beliefs as we talked and I communicated with her parents. The following year, I was invited to attend her baptism – which I did. The warmth which I received from Sarah's family and religious community was a reflection that I accepted their religion as important in their lives, and did not make them feel an oddity for so doing.

This raises suggestions that can be implemented by teachers in teaching minority pupils to help them feel that they belong, can contribute to, and are a part of the school and the wider society. In speaking of community cohesion, the DCSF (2007, p. 10) suggested that meaningful contact between individuals from different groups breaks down stereotypes and prejudice; RE teachers can play an important role in this as they seek to involve members of different faith communities. The definition of meaningful included:

1   Conversations to go beyond surface friendliness.
2   People to exchange personal information or talk about each other's differences and identities.
3   People share a common goal or interest.
4   Where contacts are sustained long-term, with one-off or chance meetings unlikely to make much difference.

While it is important to build understanding on commonalities, the differences enrich and make any contact 'honest'. While children of all ages have similar interests and goals, which can form the basis of interaction, it is important to recognise and explore differences, and allow questions to form and be discussed.

Summary

This chapter has focused on aspects of inclusion. It is impossible to cover aspects of inclusion in one chapter, thus the focus initially was on the importance of inclusion and the positive benefits this can bring. The discussion then explored differentiation in terms of pupils who have been identified as having special educational needs and those who are gifted and talented. Throughout both of these sections it was important to note that the setting of appropriate and challenging learning outcomes was at the forefront of differentiation, and the removal of potential barriers. This might include using pictures for those with low literacy levels, which inevitably will help others. The suggestions made would raise the quality of the RE experience for all pupils. In building a school that is inclusive and celebrates diversity, the last part of the chapter focused on the role RE can play in helping establish such a culture and the reasons that might be important. In being inclusive, teaching can meet one of the stated aims that it gives all students equal access to Religious Education and provides enjoyment and success.

References

Baumfield, V. (2002) *Thinking Through Religious Education*. Cambridge: Chris Kington Publishing.

Blaylock, Lat (2001) Teaching RE to Gifted, Talented and Exceptionally Able Pupils, *Resource*, *23*(3), 14–19.

Davies, L. (2008) *Educating Against Extremism*. Stoke on Trent, UK: Trentham Books.

DCSF (2007) *Guidance on the Duty to Promote Community Cohesion*. Nottingham, UK: DCSF.

DfES (2003) *Aiming High: Raising the Achievement of Minority Ethnic Pupils*. London: DfES.

Lewis, C. S. (2009 [1955]) *The Chronicles of Narnia Book 1, The Magician's Nephew*. New York, NY: Harper Collins.

Lore, Pittacus (2013) *The Rise of Nine (Lorien Legacies 3)*. London: Penguin.

Ofsted (2000) *Evaluating Educational Inclusion: Guidance for Inspectors and Schools*. London: Ofsted.

Ofsted (2012) *An Inclusive Approach to Religious Education in a Special School: Little Heath School*. Manchester, UK: Ofsted.

Orchard, Janet (2001) *Raising the Standard. Flying the Flag. Challenging Activities for all in RE at Key Stage 3*. London: National Society.

QCA (2001) *Planning, Teaching and Assessing the Curriculum for Pupils with Learning Difficulties*. Religious Education. London: QCA.

Tolkien, J. R. R. (1992 [1977]) *The Silmarillion*. London: Grafton.

Wittkower D., and Rush, L. (Eds) (2013) *Ender's Game and Philosophy: Genocide is Child's Play*. Chicago, IL: Open Court.

X, Malcolm (1968) *Autobiography of Malcolm X*. London: Penguin.

Part III

Teaching and learning in Religious Education

Chapter 7

Effective teaching and learning in RE

Chapter outline

The importance of the teacher

Pupils are at the centre of the learning and teaching process

- Bridge 1: with children's own experiences
- Bridge 2: with prior learning
- Bridge 3: between beliefs, practices and religions
- Bridge 4: with local, national and international communities
- Bridge 5: with other subjects

Focus on religions and religious understanding

Use a diversity of activities

- Enquiry-based learning
- Storytelling

It was initially envisaged that this chapter would be three; with one focusing on effective teaching at Key Stage 3, a second on key Stage 4 and a final on Key Stage 5. This would have created an artificial separation between the Key Stages, as it is the argument of this book that effective learning and teaching in RE is characterised by similar approaches across all age ranges. This is not to suggest that a pupil's experience in schools at the moment is the same across the different phases. Rather that they should be, with appropriate challenge for each age group. It is not unusual to see very different approaches between Key Stage 3 and the examination phases, it is as though what was considered effective lower down the school would not be suitable in preparing pupils for exams. One newly qualified teacher reported: 'I have freedom at Key Stage 3 to engage in active learning, but it has been made clear to me that a lecture style approach is what is expected at Key Stage 5'. Emma Davies (2013) has completed some research about the use of 'the arts' in the secondary RE classroom. Her results support the view that learning approaches to RE change across the school:

Table 7.1 Data on the use of the arts in RE lessons

	I lesson in every 4	I lesson in every 3	I lesson in every 2	every lesson	N/A	total	Average rating
Key stage 1	7.41% 2	0% 0	14.81% 4	3.70% 1	74.07% 20	27	2.57
Key stage 2	8.33% 2	0% 0	16.67% 4	0% 0	75% 18	24	2.33
Key stage 3	16.67% 10	21.67% 13	36.67% 22	25% 15	0% 0	60 .	2.70
Key stage 4	26.23% 16	24.59% 15	28.51% 18	18.03% 11	1.64% 1	61	2.40
Key stage 5	42.22% 19	8.89% 4	15.56% 7	4.44% 2	28.89% 13	45	1.75

If the data from the 'every lesson' column in [Table 7.1] is compared, there is a marked difference between colleagues applying the arts in key stage 3 (25%), key stage 4 (18.03%) and a much lower proportion at key stage 5 (4.44%). While this may be due to the perceived constraints in the exam curriculum … the disparity between key stages is interesting as the teaching styles employed clearly shifts. Is the content covered linked to exam boards that dissimilar to the syllabi suggested by SACRE and skills outlined in A Review of Religious Education in England (Religious Education Council of England and Wales, 2013) that the arts are not applicable in these later years? Or is there a perception that the use of the arts is not a valid approach to exam based models of teaching?

(Davies, 2013, pp. 37–38)

This is wrong; first, because effective teaching and learning can be effective for the exams, but also because the purpose of RE at Key Stage 4 and 5 is not solely about examination success. It is against this background that the principles outlined thus far in this book will be brought together in this chapter to suggest approaches to learning and teaching in RE that are effective in every phase of learning in striving to achieve the purposes of RE.

The importance of the teacher

The importance of the teacher cannot be overemphasised within the RE classroom:

> Great teachers bring colour, tone, and meaning to that which we read and have experienced. From them we catch something; we sense their commitment, feel their excitement, are lifted by their dedication, refreshed through their insights, encouraged through their struggles, and strengthened by [them].
>
> (McConkie, 1975, p. 51)

There is much that an enthusiastic teacher brings to the classroom. A passion for their subject and the purposes thereof does much to help to stimulate interest and enjoyment in Religious Education within the pupils. Enthusiasm is infectious and to be taught by someone who is passionate about their subject is a gift. As referred to in Chapter 1, the attitude of respect for all is crucial for an RE teacher and as pupils see the importance that the teacher attaches to the things that are being learned they in turn will begin to mirror some of those attitudes.

However, the converse can also be true; Barbara Wintersgill has highlighted this concern:

> How religious and secular philosophies are presented to pupils is critical, if the elusive qualities of 'tolerance and respect' are to be developed, and in this context the method of teaching is as important as the content, if not more so. *Religious traditions in the hands of an unsympathetic teacher, even if a certain amount of subject knowledge has been acquired, is likely to have the reverse effect.* Too often, inappropriate teaching methods foster ridicule, disinterestedness and early dismissal of the claims of religions to be taken seriously.
>
> (Wintersgill, 1993, p. 44 emphasis added)

RE can be taught very badly, and it can have a detrimental effect on pupils' view of the importance of religion in people's lives. Pupils find that a teacher's negative view of a religion, even if it is just presented in a boring way, passes on to the class (Moulin, 2011, p. 320).They do not discover the richness and diversity that is had in the lives of religious believers; rather they encounter a subject that has no relevance to them or their lives. It could be argued that such a utopian view of RE teachers is impossible when 'in nearly half of the schools that responded [to a NATRE survey], at least one in 10, and in some cases one in five, RE lessons were taught by teachers whose main time was spent in another curriculum area' (Ofsted, 2013, p. 18). This is a legitimate concern, but one that stereotypes the non-specialist RE teacher. Indeed, Jackson et al. (2010) reported on interviews with such teachers:

> With regard to expertise of staff, many non-specialists were found to be teaching religious education. Of these, most interviewed or observed were highly committed to the subject, and had clear views on resources and pedagogy. Nevertheless, many heads of department and coordinators recognised that they had to meet the needs of non-specialists, often teaching their main subject as well, and only teaching religious education temporarily; this had an impact on the choice of materials. In order to help non-specialists in one secondary school, a published scheme for Key Stage 3 was purchased plus the exam board's approved textbook for GCSE.
>
> (p. 9)

An inappropriate approach to RE is not limited to non-specialists and it is important to note that teachers of any background and expertise can become enthusiastic as they understand the nature, purpose and importance of RE. What is important is that this enthusiasm is built by teaching but also by constant learning and the recognition that teachers do not know everything. It is far better for a teacher to acknowledge the limits of their experience and knowledge:

'Miss, what religion was the Good Samaritan?'

'Well, he was middle eastern, so I expect he was a Muslim.'

RE's minimum standard for accurate information about religions is 100%. Teachers should be ashamed if they … make it up as they go along.

(Blaylock, nd, p. 1)

This approach of teachers is not limited to teachers who have a faith or those who are agnostic or atheist. A teacher's first concern in the RE classroom is to the pupils and their learning. The teacher's religious or non-religious identity should not limit or inhibit pupil learning. It is at the choice of the teacher whether they share aspects of their beliefs, but at no point should they become confessional in the way that the views are presented. One teacher has identified how it is possible to have beliefs while not declaring them:

> As I look at the students whom I teach, how does believing that they are children of God affect me? It does not mean that I tell them so as exemplified in a recent interview for a potential teacher [when] she was asked the question, 'What would you say if someone asked you the relevance of Jesus for today?'. She answered, 'I would tell them that Jesus had died for them, and that he was willing to help them in their lives'. This candidate suggested a confessional approach that saw the teacher's role to nurture in, or even to convert to, a specific religion. I would be opposed to such an approach in the school classroom, rather I suggest that a teacher's beliefs could legitimately affect their approach to, and interaction with, the pupils. As such the belief that I teach pupils who are children of God suggests that I treat each child with respect. As I believe that 'God has created [every person] with a mind capable of instruction' it is my responsibility as a teacher to find a way to teach that touches the innate desire to learn in every child. This has become known as 'personalised learning' or reflecting the imperative that 'Every Child Matters'. It means to me that every child is worthwhile and that I should do my very best to speak to them as children of God (i.e. not in a mean or coarse way) and try to help each child reach his/her potential.
>
> (Holt, 2012, p. 186)

Whatever beliefs are held by the teacher, they should enhance the teaching of RE and the ability of pupils to fulfil its purposes. In conducting some research about the representation of religion, Daniel Moulin found that some teachers strive to give a fair representation while others lacked knowledge and the ability to recognise different viewpoints (2011, p. 320). This second finding is worrying.

Pupils are at the centre of the learning and teaching process

Pupils are at the centre of all learning and teaching within RE. Throughout this book the focus has been on enabling pupils to make progress; the constructivist approach to RE suggested in Chapter 2 begins and ends with the child's own experiences, the pedagogies chosen reflect a desire to select approaches that are appropriate to help the pupils learn. The aims of RE are phrased in such a way as to ensure that the pupil's RE experience and outcomes are at the heart of everything that is done. The centrality of pupils in RE can be best summarised by the use of bridges: all learning provides children with bridges.

Bridge 1: with children's own experiences

The constructivist approach to RE and the conceptual pyramid outlined in Chapter 2 highlighted the importance of beginning with concepts within the pupils' own experiences to help them learn and make progress most effectively. If pupils are able to make links with their own experiences they will be able to engage in deeper learning and see the relevance of what they are learning. RE is not about cultures and practices that are alien; rather it is about beliefs and practices of people who are, or will be, in pupils' everyday experiences. If it is possible to make links with pupils' own experiences then RE can begin with a shared concern or life experience and then explore differences.

At the core, this bridge is finding concepts that can be explored such as celebrating or sacrifice. Over time, various religious concepts become a part of a child's own experience and the sections of the pyramid intermingle. However, it might be as pupils struggle to interpret and understand the various concepts and beliefs that the teacher needs to find things that are within the pupils' conceptual framework of understanding that they might not realise they know. For example, in exploring the cosmological argument use could be made of two things that are either explicitly in the pupils' own experience, or are a bridge between their experience and the cosmological argument.

---

1 In the pupils' own experience: putting a pair of socks on

For those involved in the philosophy of religion (and many more besides) the question of the origin and nature of the universe and why it requires an explanation is important. The cosmological argument begins with any event in your life and works backwards. For the sake of argument let's begin with me putting my socks on this morning! What on earth does me putting my socks on this morning have to do with an argument for the existence of God?

> *Question 1:* What was the cause of me putting on my socks this morning?
> *Answer:* I'd just had a shower.
> *Question 2:* What was the cause of me having a shower?
> *Answer:* I'd just got up and I was a bit smelly.
> *Question 3:* Why had I got up?
> *Question 4:* Continue this line of questioning for a while.
> *Answer:*
>
> ...
>
> *Question:* Why was I born?
> *Answer:* Because my mummy and daddy loved each other very much ...
> *Question:* What was the cause of my mummy and daddy being born?
> *Answer:* Because their mummies and daddies loved each other very much ...
> Where will this line of questioning ultimately lead?

This is the general premise of the cosmological argument. To put it in equation form:

- P1: Everything has a cause.
- P2: The universe is something.
- C: The Universe has a cause (which is God).

Whatever event we begin with, those who accept the cosmological argument will always take it back to the first cause.

---

2 A bridge between pupils' experience and the cosmological argument: a television advert

There is a car advert that ends with a flag being unfurled. The cause of this is a car on a platform dropping, which in turn was caused by innumerable car parts moving, which was all caused by a single nut rolling. The question is asked: 'What caused the flag to unfurl?' This can lead in to a discussion of the cosmological argument. In this activity pupils may not have encountered the particular advertisement before but the medium is within their experience and they are able to utilise its message in the specific situation as guided by the teacher or their own reasoning.

These bridges between pupils' own experiences and their learning are crucial to help understanding. In some cases, specific examples and concepts are within their immediate recall, but on occasion the teacher has to take the initiative in providing a bridge. An example could be used within the use of popular culture.

At this point it is important to provide the warning that any activity overused can become stale and lead to pupils switching off rather than engaging, and so all tasks should be used judiciously:

> The young people generally appreciated these resources for learning and many found them more interesting and memorable than books, suggesting 'you learn better from TV because it's made interesting', 'you remember it better' (Year 7 pupils Moorside). … There were some detracting voices, however. Increasing familiarity with these forms of learning can mean that they lack the power to engage that they once had. A Flintmead student admitted that there was a danger of 'drifting off' when DVDs were being used in lessons.
>
> (Jackson et al., 2010, p. 162)

The effective use of popular culture references is important but should not dominate, and they should be used only when they can be explicitly linked to religious concepts and teachings otherwise they serve no purpose: 'while there were plenty of good secular images and video clips to serve as an "emotional hook" for students in religious education, the links between these and religious … themes were less obvious or memorable for the young people' (Jackson et al., p. 126).

Examples include the use of series such as *The Simpsons*. This can be done effectively, but is not necessarily used with caution, sometimes a two-minute clip suffices whereas the teacher might show an entire episode. Consider the example of the episode *I'm Goin' to Praiseland*; only a small segment is truly linked to RE learning, but using that snippet can be hugely effective.

Hume could be used to support the argument that because of the incompatibility of religious belief systems who claim revelation as their basis that if they can't all be right then none of them are. Religious beliefs are therefore just what Dawkins proclaims them to be – superstitions built up over years of childhood indoctrination. Psychologists could see this as an example of classical conditioning – that people have been taught by their parents and society to behave or react in certain ways. With the loss of a loved one rather than looking at the physical evidence society/religion has conditioned people to fall upon the crutch of a life after death (despite there being no evidence for it). This would be exemplified through an episode of The Simpsons (I'm Goin' to Praiseland, Season 12 Episode 19), where the different characters all have visions of heaven according to their life views – the comic store owner, for example, going to Star Trek heaven.

This type of bridge to religious concepts and beliefs could be extended to literature, songs, newspapers, documentaries, video games and so on. All of these types of learning are within the pupils' own experiences and using their literacy with such media ensures that learning can be framed in relatable and understandable terms. In addition to linking with pupils' experiences, these types of activities and resources can also be utilised as a form of the 'arts' to highlight the vitality of religion and religious expression. Although speaking about art specifically it could be argued that Richard Yeomans' opinion about what art can bring to RE is equally true of all of the arts:

> [The] art[s] can make a contribution on several levels, and as a teaching tool provides a vivid and effective visual backing to religious education, giving concrete form to religious dogma, expression and attitudes, as well as revealing the social, political and historical dimensions of a religion. [The] art[s], while providing some insight into religion, is also something to be enjoyed for its own sake and perhaps its greatest value is its capacity to capture the imagination of the pupil or student. I would suggest that [the] arts[s] could provide a more direct and immediate stimulus for the study of religion.
>
> (Yeomans, 1978, p. 51)

One caveat might be about the assumptions that teachers can make about the popular culture or arts experiences that are in the pupils' experience. While a film might be contextualised, one RE teacher lamented that her Year 10 class had no experience of Star Wars as she spoke about the effect of choices on a person's path. An attempt might be made to 'enlighten' pupils but cultural experiences cannot always be assumed.

A further bridge should also be made between what has been learned to a pupil's own conceptual framework and experience. Teachers should first of all help pupils to understand how their learning has increased their experience and knowledge, which could be termed 'signposting' and 'reviewing learning'. Second, teachers of RE could, as appropriate, explore how the learning that has taken place can impact on a pupil – perhaps what used to be termed 'learning from religion'. This is not always necessary, but pupils can be given an opportunity to reflect on what has been learned and their response to it. Consider the pupils who read the Good Samaritan and reflect on the roads that they cross every day, and what they can do to think about the situations in which they could stop and help. As outlined in Chapter 1, a person's beliefs and practices can be transformed and enhanced through engagement with differing views, and meet the purpose of RE that 'pupils are encouraged to develop knowledge of the beliefs and practices of religions; and *informed opinions* and, further to develop pupils' own responses to questions about the meaning and purpose of life'.

Bridge 2: with prior learning

In a lot of ways this is similar to the previous bridge; however, it is important to note that in order for progress to be made pupils need to be aware of the steps they are making from lesson to lesson, and within lessons. The learning should build understanding rather than be fragmented:

> The most recent Ofsted report on English, *Moving English Forward*, noted that: 'some teachers appear to believe that the more activities they can cram into the lesson, the more effective it will be'. This was also common in many RE lessons seen. Superficially, pupils were active throughout the lesson, but the tasks did not build their understanding progressively. The purpose of, and links between, tasks were often not made clear.
>
> (Ofsted, 2013, p. 11)

Engaging activities can be planned, but they must be linked with progress. Utilising prior learning also provides the conceptual basis that was explored in Bridge 1.

Bridge 3: between beliefs, practices and religions

If one of the purposes of RE is to encourage students to develop informed opinions and an awareness of the implications of religion for the individual, as well as knowledge of the beliefs and practices of religion, then an awareness of the inter-relatedness of religious belief and practice is imperative. In some situations it is possible to teach practices without reference to the beliefs that underpin them. Moulin reports that this presents a skewed view of religions where the 'boring' observable parts are the starting point while the adherent is thinking: 'if I were telling someone about it, I wouldn't start that way. They start in the wrong place; they start with the rules of religion' (Moulin, 2011, p. 316).

What this might mean, and this is explored further in Chapter 8, is that the Five Pillars of Islam are explored without reference to the beliefs that underpin them such as the importance of submission to Allah, or the Five Ks as the observable form of Sikhism is studied with little understanding of the importance of the nature of God and service within the Sikh community. The observable aspect of religion becomes the central aspect of study; without bridges that connect belief and practice it is impossible to develop informed implications of religion.

This one-dimensional view of religion could also be evident in the study of some of the social and ethical issues within religion. Oftentimes religious texts are used to provide a grounding for religious attitudes; for example in an exploration of Christian attitudes towards homosexuality, teachers and pupils might point towards different biblical texts to support a viewpoint. These are important, but what is often missed are the underlying beliefs that contribute to the attitude and practice. In support of homosexuality it would be possible to see the underpinning belief to be the belief in the equality of humankind evidenced through the death of Christ for creation, and also the way in which Christ sought out those on the margins of society. Conversely, in opposition to homosexuality the importance of the family as instituted by God and the perpetual applicability of God's commandments are rarely explored. The impression that pupils are left with is that religious attitudes are determined by a series of proof texting activities rather than a rational outworking of deeply held beliefs. The bridge that should be in evidence is between all aspects of a religion; this could be as straightforward as asking questions such as: 'In Year 7 we explored beliefs about Jesus's atonement; how do you think this applies when we look at issues of crime and punishment?'

The other bridge within this context is the bridge between religions. It is incorrect to teach Judaism as a preparation for Christianity but to fail to make the links between the two religions would be to do pupils a disservice. Religions are not all the same but they share common features and in some cases stories and practices. This may be most evident in a thematic approach to RE where the commonalities and differences are concentrated into a unit of work, but even in a systematic approach links can be made and similarities and differences can be explored. Two such examples might be in the exploration of the role of Abraham in Judaism; if this story is compared with the Qur'anic version then important differences can be found and the implications for Jews and Muslims today can be developed. Thus, a story of a man from 4,000 or so years ago can be seen to have real-world relevance today as it does for religious believers worldwide.

In discussing the person and life of Jesus it might be interesting to explore the number of interpretations about him throughout the world's religions. For example in relation to Judaism where Segal confirms that today many Jews are 'intrigued by Jesus and would like to see him as a member of Jewish tradition, but don't know exactly how to do so (Walshe and Copley, 2001, p. 37). Or his prophethood in Islam, where it is asserted 'that more sayings are attributed to Jesus in Arabic than in any other language and that today, there are probably more Muslims than Christians who accept the doctrine of the virgin birth at face value' (Walshe and Copley, 2001, p. 38). Within Hinduism it may be possible for Jesus to find a place as an avatar. Walshe and Copley argue that 'The implications for religious education are clear. The understanding of Jesus promoted in RE should be broadened to include his significance for a number of world faiths in order to do justice in the classroom to the traditions about him' (2001, p. 39).

These bridges are important to build understanding of religions for pupils. A focus on linking different aspects of religions within the tradition enables a more coherent picture to be built up. Bridges between religions allow discussion to takes place that will explore the commonalities, but also build understanding of the individual religion as they are seen in distinction to one another.

Bridge 4: with local, national and international communities

One of the stated purposes of RE in Chapter 1 is to prepare pupils to be informed, respectful members of society who celebrate diversity and strive to understand others. What is important within RE is to explore the various levels of society to which pupils belong.

- School
- Local
- National
- Global

The vast majority of pupils' lives are spent building their identity within the first two levels of society (with school being replaced by work). However, it is possible for RE to have as its focus the global society. Religion becomes an esoteric phenomenon that happens beyond the pupils' own experiences. To some extent this can build up a caricatured and irrelevant view of religion that remains alien to the vast majority of pupils. Consider that pupils only learn about the general way in which religion is practised, this might be termed 'the chocolate box view of religion', a view that is static and unchanging. If, as the ethnographic approach to RE suggests, the pupils are exposed to the practice of religion by individuals, particularly in their local community, then its relevance and applicability is undeniable. For this reason RE should use authentic voices within the classroom, but also explore religion in the local community. Jackson et al. (2010) suggested this as one of their key recommendations: 'School leaders and RE teachers should develop community partnerships between the school and local faith communities, particularly those with an orientation towards social action, so that pupils can learn about the role of religions in society' (p. 13). Following this, RE can then move out from there to the national and global implications of religion. One training teacher of RE lamented that he could not take pupils on exciting visits to Bethlehem or India. To some extent, as interesting as those visits would be, much more important are visits to/from local faith communities that explore with pupils the way that religion is lived within their communities. This will break down far more barriers than a global tourist activity. Consider this observation by Ofsted (2010):

> A school decided to invite representatives from the local faith communities to its training on RE where they were introduced to the process of enquiry-based learning. As a result, they gained a greater appreciation of their role in supporting the overall programme for RE and were therefore able to make a richer contribution to it. Instead of simply imparting information, their meetings with pupils became conversations and discussions where they shared their experiences and views and contributed to the process of research and enquiry. Pupils' visits to local places of worship focused less on facts about the building and more on religious commitment and living.
>
> (p. 48)

Thus bridges are built within communities that will prepare pupils to be informed and respectful.

Bridge 5: with other subjects

Often in schools subjects are allowed to exist in splendid isolation without any communication with other subjects. However, for this to be the default position for all subjects is a concern. There is much to be gained through the integration of certain topics with other subjects. In some situations a co-operative organisation of the curriculum enables more time for an in-depth focus of peculiarly religious aspects of the topic.

Consider the exploration of the importance of Martin Luther King; usually this would be done without consultation with other subjects, but if history were to focus on the historical context and events of his life, English to focus on the structure and content of his speeches, drama to explore different events in his life, PSHE to include his responses to bullying, then RE could legitimately spend a great deal of time exploring his religious beliefs and how they were exemplified throughout his experiences. The learning experience for pupils would be far greater than if these things were covered superficially by each department independently of one another.

Ofsted (2013) gave a specific example of how this works in practice:

> In history … pupils had been studying the impact of a sea disaster on a fishing community. In RE they used a worry box to record any things that distressed them about life today. This led to a discussion about bereavement and how different religions make sense of death. The teacher used a range of resources (such as Michelangelo's Last Judgement) to stimulate questions about life after death. One pupil said, 'I thought heaven was supposed to be nice!' Pupils investigated the response of two religions (Christianity and Hinduism) to the question: 'What happens when we die?' They showed exceptional independence in completing the task, quickly gained a good range of viewpoints about life after death, and engaged seriously and sensitively when sharing their ideas and findings.
>
> (p. 24)

A linking with other subjects can also enhance an RE teacher's ability to use different learning approaches. A piece of art might be used to add colour to a worksheet, or provide decoration to the classroom. Sacred objects, themselves an artistic representation of the spiritual, are perhaps the best used of all of the art forms in the classroom, but much must be done to move the lesson beyond the illustrative nature of such art. The use of art as a pupil activity is done in much greater frequency but can be done very badly and with no educational or religious purpose. This example of the use of art could be extended to the creation of short plays to complete 'drama' activities in the classroom. This type of activity usually entails six plays of the same story (or variations on a theme being produced). There must be a better way to utilise both approaches to the use of art in the RE classroom. An art/drama/other teacher would not ask a pupil to produce a piece of work without meticulous planning and investigation on the part of the pupil. Yet, sometimes this is what RE teachers do. It may mean that a teacher has to take more time than they actually wanted but it ensures that the piece of work produced is not just reflective of a vague religious understanding but also is a good piece of art.

One further example is the use of process drama within RE. Bowell and Heap (2013) have described process drama as focusing 'on developing a dramatic response to situations and materials from a range of perspectives. In other words, participants in process drama take on roles that are required for the enquiry, investigation or exploration of the subject matter' (p. 6). Simplistically, this is where pupils are a part of the evolution of a story, perhaps acting out excerpts or freeze frames. A group is chosen and individual characters can be interviewed to check learning or move it along. These do not have to be traditional religious stories, but can also be stories with a religious theme. 'The task of the teacher is to find ways in which to connect the students with the content and enable them to develop responses to it through active engagement and reflection' (Bowell and Heap, 2013, p. 6).

Building bridges with other subjects enhances the pupil experience in two ways:

1   The depth of learning can be improved as more time can be given to specifically religious concepts.
2   The array of learning approaches a teacher can use increases as they interact with other subjects.

Focus on religions and religious understanding

One of the key findings of the Ofsted report of 2013 was that the depth of pupils' religious understanding was insufficient and that teachers should 'ensure that learning in RE has a stronger focus on deepening pupils' understanding of the nature, diversity and impact of religion and belief in the contemporary world' (p. 7). Greater development of this will be made in the remaining chapters of this book, but thus far it should have been evident that understanding the central concepts in individual religions should be at the core of good RE. It is insufficient for pupils to have knowledge of religions that is only good for a pub quiz, the central concepts should be explored and from there the impact of them on the lives of individuals. This does not mean that learning cannot be fun because pupils have to be constantly plumbing the depths of religious experience. Rather, the way that religious concepts are presented enables pupils to gain a depth of understanding. In conversation with some teachers it is evident that they feel that this understanding is shown purely through written work. Written work has its place, but a pupil's engagement with the concepts can be shown in many different ways, and if the learning activity is engaging it is more probable that the concepts taught will be remembered. Consider the following two activities.

Year 7: Reincarnation/cycle of samsara

Pupils had previously studied Hindu beliefs about the nature of God, worship, scriptures and elements of caste. In this lesson pupils were to explore the concepts of karma, the atman, Reincarnation and the cycle of samsara. After a brief introduction, pupils were to design their own moksha chitram (similar to snakes and ladders) game by:

*   Numbering a matrix 1–100
*   Making 100 moksha
*   Listing ten animals in order of improvement (completely subjective)
*   Placing these ten animals on different squares between 1 and 40
*   Placing humanity, and possibly different castes between 40 and 60
*   Adding ladders with positive actions at the bottom
*   Adding snakes with negative actions at the top.

Pupils were then to play the game and keep a diary of the 'Journey of the atman' to facilitate a piece of creative writing that explored these beliefs' impact on an individual. This lesson was observed by a university lecturer in Hinduism and the teacher commented that 'she noted that the Year 7 pupils acquired an understanding of the concepts of karma, atman and rebirth much better than the first year undergraduate students she had been lecturing to the week before'.

Year 13: The ontological argument

This activity explored Anselm's first ontological argument and laid the groundwork for students to be introduced to Gaunilo's criticisms. The structure of the lesson was as follows:

- On entrance pupils should design their perfect island (10)
- On completion pupils should display – they should discuss what makes them perfect. Is there any way to make them more perfect? (Or is that an impossibility?) (5)
- Building on this, pupils should be introduced to Anselm's First Ontological Argument. They should explore the various nuances through the answering of questions (especially the concept it is better for something to exist in actuality than just in the mind – formal and intentional existence) (10)
- Pupils will then be asked to summarise the Ontological Argument (5)
- They will then check one another's summary and suggest changes (5)
- Students should brainstorm (in pairs) any problems they see with the Ontological Argument – using their prior knowledge of Religious Language and the starter activity (5)
- Students should read Gaunilo's criticism – and reconstruct the Ontological Argument for the existence of an Island (10)
- Students should play a game of corners based on the Ontological argument (5)

Both of these activities could potentially be described as lacking depth with a cursory examination, but in actuality the depth of learning that was experienced by pupils was substantial. This was also supported by challenging support notes in the case of Year 13, which utilised the original words of Anselm. In some cases original texts are provided with no support to decipher the meaning; at other times the summary of the text is the only thing provided. The role of the teacher is to challenge pupils using 'authentic' material but also to provide them with the skills/commentary to decode what is meant and its importance.

Use a diversity of activities

As was evident from the kaleidoscopic approach outlined in Chapter 2, and the various activities provided throughout, it is imperative that the RE teacher utilises different learning activities across their teaching. It is for the teacher to decide which activities will help their pupils make progress and fulfil the aims and purposes of RE. The key questions that a teacher should have in mind when planning RE are:

- What are the learning objectives?
- What concepts in a pupil's own experience could provide a bridge to the learning?
- What religious concepts do I want pupils to understand?
- What activities and resources will be engaging?
- How will these activities help the pupils make progress and meet the learning objectives?

Accompanying the introduction of the 2007 National Curriculum was the idea of a compelling learning experience. This is an experience in which the pupil is carried along on the crest of a wave, they are so engaged with the learning that they almost cannot help but make progress. It is these types of activities that will help pupils make progress.

Enquiry-based learning

In addition to the various activities already explored there are many others that could be utilised. One such example is the use of enquiry-based learning. Both Ofsted reports of 2010 and 2013 highlighted an enquiry-based approach as a way forward within RE, enabling pupils learning to be deepened and go beyond comprehension. Enquiry has been defined as: 'a term which is generally perceived as referring to the process of questioning and research. Ultimately this is with a view to reaching a reasoned conclusion, although the process of enquiry itself is also of significance to the learner' (Pickford, Garner and Jackson, p. 1).

Placing enquiry at the heart of RE engages pupils on a voyage of discovery. One possible cyclical model could be:

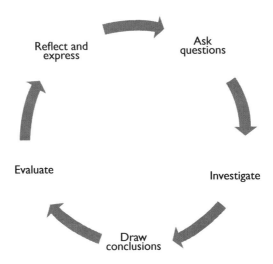

Figure 7.1 Cycle of enquiry (see Ofsted, 2013)

There are many ways in which enquiry-based learning could be integrated into RE. The questions can be determined by the teacher or by the pupils. The process as a whole enables pupils to express informed and reasoned opinions rather than superficial responses. Consider the question: 'Why is the death of Jesus important to Christians today?'

- Pupils investigate statements by Christians; these could be interviews, web resources, or statements provided by the teacher.
- Pupils draw tentative conclusions based on their investigation.
- Pupils discuss these conclusions with one another to evaluate their tentative positions.
- Pupils produce work that answers the original question.
- Pupils raise any questions that come out of the investigation.

Or utilising a murti of Ganesh with the question: 'How is the importance of Ganesh shown through his murti?'

- Pupils investigate the murti and explore the various symbols that they find.
- Pupils draw tentative conclusions based on their investigation.
- Pupils discuss these conclusions with one another to evaluate their tentative positions.
- Pupils produce work that answers the original question.
- Pupils raise any questions that come out of the investigation.

It should be noted that the initial investigation and the work pupils produce can be vastly different types of activities that are designed to suit the question. In response to Ofsted, this enquiry-based approach should utilise:

> an appropriate repertoire of approaches to learning that match different types of enquiry, for example:
>
> - using experiential and creative activities where pupils need to develop their insight into the 'experience' of religion
> - using reasoned argument and debate when pupils are exploring controversial issues
> - using investigative and interpretative skills when pupils need to gather, analyse and present information.
>
> (Ofsted, 2013, p. 27)

In this way, pupils are placed at the centre of learning and understanding is enhanced.

Storytelling

Storytelling is an activity that is used abundantly within primary RE but perhaps disappears from view in the secondary classroom. Storytelling in Religious Studies can be effective if it is utilised correctly and enthusiastically by the teacher. It goes beyond expecting pupils to be able to recall what they know about religious stories, but it encourages creativity, deep level thinking and high order questions through engagement and imagination. Baumfield suggests 'storytelling is an oral activity that enables pupils at all levels of ability in reading to participate. It promotes listening skills and builds confidence in speaking as well as developing thinking skills' (2002, p. 86). This highlights the potential storytelling has to be an inclusive tool to challenge all students and help them make progress.

Trevor Cooling suggests that stories are 'big ideas sometimes referred to as a meta-narrative, which express our whole understanding of the whole world and help people to make sense of their lives' (2002, p. 45); here he could be seen to suggest their use for personal development. Stories can also be used to explore difficult issues. Dyson (2009) suggests that stories provide a safe place to discuss topics that are upsetting or controversial, thoughts and feelings are explored in the context of characters rather than in a personal way.

Robin Mello (2001) highlights the deepening of learning that can take place through the use of story. She supports her research by suggesting that stories provide 'the link that connect[s] the learner with both interpersonal and intrapersonal realms. Therefore, narratives are found to be seminally important to the learning and development of children'. Stories also have many levels and depths that need to be analysed and studied for academic understanding in addition to exposing the audience to the culture of the story, its language and heritage. Miller Mair echoes this in suggesting that 'All our stories are expressions of ourselves even when they purport to be accounts of aspects of the world. We are deeply implicated in the very grounds of our story telling' (1989, p. 257). Religions can therefore be experienced through their stories.

John Hammond suggests that the use of storytelling in Religious Education can link closely to personal enquiry: 'like ritual, the disciplined use of silence, the encounter with symbol, the telling and hearing of narrative are within and outside of religion and can act as bridges between the world of religion and the experience of the student' (2002, p. 197). The use of stories within Religious Education can break down the illusory barriers of 'them and us' and allow students to be able to build bridges with religions outside of their own. This is enabled because storytelling allows pupils to personally connect with an unfamiliar concept on a direct level utilising a familiar framework.

> Through stories and storytelling, children were exposed to long-standing archetypal models that engaged their imaginations. Storytelling stimulated sympathetic responses as well and caused students to think more deeply about their social world.
>
> (Mello, 2001)

Storytelling thus has huge value as an inclusive tool throughout the Key Stages as pupils are able to engage with the themes. Storytelling is, however, a skill that requires practice and preparation. In using a story, teachers should be aware of what they are trying to achieve, and how their telling can help pupils make progress.

The story of the Good Samaritan is an incredibly evocative story but can come across as bland and uninspiring. It could be told in this way:

- A Jewish man is walking from Jerusalem to Jericho.
- He is robbed, beaten and left for dead.
- A priest comes along, crosses the road and carries on his way.
- A Levite comes along, and does the same.
- A Samaritan comes along, he stops and helps the man and takes him to an inn and pays for his care.

Even with enthusiasm this has little to engage the pupil, and changing it to reflect football teams might not enhance a depth of learning. Consider now the same story but told using enthusiasm and questions, perhaps pitched using specific stepping stone progress:

- A Jewish man is walking from Jerusalem to Jericho.
- He is robbed, beaten and left for dead.

- A priest comes along [question: what would you expect the priest to do?], crosses the road and carries on his way [question: why do you think the priest crossed over the road and carried on? Are these good reasons?].
- A Levite [question: what is a Levite?] comes along [question: what would you expect him to do? Surely two priests in a row would not walk past], and does the same.
- A Samaritan comes along [question: what is a Samaritan? Discussion of the relationship between Jews and Samaritans. [Question: what would you expect him to do?], he stops and helps the man and takes him to an inn and pays for his care [question: why did he do this?].
- Questions: What was Jesus teaching in this parable? How does this link with others of Jesus's teachings? In what situations do we see people who are battered and bruised (physically or emotionally)? What are some reasons we do not stop and help? What can we do to be like the Samaritan?

The understanding of the story and Christian belief is deepened, and the level of empathy and informed response is enhanced.

Summary

This chapter has explored various activities and factors that contribute to the effective learning and teaching of RE. It began with the importance of the teacher; this cannot be overestimated, the teacher can make or break a person's attitude towards a subject. RE is incredibly exciting and engaging but when done badly it is boring and monotonous. To assist the teacher, the bridges with pupil experience (between religions and beliefs and with other communities) will help pupils make links and see the relevance of learning. The diversity of activities that are available to the RE teacher can similarly help engage and enthuse the learner.

References

Baumfield, V. (2002) *Thinking Through Religious Education*. Cambridge: Chris Kington Publishing.

Blaylock, Lat (nd) *Rubbish RE: The Ten Worst Examples We Could Find*. Available at www.natre.org.uk/docstore/Ten%20ideas%20for%20rubbish%20RE.pdf (accessed 1 May 2014).

Bowell, Pamela and Heap, Brian (2013) *Planning Process Drama. Enriching Teaching and Learning*. Abingdon, UK: Routledge.

Cooling, T. (2002) 'Commitment and Indoctrination: A dilemma for Religious Education?'. In L. Broadbent and A. Brown (Eds), *Issues in Religious Education*. Hove and New York: Routledge (ch. 4).

Davies, Emma (2013) *A Critical Reflection Upon the Use of the Arts Within Secondary Religious Education*. Unpublished MA Thesis. Chester, UK: University of Chester.

Dyson, J. (2009) What's the Use of Stories? Exploring the Place of Personal Stories and Grand Narratives in RE (and Life in General), *Resource*, *32*(1), 14–17.

Hammond, J. (2002) 'Embodying the Spirit: Realising RE's Potential in the Spiritual Dimension of the Curriculum'. In L. Broadbent and A. Brown (Eds), *Issues in Religious Education*. Hove and New York: Routledge (ch.15).

Holt, James D. (2013) 'Faith Based Practice? The Impact of a Teacher's Beliefs on the Classroom'. In D. Morris (Ed.), *Re-Imagining Christian Education for the 21st Century*. Chelmsford, UK: Matthew James (pp. 183–192).

Jackson, R., Ipgrave, J., Hayward, M., Hopkins, P., Fancourt, N., Robbins, M., Francis, L. J. and McKenna, U. (2010) *Materials Used to Teach about World Religions in Schools in England*. London: Department for Children, Families and Schools. Research Report.

McConkie, Joseph Fielding (1975) *Teach and Reach*. Salt Lake City, UT: Bookcraft.

Mair, M. (1989) *Between Psychology and Psychotherapy: A Poetics of Experience*. New York, NY: Routledge.

Mello, R. (2001) The Power of Storytelling: How Oral Narrative Influences Children's Relationships in Classrooms. *International Journal of Education & the Arts*, 2 (1) www.ijea.org/v2n1/

Moulin, Dan (2011) Giving Voice to 'the Silent Minority': The Experience of Religious Students in Secondary School Religious Education Lessons, *British Journal of Religious Education*, *33*(3), 313–326.

Ofsted (2010) *Transforming RE*. Manchester, UK: Ofsted.

Ofsted (2013) *Religious Education: Realising the Potential*. Manchester, UK: Ofsted.

Pickford, T., Garner, W. and Jackson, E. (2013) *Primary Humanities. Learning Through Enquiry*. London: Sage.

Walshe, K. and Copley, T. (2001) The Jesus of Agreed Syllabuses in Key Stage 1 and the Jesus of Theology and Religious Studies. *British Journal of Religious Education*, *24*(1) 32–40.

Wintersgill, B. (1993) 'Learning about World Religions in the Basic Curriculum'. In C. Erricker (Ed.), *Teaching World Religions. A Teacher's Handbook Produced by the SHAP Working Party on World Religions in Education*. Oxford: Heinemann (pp. 42–44).

Yeomans, Richard (1978) 'Religious Education Through Art'. In R. Jackson (Ed.), *Perspectives on World Religions*. London: University of London, School of Oriental and African Studies (pp. 51–72).

Chapter 8

Teaching world religions

Chapter outline

Religion at the heart of RE

Issues of diversity within traditions

Using 'insider' voices

Standing on sacred ground

Focus on beliefs and then practices

Dealing with controversy

Subject knowledge

Teaching about the world's religions and helping pupils understand about the impact, influence and practice in believers' lives is the central task of Religious Education at any Key Stage. While the beginning point is the children's own experiences, RE links these to the beliefs and practices of the world's religions. What is meant by world religions? They could be described as a system of beliefs and practices that are followed by a group of people; indeed Jackson et al. recognise the problems associated with the terminology 'world religions' but also recognise its value:

> Many scholars view the terms 'religions' and 'world religions' critically, but find them to be useful categories to encompass sets of beliefs, practices, experiences and values dealing with fundamental existential questions, such as those relating to birth, identity and death. Some scholars look for looser ways to describe world religions – as broad religious traditions, for example – rather than as completely homogeneous systems of belief.
>
> (Jackson et al., 2010, p. 21)

The major religions of the world are generally listed as:

- Buddhism
- Christianity
- Hinduism
- Islam
- Judaism
- Sikhism

This is not to suggest that RE should be limited to these religions, but Agreed Syllabi and exam specifications focus on these as the religions that can and should be covered. The 2011 UK census highlighted the breakdown of religions in the UK:

Table 8.1 Breakdown of religions in the UK (from 2011 UK census):

Religion	Number of people in UK	Percentage of UK population
Christian	33.2 million	59.3
No religion	14.1 million	25
Muslim	2.7 million	4.8
Hindu	817,000	1.5
Sikh	423,000	0.8
Jewish	263,000	0.5
Buddhist	248,000	0.4
Other*	240,000	0.4

*Note: this included those identifying as Jain with 20,000 people and Ravidassia with 11,000 people.
Source: Office for National Statistics (2012).

Other religions such as Baha'i and Jainism could find a place in the RE classroom as appropriate. One of the issues surrounding the inclusion of other religions is the pressures that are already placed on curriculum time. This is why, perhaps, the religions outside of the 'Big Six' have a place within the RE classroom as appropriate rather than by default. For example, if a school or local community has a significant presence of a particular religion outside those listed above, then they should be covered. This is particularly the case if pupils from that faith tradition are represented in the classroom. Further discussion of this, and also the place of the 'silent majority' (Rudge, 1998, p. 155) of those who do not identify with a religious tradition outlined above, which would include those from a non-religious background, is needed as these groups grow in number.

Religion at the heart of RE

There has been an increasing trend to rebrand RE into 'Philosophy and Ethics'. The most common reason for this change is to appeal to the children and parents, because they have a negative view of RE. To some extent this has also been reflected not just in the name but also in the teaching of RE; Ofsted have reported that:

> an increasing number of departments visited were moving towards a Key Stage 3 curriculum which concentrated more heavily on GCSE-style, 'issues-based', social, moral or philosophical topics such as 'Rights and Responsibilities' or 'The Environment'. … In practice, it meant that pupils were not developing a sufficient level of knowledge and understanding of religion and belief. As a result, when they came to try to apply religious perspectives to various moral or social issues they did not have the depth of knowledge they needed.
>
> (2013, p. 14)

This does not need to be the case; RE, with religion at its heart, is engaging and does not need to be watered down to philosophy and ethics. These two subject areas play an important role in RE, but they are expressions of beliefs, and as such these beliefs need to be explored in depth to provide context for their study. If RE is made relevant and challenging, and pupils can see the purpose of it, then no apology needs to be made for its inclusion in the curriculum.

Issues of diversity within traditions

One of the major contributions of the ethnographic approach to RE is the recognition that the representation of a religion as a homogenous group is artificial and potentially dangerous. In some cases RE teachers teach a 'chocolate box' view of a particular religion. What is meant by 'chocolate box' is a presentation that is sanitised, static and 'one size fits all'. This is the approach that describes all Christians as believing in the Trinity; all Orthodox Jewish people wearing Hasidic style clothing; all Muslims wearing the burkha or the shalwar khameez. This approach provides a univocal view of religion that can serve to reinforce stereotypes, be out of step with pupils' experiences of religion; most crucially this presentation may be at odds with the beliefs and practices of the pupil themselves (see Moulin, 2011). Consider the Jehovah's Witness child in the classroom who is told that a Christian is someone who believes in the Trinity; she is aware that she does not believe in the Nicene view of the Trinity yet she believes she is a Christian. Or the Muslim child who is presented with a view of Islam that presents Sunni as normative, and also the original form of Islam with other forms being schismatic; whereas as a Shi'a Muslim they believe that Shi'a is the original form and Sunni is schismatic. The RE teacher might have particular views about the validity of these beliefs, but these need to be secondary to the recognition that what is being taught is a particular expression of the religion rather than the normative view. If RE is to be truly inclusive and representative of religion then there should be the recognition that a 'major focus of RE is the study of diversity of religion and belief' (DCSF, 2010, p. 8). This does not just mean between religions, but also within religions.

An analogy that can be used to illustrate this point is the traditional Indian tale of the blind man and the elephant. In this story a man comes across six blind men engaged in an argument. The argument is based around the question: 'What is an elephant like?' The first has been feeling the side of the elephant and describes it as like a rough wall; the second has focused on the tusk, suggesting a sword; the third describes it as like a snake, after focusing on the trunk; the fourth, a palm leaf as his area of investigation, was the ear; the fifth describes the leg as like a tree trunk; and the final blind man describes the elephant as being like a rope because he focused on the tail.

Sometimes this story is used to explore RE as a whole and suggest that religions are merely limited expressions of the same larger truth. This is problematic as a pluralistic and syncretistic view of religion. The 'better' interpretation in the context of RE is that the elephant is a particular religion and that, as RE teacher, we can only describe part of the experience of the followers of religion. What is important, however, is that the existence of the elephant (wider experience of religion) is recognised so that there is room for diversity of belief and practice. In this sense, some of the teacher's most important words to use are 'some', 'many' and 'most'. Blaylock suggests that 'In RE, where learning that sentences that start "All Hindus …" or "All Christians …" are mostly false' (2004, p. 61).

This is not to suggest that every element of diversity needs to be explored, only that the possibility of it existing should be recognised. For example, in discussing the Christian view of God, the creedal view of the Trinity is that which is expressed in the majority of Christian denominations. As such, when exploring this belief in the RE classroom, mention could be made that 'Most Christians believe in the Trinity …' without further recognition of other beliefs unless it is necessary to do so in the context of the class being taught or the questions asked. In discussing the issue of New Religious Movements it has been argued that this diversity of expression is one of the places that these religions can legitimately find a place within the RE classroom outside of a unit of work, which seems rather implausible in most schools:

> Within Christianity, for some issues, such as the use of legal drugs, there is no diversity except for personal application of principles (for example a Christian might decide to avoid the use of alcohol through personal choice and an interpretation of their body as a temple; but there tends to be no specific condemnation). However within the Church of Jesus Christ of Latter-day Saints there is a strict prohibition on tobacco, alcohol, and tea and coffee which could be explored in examining moral issues.
>
> (Holt, 2010, p. 81)

The diversity of belief and practices presents a much more honest view of the world's religions, and goes beyond the chocolate box view that does not go far enough in developing pupils' understanding of religions or in preparing them for a diverse society of religions and expression of those religions that goes beyond a one-dimensional and slightly caricatured picture.

Using 'insider' voices

If diversity is to be recognised and the varieties of experiences within a tradition are to be recognised it is important that authentic voices from within religions are included within RE. The teacher's role is crucial in the facilitation of this, as insiders' voices, while being authentic, are only such for their own experience. It would be interesting for the pupils to consider the contrast between the individual's experience and what they have been taught. For example, the one-dimensional view that all Roman Catholics disagree with contraception could be viewed in light of the believer who feels that, for reasons of individual conscience and family planning, it is perfectly acceptable for them. This is not only a difference of practice, but also could raise important discussions about the role of moral authorities within Roman Catholicism: is the individual conscience more important than the teachings of the Church?

The authentic voices can be experienced in a variety of ways:

- Visitors
- Visits to places of worship
- Video clips
- Video conferencing
- Books written from an insider's perspective.

All of these experiences are valuable, though some may prioritise the face-to-face meeting over the other forms as they are more immediate and interactive. One teacher suggested that: 'They are talking to real Muslims and they are putting across their faith as they practise it, so you've got some spirituality there … I want the real feelings of what it means to believe' (in Jackson et al., 2010, p. 137).

However, there are advantages of using prepared material that can be built into the lesson with the teacher knowing exactly what is going to be said. In using these voices it is important that the people are as local as possible so that pupils can see the expression of religion within the UK context. There are exceptions to this, for example someone who is describing their experience of the Hajj necessarily does so in the context of Makkah and the surrounding area. Consider, for example, the teacher who in exploring Hindu funerals shows a clip of a funeral taking place on the banks of the Ganges. This is interesting, but could have sent the message of an 'alien' religion that is practised within India. What may have been better is an interview with a British Hindu about how funeral rites are performed within this country, for example.

Care should be taken in using these insider voices but doing so ensures a study of RE that goes beyond the facts. Pupils are able to see and ask questions of practising adherents. The teacher necessarily stands one step removed from religion as an 'outsider' but the bridge to religious understanding can be provided by these authentic voices.

Standing on sacred ground

W.B. Yeats wrote:

> I have spread my dreams under your feet;
> Tread softly because you tread on my dreams.

(2010, p. 26)

It is in this position that RE teachers find themselves. In exploring religious beliefs and practices, teachers and pupils are handling the most sacred and deeply held beliefs of adherents to religions from around the world. Some of these beliefs and practices will seem alien, and perhaps odd, to people who are unfamiliar with them; however, for religious believers, they are an expression of something sacred and incredibly important. How religious beliefs and practices are presented is crucial if they are not to be held up for scorn or ridicule. Dan Brown, in his book *The Lost Symbol*, has his character describe Communion in the Roman Catholic Church in such a way as to shock: 'Don't tell anyone, but on the pagan day of the sun God Ra, I kneel at the foot of an ancient instrument of torture and consume ritualistic symbols of blood and flesh' (2009, p. 58). In doing so, he illustrates the point that any religious practice can be presented negatively if the teacher is not careful.

As such, the RE teacher needs to be very careful how they present such beliefs and practices. One such example is in the use of objects that are held to be sacred or important within religions. The term 'artefact' has been avoided here in light of the most accepted use of the term in films, usually depicting Indiana Jones. Roger Homan (2000) suggests that 'The use of the term "artefacts" frequently conveys a sense of a distant and even dead culture whose human participants are to be understood from the analysis of physical traces' (p. 28). This may be oversensitivity, but the objects associated with religions are living and sacred. The use of artefacts is seen to be important within RE, indeed Pamela Draycott argues that 'artefacts are not an optional extra in terms of religious education but a necessity' (1997, p. 2). However, they should not be used uncritically. In having children handle them and ask questions of them, or even using them to provide decoration, is it possible that the teacher is making the sacred mundane?

It is impossible for a religious object to have the same meaning outside of its context or when used by someone for whom it does not hold significance. Does this mean then, that they should not be used within the classroom? Jackson et al. (2010) suggest that their use can 'encourage empathy with the people for whom these artefacts hold religious significance, and ... generate responses of awe and wonder' (p. 205); while acknowledging that the boundaries are sometimes blurred between '"hands-on" learning [and] respect for other people's sacred objects and religious devotion' (p. 205). If such objects are to be used then careful consideration should be made: 'Teachers will need not only to sort out the appropriate uses for different objects of religious devotion but also to clarify the extent to which they are prepared to use these objects as a vehicle for experience' (Homan, 2000 pp. 28–29). Homan (2000) suggests that part of this is through their appropriate use, but also by recognising that, in following these conventions, recognition is given that non-believers are showing respect rather than giving reverence to the objects. This is important, as they may handle them in a similar way to a believer but without the associated beliefs.

It is possible to utilise religious objects without much thought other than to illustrate. The teacher needs to be fully aware of the rationale behind the use they are making of such objects. For example, the dressing up of a child in the 5Ks for some teachers would be seen to be educationally unjustifiable. The 5Ks will probably not have significance for the child, as such their sacredness and importance within the Sikh community will not be understood fully and could potentially be opened up to ridicule.

It is not just religious objects that should be treated with care, but also the beliefs and practices that are within religions. There are many practices, as outlined earlier, that may seem odd outside of their specific context of belief. It is important for the teacher to help pupils understand the context so that the resultant actions are not demeaned.

Extending to beliefs and how they are presented; consider the story of the Feeding of the 5,000 and how that is presented within the RE classroom. It is increasingly common to hear that on being offered five loaves and two fish that Jesus began to share them out. On seeing this sharing, the crowd of 5,000 men (women and children were extra) were motivated to share the food that they had brought with those around them. Thus everybody was able to eat and be filled, with twelve baskets of leftovers. This is a very good way of presenting the message of sharing and will be acceptable to a number of Christians. However, the message of the miracles of Jesus is not just in their parabolic meaning; much more important for a large number of Christians is recorded in the Fourth Gospel:

> And many other signs truly did Jesus in the presence of his disciples, which are not written in this book: But these are written, that ye might believe that Jesus is the Christ, the Son of God; and that believing ye might have life through his name.
>
> (John 20: 30–31)

Making sharing the main theme of the miracle reduces it to a parable. It misses the point for most Christians that Jesus's miracles show that he is the Son of God. The central beliefs of Christianity are removed from this retelling of the story. In exploring beliefs it is important that the beliefs are shared honestly according to the religion, with diversity being recognised as appropriate.

Focus on beliefs and then practices

Sometimes RE can focus on the outward expression of religion rather than the inner beliefs and commitments. As such, the connection between beliefs and practices is lost, as practices are the first thing to be explored. Consider, for example, the Five Pillars being studied without an understanding of the Articles of Faith within Islam; Shabbat laws being explored without understanding the nature of the Almighty and the covenant relationship within Judaism. A further example might be the knowledge of the 5Ks within Sikhism with little or no reference to the Japji and the underlying beliefs. Jackson et al. (2010) noted the problems this might cause:

> A text had good explanations of the 5 Pillars of Islam but its omission of the seven cardinal tenets of belief skewed the representation of the faith. ... At the level of smaller details, an example where a resource explained that some Jewish men strap straps and boxes to themselves when they pray, but failed to mention that these contained texts of the Torah, showed how such omissions can take away the meaning and significance of what might, without them, seem strange religious practices.
>
> (p. 91)

In a Key Stage 4 discussion, religious attitudes to social and ethical issues may be explored in great detail but without a linking with, or underpinning by, the beliefs of the religion. Although there may be 'no right way' to teach moral issues, what happens is that pupils might learn that Muslims oppose abortion and then explore the reasons why. Perhaps a more effective way might be to explore the nature of humanity and its relationship to God, and from there ask pupils to suggest possible responses of Muslims to issues such as abortion and euthanasia. Thus links are drawn between beliefs and practices. Sometimes it is possible to begin with the observable and explore why, but this should be for the purpose of deeper learning and drawing connections, rather than proof texting and mere illustration.

At Key Stage 5 it is possible to explore arguments for the existence of God; for example, without reference to the underpinning beliefs about God. It is not, however, advisable. An understanding of who Christians, for example, believe God to be is a crucial precursor to understanding arguments for his existence. Without an understanding of God as benevolent, omnipotent or as creator it is impossible to understand the design argument with such aspects as aestheticism. These topics across the Key Stages are usually studied in isolation to religious beliefs; whereas it could be suggested that a deep underpinning of learning with an understanding of religious beliefs will help pupils make links with other aspects of their study.

Dealing with controversy

Religion can sometimes be presented as a utopian collection of beliefs and practices. However, religions are not without flaws. To present a chocolate box view of religions is to provide pupils with a view that is at odds with their experience. Pupils are aware that conflicts within and between religions happen. They are also aware that there are aspects perhaps in the beliefs, perhaps in the history, of religions that are challenging and go outside of the chocolate box view. Consider the response of one secondary school teacher to the teaching of Islam:

Thrust into a classroom situation I began to teach the 'chocolate box' view of Islam. What I mean by this, is the sanitised bare facts – the Five Pillars and the ideal of how a Muslim should live. I perhaps would have continued along this path had it not been for the events of September 2001. I walked into school on 12th September to be faced by a colleague who announced that he was no longer going to teach about Islam, and throughout that week a number of Islamaphobic comments from students. After challenging these individually I was asked by the school to meet with each year to discuss the events of the past few days. Some of the comments I made include:

> Due to recent tragic events, comments in the media, and even comments within school it is felt that it may be appropriate to say a few words about the religion of Islam.
>
> You may have heard the terms 'Muslim terrorist' or 'Islamic Jihad' as you have listened to the news. It is possible that the terrorists who carried out these evil acts were Muslims, but their actions do not reflect the attitudes or beliefs of individual Muslims or the religion of Islam as a whole.
>
> Islam is a religion that teaches peace and brotherhood. Unfortunately, some people have interpreted certain beliefs to mean that they can kill and terrorise people. This is far from the message of Islam that most people would accept.
>
> Just as it would be wrong to blame a whole class for the actions of one person, so it is wrong to blame a whole religion for the actions of a few people. Last week, we saw in the news so called Christian people in Northern Ireland, shouting at or throwing things at schoolchildren – does this mean that all Christians support this act? – Of course not.
>
> These acts of terrorism were evil, but we must make sure we do not add to the suffering by blaming innocent people. We must treat each other, irrespective of religion or colour, with respect and tolerance.

However, these events meant that a chocolate box view of Islam was no longer enough either for me or my students. There were real controversies that needed to be discussed or they would not be able to understand the basic message of Islam and what a positive force it could be. They would be left to the newspapers to find out what a negative force it can be. This was not acceptable to me. Now, when I teach Islam I tackle the issues head on. Sometimes I get complaints – some from Muslims that I am not truly representing Islam. I accept this but in teaching the Islamic view of women I have to build on the traditional stereotype to challenge it from the Qur'an and the Hadith. If I don't include the negative – I am glossing over it. I will always teach that it is a minority view and out of step with Qur'anic teaching because sometimes the chocolate box is not enough.

This type of controversy is not limited to a teaching of Islam; all religions can be seen to have areas of controversy. Only by having pupils engage with them in light of the beliefs of the wider religion, can they hope to understand the variety of expressions and disagreements.

A further example might include the Holocaust within Judaism. This is an incredibly challenging topic to approach from an RE perspective. If Jewish people believe that they are the Almighty's chosen people, and that he has been intimately involved in their history through examples such as the Exodus and Judah Maccabee, why did this happen? Controversial issues are not just outward expressions, but can be internal conflicts within a person. To have faith is a challenging position and to engage with some of these controversies and recognise how religious people might respond will help pupils understand others, and formulate their own responses to questions of meaning.

Subject knowledge

It might be interesting in teaching RE to imagine that a person from a particular religion is at the back of the classroom when that religion is being taught. Returning back to the example of the Feeding of the 5,000, would the teacher be comfortable explaining why they have taken such an approach in the telling of the story? This suggestion is not meant to shackle the teacher to an uncritical exploration of religion, but seeks to ensure that the religion is represented accurately. Lat Blaylock has suggested that '100% accuracy is the standard', indeed 'settling for less than 100% accuracy is a dereliction of professionalism' (2004, p. 61). This standard of accuracy is demanding but if it is not met it is usually because of two reasons:

1   Lack of knowledge.
2   Assumption of knowledge.

The first is probably the least common and the most easily remediable. If a teacher recognises that they do not know about an aspect of a religion then it is possible to gain an understanding of the topics to be taught in a number of ways. This could be through interaction with members of the faith community, professional development or independent research. Every teacher of RE has aspects of their subject knowledge that need enhancing and recognising that ensures that the teacher continues to study and learn. The next six chapters of this book are designed to provide a brief introduction to the major religions of the world and to begin the teacher's development of knowledge. What should be guarded against, however, in this case, is the making up of knowledge when faced with a question to which the teacher does not know the answer. Sometimes 'I don't know' or 'Let's explore that together' are the best answers that can be given; they are certainly more preferable to a guess.

The assumption of knowledge is dangerous because the teacher does not know that they do not know. Perhaps the main focus of elements of their experience has been in the studying of Christianity. As such, they may feel that they know all there is to know. Consider the student teacher who teaches that 'most Christians believe in the Trinity' is to be pulled up by her school mentor for her subject knowledge. She is told 'all Christians believe in the Trinity'. When she replies that there are groups that do not, she is told dismissively that those groups do not even believe in Jesus. It is important that teachers at every stage of their career are open to learning. It is impossible to know everything about a religion; similarly if a teacher has a particular religion they cannot assume that theirs is the only interpretation.

Summary

This chapter has outlined the importance of placing world religions at the heart of RE in the secondary school. It is this that will enable the aims and purposes of RE to be met fully. In doing so, however, it is important to recognise the diversity within and between religions. One way to facilitate this is to allow religious insiders, or authentic voices, to speak for themselves. These voices need to be contextualised and placed in the wider aims of RE by the teacher, but this will help not just a more 'real' experience of religion but also diversity to be explored. Also of benefit when teaching world religions is the sensitivity that is necessary when teachers are exploring the most sacred aspects of a person's beliefs. Care should be taken, while also recognising the challenging and controversial nature of belief. The experience of religions that is given to pupils should be varied but also reflect the honesty of the different facets of the tradition and practice, beginning with the central beliefs and concepts of that religion. All of this is underpinned by subject knowledge of the highest standard, and openness to learning more on the part of the teacher. If these aspects are explored then pupils will recognise the value of RE and also be able to engage at a deep level with religious belief.

References

Blaylock, L. (Ed.) (2004) *Representing Religions: Teachers of RE from Six Religions Explain how to Represent Their Religions in Your Classroom.* Birmingham, UK: RE Today.

Brown, Dan (2009) *The Lost Symbol.* London: Bantam.

Department for Children, Schools and Families (DCSF) (2010) *Religious Education in English Schools: Non-Statutory Guidance 2010.* London: Department for Education.

Draycott, Pamela (1997) *Religious Artefacts: Why? What? How?* Derby, UK: Christian Education Movement.

Holt, James D. (2010) 'Beyond the Big Six: Minority Religions in the Secondary RE Classroom'. In Schmack et al. (Eds), *Engaging RE.* Newcastle upon Tyne, UK: Cambridge Scholars (pp. 76–91).

Homan, Roger (2000) Don't Let the Murti Get Dirty: The Uses and Abuses of Religious 'Artefacts', *British Journal of Religious Education, 23*(1), 27–37.

Jackson, Robert, Ipgrave, Julia, Hayward, Mary, Hopkins, Paul, Fancourt, Nigel, Robbins, Mandy, Francis, Leslie and McKenna, Ursula (2010) *Materials Used to Teach About World Religions in Schools in England.* London: DCSF.

Moulin, D. (2011) Giving Voice to 'the Silent Minority': The Experience of Religious Students in Secondary School Religious Education Lessons, *British Journal of Religious Education, 33*(3), 313–326.

Office for National Statistics (2012) *Religion in England and Wales 2011.* Available at: www.ons.gov.uk/ons/dcp171776_290510.pdf (accessed 1 May 2014).

Rudge, Linda (1998) 'I Am Nothing' –Does It Matter? A Critique of Current Religious Education Policy and Practice in England on Behalf of the Silent Majority, *British Journal of Religious Education, 20*(3), 155–165.

Yeats W. B. (2010) *The Wind Among the Reeds.* Pakenham, Ontario: FQ Books.

Teaching Buddhism

The categorisation of Buddhism

In beginning any discussion of Buddhism it is important to ask the question: 'Is Buddhism a religion?' This question can be asked because it challenges traditional assumptions about the characteristics of a religion. Buddhism is generally an atheistic religion; a religion without God. As such some would categorise Buddhism as not being a religion.

There are other reasons for this, and also reasons why people would accept Buddhism as a religion. The Buddha is not a representation of God for Buddhists, rather he is an exemplar who set the example, and he has no supernatural abilities that set him apart from others. Buddhists are seekers of truth as exemplified in the Buddha's life. The Buddha in some ways fits the mould of religious leaders, but in the rejection of him being a spiritual manifestation or messenger of a supreme being he could be seen to stand alone; though other figures in religion might be seen to fulfil a similar role without a divinely appointed role such as Martin Luther King in Christianity and the Rightly Guided Caliphs within Sunni Islam.

It is taught that Buddhists do not worship the Buddharupa with any expectation of reward; they are paying reverence to what it represents. By sitting in front of the Buddha and making offerings, a Buddhist might believe that they are in the presence of the Buddha and gain inspiration from his example. While the object of worship may not be divine, the belief that a devotee is paying devotion of something or someone beyond the immediate context is very religious in nature.

Narada Mahathera recognises the issue that is faced in the classification of Buddhism:

> Buddhism cannot, therefore, strictly be called a religion because it is neither a system of faith and worship, nor 'the outward act or form by which men indicate their recognition of the existence of a God or gods having power over their own destiny to whom obedience, service, and honour are due.'
>
> If, by religion, is meant 'a teaching which takes a view of life that is more than superficial, a teaching which looks into life and not merely at it, a teaching which furnishes men with a guide to conduct that is in accord with this its in-look, a teaching which enables those who give it heed to face life with fortitude and death with serenity,' or a system to get rid of the ills of life, then it is certainly a religion of religions.
>
> (1995, p. 9)

Buddhism is often termed a way of life rather than a religion. However, all religions could be seen to be ways of life. The categorisation of Buddhism is largely moot as it is accepted by most as such, however, it is important for teachers and students of RE to understand that it challenges and perhaps expands the definition of religion. Its place as a non-theistic religion was used as a precedent by the Supreme Court in the United Kingdom to accept the argument of Scientology that it can be similarly categorised (see Bingham, 2013).

As highlighted in Chapter 8, no religion is a monolithic block. There are many different manifestations of it, even within the UK. Consider the experience of one teacher:

The problem of Buddhism in Britain and its relation to the various interpretations was highlighted for me in a parents evening where I asked a parent if she followed the Theravada or Mahayana school of Buddhism. She looked quizzically at me and said she didn't know either of those schools, they were Tibetan Buddhists. I asked which would be considered to be 'British Buddhism'. There is no such thing, I was told. After being rather disparaging about what she saw as diluted westernised teaching of another local Buddhist community, she then asked me how someone could be a true Buddhist without a Lama. This highlighted for me the concerns that face a teacher of Buddhism as much as a teacher of Hinduism or Christianity; the diversity is so big that we have to acknowledge it while we teach 'classroom Buddhism'.

Out of the teachings of the Buddha it is believed that three ways or 'vehicles' (yanas) were developed to help different types of people on the path to enlightenment. The different forms of Buddhism are manifold but the main schools include:

- *Hinaya/Nikaya Buddhism*: *the common vehicle.* Theravada, or Way of the Elders, is the only surviving school of Nikaya Buddhism and is to be found mainly within South and Southeast Asia. Hinaya can be translated as the lesser or lower vehicle, which is seen as a derogatory term coined by some in the Mahayana school and should be avoided. The idea of the three vehicles is rejected by Theravada Buddhists. Nikaya Buddhism is the oldest surviving form of Buddhism. Theravada Buddhists only accept the historical Buddha and teachings that can be historically linked to him. The beliefs about the Buddha reflect his place as the main focus of devotion and as a guide, teacher, and exemplar.
- *Mahayana: the great vehicle.* This developed in India somewhere between the Second Century BCE and the first century CE. Mahayana Buddhism accepts the early teachings of Buddhism; and renunciation of the world is important as in Theravada. Mahayana Buddhism expands the concept of the historical Buddha to include it as a cosmic presence that influences the world; as still active in the world and can be experienced in visions and through meditation; a source of blessings to Buddhists. Zen is a form of Mahayana Buddhism.
- *Vajrayana: the diamond vehicle* (also known as Tantric Buddhism). This developed in India in approximately the fifth century CE. Vajrayana can be seen to be a part of Mahayana Buddhism; and the four main schools of Tibetan Vajrayana Buddhism identify themselves as belonging to Mahayana. Mahayana itself can be seen as a precursor for the practice of Vajrayana. Vajrayana highlights the importance of the teacher who shows the student the path to enlightenment.

A further school could be added who were known as the Western Buddhist Order. They are now called Triratna Buddhism to recognise that this school is spreading in India as well as in the West. The Western Buddhist Order was founded by the Venerable Sangharakshita in 1968. It is an organisation that explores the living of Buddhist principles in modern society.

The message of Buddhism

The message of Buddhism as a way of life is the search for enlightenment through the application of the Four Noble Truths. The Buddha used a well-known Indian medical formula to help explain the Four Noble Truths. Buddhists believe that the Buddha's teaching is a cure for the world's illnesses and the way to enlightenment.

- What is the illness?
- What has caused the illness?
- Does a cure exist?
- The remedy – what does the patient need to do in order to be cured?

- *The First Noble Truth* is that suffering is a part of everyday life (dukkha). Instead of running smoothly, life is filled with the miseries of birth, old age, sickness and death. If a person is happy with a friend, for example, then when that friend goes that person will be sad. Humanity will never be happy if their happiness is based on things that change.
- *The Second Noble Truth* is the cause of suffering is craving or desire (tanha). People tend to want more and more of everything. They become unhappy with what they have. There is always something else that is going to make them better. In the example of the friend, the suffering is caused because the person craves their friend's company.
- *The Third Noble Truth* is that suffering can be ended by stopping desires and cravings (nirodha). This state of perfect freedom and happiness is the same as enlightenment.
- *The Fourth Noble Truth* is that enlightenment and nibbana can be achieved, and suffering can be ended by the living of the Eightfold Path or the Middle Way (magga).

Everything within life is impermanent, and the recognition of this will help a person achieve enlightenment. This impermanence is shown through the Three Marks of Existence:

1 Impermanence (Anicca) teaches that there is nothing that is permanent– everything changes. There is no exception to Anicca. Everything needs to begin to exist, therefore if it begins to exist it will one day cease.
2 Suffering (Dukkha).
3 No permanent self (Anatta). There is no permanent part of the self (perhaps defined as a soul in other religions). There is no personal soul that goes from one body to the next. The personality and experiences of this life are restricted only to this life.

When a person accepts the Marks of Existence they are on the path to enlightenment – only by a recognition of these truths can a person hope for the transcendence over earthly things necessary to achieve nibbana.

The overall message of Buddhism as seeking freedom from suffering through a recognition of the impermanence of everything and the removal of craving and desire, is very counter cultural in the United Kingdom. As such, it may be that part of Buddhism's appeal is its seeming rejection of the prevailing culture of materialism and its search for equanimity and peace.

The life of the Buddha

Having focused on concepts such as the grounding of all religious teaching and expression throughout this book, it may seem strange to begin a discussion of Buddhism surrounding the historical life of the Buddha. However, the life of the Buddha gives concrete examples of the central concepts and beliefs of Buddhism and he is the first of the Three Jewels or Refuges of Buddhism.

Early life

Siddhartha Gautama was born in Nepal in the seventh century BCE. He was born as a prince. There were auspicious signs surrounding his birth. Prior to her pregnancy, his mother dreamed of a white elephant entering her womb. White elephants were very rare and honoured, and this event was taken as a sign that her baby would be great. Upon Siddhartha's birth, his father was visited by a holy man who told him that Siddhartha would either be a great ruler or a great teacher. Determined that his son would be a great king, Siddhartha's father went to great lengths to provide him with the upbringing that would be suitable for a leader. Part of this entailed Siddhartha having every luxury and experiencing no suffering. To ensure this, Siddhartha was not allowed to leave the palace grounds. One suggestion is that if plants showed signs of dying, they were replaced; if servants showed signs of getting old, then they were also replaced. Siddhartha's life was one free of suffering. On one occasion Siddhartha's father allowed him out of the palace but this was carefully choreographed to show life outside of the palace in a positive light.

The Four Sights

Siddhartha, however, was not happy. Despite having a lovely wife and child he was left yearning for more. One day he escaped the palace and encountered some very strange sights. Within Buddhism these are known as the Four Sights. He saw:

*   A wrinkled person who was walking slowly (an old man).
*   A person who was coughing and sneezing (an ill person).
*   A person lying perfectly still on a stretcher (a dead person).
*   A skinny man meditating under a tree (an ascetic).

The Four Sights are an important event in the Buddha's life. It was through these that he realised that there was lots of suffering in the world. That the way of living where everything was provided was not the way to overcome suffering and have a happy life. A person is only deceiving themselves that suffering does not exist; there was no true freedom and happiness. These thoughts helped Siddhartha realise there was a problem that needed to be solved and thus began his path to enlightenment.

In a similar way to Siddhartha, Buddhists today begin their path to enlightenment when they realise there is a problem in the world and recognise the truth of suffering.

Siddhartha decided to leave the palace and his family to seek a way to find happiness and overcome suffering. Although he left his family behind, he recognised that he could not be truly happy because he realised that someday he would lose them. He needed to find the solution.

Life as an ascetic

Siddhartha met a group of holy men – ascetics who had renounced the world. As this was the complete opposite to the way that he lived in the palace, he thought this might provide the answers he sought. Siddhartha lived like this for a number of years, sometimes living on a grain of rice a day but he came no closer to finding the answers to life's questions. He therefore gave up this life. Although some may see this period of Siddhartha's life as a failure, it is seen as an important step within his search for enlightenment. The self-denial and meditative practices of the ascetics, while imperfect, helped the Buddha develop attributes and practices that would be important in the development of the Middle Way. Having lived a life of luxury, and a life of denial, he realised that neither provided him with contentment. He decided to live a 'middle way', a life that was not luxurious neither was it ascetic. Utilising Siddhartha's example, Buddhists are able to avoid the pitfall of self-denial and strive for enlightenment without the trial and error.

The Bodhi tree and enlightenment

Siddhartha continued his search and meditated under the Bodhi tree to seek enlightenment. After sitting cross-legged with his back towards the tree, he determined to continue in meditation until he had found enlightenment. He meditated on his breathing in and breathing out. It was an evening of a full moon.

During the night he was assailed by the daughters of the demon Mara. Many evil thoughts, said to be the daughters of the evil god Mara sent to dance for him, crept into his mind. These thoughts of desire, craving, fear and attachment arose, yet Siddhartha did not allow these thoughts to disturb his concentration. He sat impassive. The Middle Way was evident in his reaction to the temptations, whether real or within his mind; he was neither interested or repulsed — both extremes of a possible reaction that would have distracted him. He was impassive and focused on his own meditation.

Siddhartha felt calm and found the power of seeing his own past lives. In the second part of the night, Siddhartha realised the impermanence of life and how living beings die only to be reborn again. In the third part of the night, he realised the cause of all evil and suffering and how to be released from it. He understood how to end sorrow, unhappiness, suffering, old age and death.

The Buddha (Enlightened One) passed into a deep meditation, passing beyond the limits of ordinary human understanding, seeing the world as it is, and not as it appears to be. And having understood the world as it is, the Buddha was perfected in wisdom, never to be reborn. Craving and desire had been completely eradicated and he had found the state of perfect peace.

The enlightenment under the Bodhi tree is central in Buddhism. Through the Buddha's example, a Buddhist can follow the meditation necessary to achieve enlightenment. In renouncing worldly attachments, the Buddha shows Buddhists how important detachment is in gaining enlightenment.

The founding of the Sangha

Following his experience of the Bodhi tree, the Buddha travelled to the Deer Park near Varanasi in northern India. Here he delivered his first sermon to a group of five companions with whom he had previously sought enlightenment. In this sermon the Buddha taught them the Four Noble Truths and the Middle Way (Eightfold Path). The six of them formed the first sangha (community of Buddhist monks). All five become arahants (in Theravada this means those who have achieved enlightenment). The sangha continued to grow. These were then sent out to explain the teachings of the Buddha (dhamma) to the wider population.

At first the sangha was limited to monks (bhikku) but after five years it was extended to include nuns (bhikkunis) at the request of the Buddha's aunt. Initially the Buddha had refused her request for ordination three times. To convince him she cut her hair, put on yellow clothes and walked 150 miles to Vesali. Her feet became swollen; in tears she waited outside where the Buddha was staying. Ananda (one of the companions of the Buddha) saw her like this and offered to ask the Buddha on her behalf. Ananda petitioned the Buddha three times, each time being refused. Ananda asked if women could become enlightened. When the Buddha answered positively, Ananda asked if women could be ordained as nuns. The Buddha replied that a woman could only be ordained if she was willing to live the Middle Way. Maha Pajapati Gotami agreed and became a nun (bhikkuni) and, not long after, an arahant.

These events are important today because they began the codification of the Buddha's experiences into teachings (dhamma) and showed the crucial things that a person should do to achieve enlightenment. For some Buddhists they show the importance of a teacher. Most importantly, they mark the beginning of the sangha, the second of the three Jewels/Refuges.

The Buddha's death and parinibbana

When he was 80, the Buddha told his followers that he would soon achieve parinibbana (final and complete nibbana at the passing away of a Buddha). Soon after this the Buddha ate his last meal provided by Cunda, the blacksmith. He soon became rather ill. In Mahayana Buddhists some believe that the Buddha was not really ill but was merely teaching people about the suffering and impermanence of this life. Buddhists believe that he did not die in the normal sense of the word but achieved nibbana, which is deathless and the state when craving ceases and kamma stops being generated. He died lying on his right side with his right hand under his head (some rupas of the Buddha can be seen in this position). His death was the final teaching on impermanence.

The Buddha was cremated; elements of his body (teeth and bones) did not burn and were placed into eight stupas which have since become places of pilgrimage to Buddhists. The stupas' locations include:

- Sri Dalada Maligawa or The Temple of the Sacred Tooth Relic in Kandy in Sri Lanka
- Sarnath
- Sanchi

Whether these stupas were of the original eight is a matter of debate but they are places of pilgrimage with relics associated with the Buddha.

The life of the Buddha as central to RE teaching

While most Buddhists would accept the story of the life of the Buddha as accurate, it can also be seen as a parable for the Four Noble Truths and the path that every person travels in the world. It evidences how a Buddhist should live their lives in seeking enlightenment. It also shows some of the questions that lie at the heart of human existence, all of which form the basis of Buddhism. In exploring the life of the Buddha in the RE classroom, the events can be explored to discuss how a Buddhist could live their life; or conversely the way that a Buddhist lives their life can be explored to construct elements of the Buddha's experience and the answers he provided.

Aspects of these events are shown in the various rupas associated with the Buddha. By focusing on the rupas, the pupils can explore the various examples of the Buddha's teachings and example.

The Noble Eightfold Path

The Buddha taught that following the Middle Way, or the Eightfold Path, is the way to escape suffering in life and achieve enlightenment. He taught that by treading this Noble Path a person might achieve a state of bliss, happiness and peace, free from suffering (dukkha) and achieve nibbana.

The Eightfold Path is:

1   Right Understanding
2   Right Attitude
3   Right Speech
4   Right Action
5   Right Livelihood
6   Right Effort
7   Right Awareness
8   Right Concentration.

The path could also then be split into three ways: wisdom (prajna); morality (sila) and meditation (samadhi). While artificially separating them into groups here it is important to note that all are interlinked with other aspects of the Eightfold Path. It is impossible to have a morality without wisdom, and it is impossible to develop that wisdom further without morality.

The way of wisdom (prajna)

Right Understanding and Right Attitude (or Intention) are in this section. Wisdom, for Buddhists, is the understanding of how to see the world and an individual's place in it.

Right Understanding

In this way a Buddhist is able to see the world as it is and understand that there is a path to freedom. Having understood that life is full of suffering, this step aims at letting go of all desires and cravings and so to stop suffering.

Right Attitude

A Buddhist believes that a person's mental attitude to life affects what they get out of life. Developing right attitudes and thoughts is important on the path to enlightenment.

The way of morality (sila)

The way of morality incorporates Right Speech, Right Action and Right Livelihood. Buddhist morality could be seen to be different from that found in other religions of the world. Most other religions, it could be argued, guide ethical conduct based on rules that have been laid down; whereas for Buddhism, morality is a way for a Buddhist to try to develop compassion (metta), which is the ultimate goal. The morality that is adhered to in Buddhism should be based around what is the best way of developing a harmonious relationship with the individual, others and the natural world.

Right Speech

If Buddhists are governed by compassion, this means that we will speak kindly to people. They will not speak to another with a desire to hurt or humiliate. A Buddhist should ensure that they are honest. If none of this is possible then it may be necessary to remain silent.

Right Action

Just as Right Speech is ensuring that nobody is harmed through speech, Right Action is about not harming others through actions. It is acting with compassion and wisdom in each situation. This action could be seen to link to the five precepts (pansils):

1   A Buddhist should care for all living beings.
2   A Buddhist should never take anything that does not belong to them and instead share what they have.
3   A Buddhist should avoid sexual misconduct.
4   A Buddhist should avoid harmful speech.
5   A Buddhist should not misuse drugs and alcohol.

As these would distract from the path to enlightenment, these prohibitions are associated with five positive actions that would help a Buddhist live the Middle Way:

•   kindness and consideration for all beings
•   generosity
•   commitment and fidelity to one's partner
•   honesty and fair-dealing
•   developing clarity of mind.

Right Livelihood

Whatever career or vocation is pursued, it should not be done if it causes harm to others. Therefore, the job that a Buddhist chooses to do should not cause harm to others. Although some jobs may be obviously restricted, the way that people carry out their jobs may also be seen to fall under this aspect of the Eightfold Path. For example, if a teacher is aggressive or uncaring with their students then, combined with Right Speech, they are not fulfilling Right Livelihood.

The way of meditation (samadhi)

The way of meditation includes Right Effort, Right Mindfulness and Right Concentration and is often called mental concentration. In order to receive enlightenment and escape the cycle of samsara, a Buddhist must focus on the things that are important.

Right Effort

Right Effort suggests the effort necessary to keep the mind clear of anything that might draw a person away from meditation on the Four Noble Truths and the path to enlightenment. This is shown in the Buddha's struggle with the four daughters of Mara and the thoughts of desire, craving, fear and attachment. He did not allow these thoughts to disturb his concentration. This enables a person to maintain right mindfulness.

Right Mindfulness

Right Mindfulness is the ability to focus on the here and now rather than the uncontrollable future. It, similarly, impacts on Right Action. The only way to have compassion is to have the right mind-set and an idea of how everybody and everything fits into the universe. Without Right Mindfulness, Right Effort could be disorganised and ineffectual.

Right Concentration

The ability to concentrate and maintain attentiveness is fundamental within Buddhism. Buddhists concentrate on meditation while other things strive to distract them. Buddhists concentrate and follow the Eightfold Path while other things seek to divert them from it. It is the ability to concentrate on dhamma at the expense of short-term pleasure. The way that this concentration is maintained through meditation is different according to the individual and possibly the tradition of Buddhism that they follow.

Elements of the Eightfold Path are an expression of Buddhist spirituality, but they are also an integral outworking of the Four Noble Truths. As outlined earlier, Buddhism is often described as a way of life. As such, the Eightfold Path forms the basis of this way of life, but it is grounded in the concepts of impermanence, rejecting desire and seeking enlightenment that are evidenced through the Buddha's life.

The nature of humanity

As suggested by one of the Three Marks of Existence (anatta), there is no permanent self. Rather, most Buddhists believe a person is made up of five constituent parts known as khandas. The self is an illusory name attached to the five khandas:

1   Form (rupa): the physical body.
2   Feeling (vedana): the sensations and feelings experienced as part of the physical world. There are generally seen to be six senses in Buddhism: sight; hearing; smell; taste; touch; and mind.

3   Perception (sanjna): This helps people to recognise, identify, classify and put their sense experiences into words; for example, we can tell the difference between chocolate and lemon.

4   Mental formation (samskara): the way that the mind develops impressions based on feelings and perceptions.

5   Consciousness (vijnana): the awareness of and sensitivity towards objects around an individual.

In the world everything is impermanent and in a state of constant change. Every element of the person is subject to change, for example, within the feeling khanda something that might cause pleasure one day may cause displeasure the next. The impermanence of the self and the khandas help Buddhists construct a worldview that is not dependent on the self. Through achieving this they can rid themselves of suffering. By acknowledging the khandas, a person may live a more balanced life; recognising that fear and suffering are just the result of the khandas, which are impermanent. The experience of pain may not be able to be reduced just by recognising its impermanence; however, it could be reduced by knowing that it will end and change.

This belief extends into the Buddhist beliefs of kamma and rebirth. While it could be suggested that the accumulation of kamma and rebirth constitute an eternal part of the self, this is not the case. Rebirth can be described as the blowing out of a candle, and the relighting of another. There is no transmigration of the soul from one life form to the next.

Although the purpose of life could be seen to be enlightenment, within Mahayana Buddhism it is taught that every being has a Buddha nature (tathagatagarbha), which means that they have a potential for enlightenment. Therefore, the process for the individual of attaining enlightenment is a search within to discover whom they really are. The purpose of life for most Mahayana Buddhists is to become a bodhisattva. Bodhisattvas, having achieved Buddhahood, delay nibbana to show others the way, and are reborn in different forms. Nibbana is a lesser goal for those whose main desire is to escape suffering.

It is important to note that within Theravada Buddhism, Siddhartha Gautama is the exemplar and guide; whereas within Mahayana, he is known as *the* Buddha but there are other bodhisattvas who are used both in worship and in guides. As one example, The Dalai Lama, in Tibetan Buddhism (a part of Vajrayana, and consequently can be seen to be part of Mahayana), is traditionally thought to be the rebirth of a bodhisattva.

Religious expression

This chapter has necessarily focused on aspects of the conceptual centre of Buddhism. While their outworkings into elements of Buddhists' practice have been explored, the bulk of a Buddhist's religious expression has been left unexplored. There will be aspects of populist Buddhism in some areas of the world that will not seem to link with the teachings above, as traditional beliefs are fused with Buddhist concepts. However, even outside of these expressions there are outward practices found in the way that Buddhists worship, the design of the viharas and the celebration of festivals that will help a pupil explore the central beliefs that have been outlined. The Three Jewels/Refuges can be seen to be central to most Buddhists:

- I take refuge in the Buddha.
- I take refuge in the dhamma.
- I take refuge in the sangha.

If the final refuge is taken as an example, while that might be a unifying force, the understanding and expression of how it functions may be different within the schools of Buddhism. Sometimes the community (sangha) is seen to be divided into two distinct groups: the ordained and the laity. Here, the specific functions of each are separate and distinct but both laity and the monks and nuns gain merit (kamma) by fulfilling their duties towards one another. The monks and nuns would adopt the five additional precepts (pansils) (Theravada monks actually have 227 rules (vinaya) in total):

- Refraining from eating after midday (though they can drink).
- Refraining from unsuitable entertainments.
- Refraining from using scents and personal adornments.
- Refraining from sleeping on a luxurious bed.
- Refraining from handling gold, silver and money.

The sexual misconduct precept is replaced by a vow of celibacy.

In other interpretations of Buddhism, particularly Triratna, there is no separation in the sangha. The sangha itself is self-sufficient and does not adopt a vow of poverty – this enables the work of order to be carried out in a simpler and more effective way. The sangha has been extended to all of those who have gone for refuge and it could be seen to be much more inclusive than in other forms of Buddhism.

As teachers of RE, it is necessary to explore these different expressions not just about the sangha but means of worship, attitudes to various aspects of the world and many others. In doing this students are able to develop informed opinions about them as expressions of faith. It would be an interesting task for pupils to begin with certain practices and through the enquiry process explore the relationships between beliefs and practices within Buddhism.

References

Bingham, Jon (2013) 'Scientology is a Religion, Rules Supreme Court'. In the *Daily Telegraph* 11 Dec 2013. Available at: www.telegraph.co.uk/news/religion/10510301/Scientology-is-a-religion-rules-Supreme-Court.html (accessed 1 May 2014).
Mahathera, Narada (1995 [1982]) *Buddhism in a Nutshell*. Kandy, Sri Lanka: Buddhist Dharma Education. Available at: www.buddhanet.net/pdf_file/nutshell.pdf (accessed 1 May 2014).

Further reading

Bechert, H. and Gombrich, R. (1991) *The World of Buddhism*. London: Thames and Hudson.
Chryssides, G. (1988) *Introduction to Buddhism*. Cambridge: Cambridge University Press.
Cush, D. (1990) *Buddhism in Britain Today*. London: Hodder.
Hawkins, B. K. (1999) *Buddhism*. London: Routledge.
Keown, D. (1996) *Buddhism: A Very Short Introduction*. Oxford: Oxford University Press.
Kulananda (2001) *Buddhism*. London: Thorsons.
Schmidt-Leukel, P. (2006) *Understanding Buddhism*. Edinburgh, UK: Dunedin.

Chapter 10

Teaching Christianity

Chapter outline

What is Christianity?

The message of Christianity

The nature of God

- God as Creator
- God as Judge

The life of Jesus Christ

- The Incarnation
- The Baptism of Jesus
- The temptations of Jesus
- The miracles of Jesus
- The teachings of Jesus
- The Last Supper
- The death and resurrection
- Pentecost
- The Life of Jesus as Central to RE teaching

The nature of humanity

Religious expression

What is Christianity?

An agreed syllabus should 'reflect the fact that the religious traditions of Great Britain are, in the main Christian, while taking account of teachings and practices of the other principal religions represented in Great Britain' (Education Reform Act 1988, Section 8 (3)). Therefore, the teaching of Christianity should be found within every Key Stage. Christianity is a religion with many different expressions and, as such, when teachers are teaching Christianity the question could be asked 'Whose Christianity?' Indeed, in 2001 it was suggested that there are over 33,000 different Christian groups (Barrett, Kurian, and Johnson, 2001). There are traditionally seen to be three main groupings of Churches: Orthodox, Catholic and Protestant. However, there are groups who would find themselves outside of those umbrella groups; Barrett et al. categorise them as Independents and Marginals (2001).

The borders of Christianity are hard to define, and depend very much on the person who is drawing them. It is for this reason that before exploring any of the central beliefs of Christianity it is important to establish who is a Christian, and what the defining beliefs are. One example of the problems associated with establishing a definition is highlighted using the example of Jehovah's Witnesses who would self-identify as Christian supported by a belief in Jesus and the use of the Bible, but other Christians may address their Christianity 'by referring to Trinitarian doctrine: those who hold the idea of God in Trinity are Christians, but those (like the Witnesses) who do not hold this belief place themselves alongside, but separate from, the main stream of Christianity' (Holt, 2004, p. 17).

The problem arises for any teacher or student of Christianity when determining who to include in the family of Christian Churches. Whatever definition is used might offend somebody by either leaving somebody out who feels they should be in, or including somebody that others feel are outside of the family of Churches. It can be suggested that there are three reasons why a group might be excluded based on definition. Christian Churches are:

- members of the World Council of Churches.
- founded before the nineteenth century.
- accept the Trinity (see Holt, 2005, p. 34).

These criteria seem to be designed to exclude; but it is right that there should be a definition otherwise there is no difference between religions. It is possible to define Christian groups as Trinitarian and non-Trinitarian as the Trinity, and belief in the creeds, seems to be one of the criteria that is used often and is a unifying doctrine among many denominations of Christianity. It was suggested by one of the early Church Fathers that only those who act in a Christian way, and are living their religion to the fullest can be considered to be Christian:

> Those who are found not living as he taught should know that they are not really Christians, even if his teachings are on their lips, for he said that not those who merely profess but those who also do the works will be saved.
>
> (Martyr, 1999, pp. 37–38)

This definition that Justin Martyr puts forward is a high standard for Christians and the Churches to live up to. Maybe if he suggested that people were trying to live their lives as Christians this might be more embracive. It could be argued that what constitutes a Christian is: 'somebody who considers themselves to be a Christian. If there has to be a criterion against which they can be judged, it would be a belief that Jesus is the Christ, the Son of God' (Holt, 2005, p. 34). This definition, while being inclusive, might be a reflection of the author's self-identification of a person on the periphery of 'traditional'

Christianity. However, it does provide a workable basis for teachers of RE who are going to encounter people who self-identify as Christian. The self-definition and identification of Jesus as the Son of God raises issues in certain situations; for example, the Unification Church identify as Christian yet would see Jesus as the Messiah, but son of Zacharias. This would also raise issues within some parts of Rastafarianism; there are elements who in no way consider themselves to be Christian, while on the other hand members of the Twelve Tribes of Israel consider themselves to be completely Christian. Therefore, perhaps a definition such as the above would not suit an exercise in pigeon-holing groups, but is perhaps the only workable one in the classroom. One Latter-day Saint Christian offered his own view on Christianity as part of a plea to be accepted:

> As a Christian I feel Christ's message is inclusive not exclusive. I have no problem in being seen as outside of the mainstream of Christianity, my problem is being seen as outside the whole of Christianity. We are free to disagree with a person's definition and practice of Christianity but we are not free to tell them who they are.
>
> (Holt, 2005, p. 34)

Using the above as a background, this chapter will explore some of the central beliefs of Christianity to introduce the religion, though it will not cover every nuance of interpretation. This will form an important basis for further reading and study.

The message of Christianity

The overall message of Christianity is one of reconciliation. Through sin humanity is in a broken relationship with God. The purpose of this life can be seen to be to overcome sin and rebuild this relationship. This is a task that is outside of the realm of human capability; as such, most Christians believe that God became flesh (incarnate) in his Son Jesus Christ. As God incarnate Christ was able to broach this gap through his sinless life and atonement on the cross of Calvary. Through the grace of Christ humanity, and especially individual humans, is able to be reconciled to God. In response to this grace Christians strive to follow Christ's example in the way that they live their lives. Christianity, therefore, is as much a way of life as other religions that are usually described as such. A common adage is 'What would Jesus do?' and, as such, every aspect of a Christian's life is affected by their relation to God. This is, of course, the ideal and such is the nature of humanity that all fall short of this ideal and are in constant need of reconciliation.

The nature of God

Within Christianity some of the characteristics of God might be identified as:

- Omnibenevolence: God is all loving
- Omnipotence: God is all powerful
- Omniscience: God is all knowing
- Omnipresence: God is everywhere.

With the basis of these characteristics, most Christians believe that God is creator and judge, God answers people's prayers and controls the universe. Some Christians describe

God as transcendent, meaning he is above and beyond everything, and cannot be completely understood. God is also seen to be immanent, meaning God is intimately involved in people's lives seeking the best for all people.

Most Christians would identify God in the doctrine of the Trinity. The Trinity is outlined in the creeds (statements of the Church councils). In the Nicene Creed it says:

> We believe in one God, the Father, the Almighty, maker of heaven and earth, and of all that is, seen and unseen.
>
> We believe in one Lord, Jesus Christ, the only Son of God, eternally begotten of the Father, God from God, Light from Light, true God from true God, begotten, not made, one in Being with the Father. Through him all things were made …
>
> We believe in the Holy Spirit, the Lord, the giver of life, who proceeds from the Father and the Son. With the Father and the Son he is worshipped and glorified.
>
> ('Credo', nd)

This shows that Christians believe God has three ways of being known:

- Father
- Son
- Holy Spirit

Each has a different role:

- The Father is the Creator.
- The Son is the Redeemer.
- The Holy Spirit is the Sustainer.

The Nicene Creed teaches that these three persons are homoousios (of one substance). God is at the same time Father, Son and Holy Spirit. To some extent this belief is seen to be a mystery and as such humanity is not meant to understand God.

A Christian will go to God for many reasons, and sees God as a listening ear, a protector, a comforter, a strength and many more things besides. They will strive to build a relationship through prayer, worship and a study of God's word. Two ways in which they know God are as Creator and Judge.

God as Creator

The Christian creation stories are found in Genesis 1–2. God in Christianity is believed to be omnipotent (all powerful) and omniscient (all knowing). In the story (whether literal or metaphorical), God created by saying: 'Let there be light' (Gen 1:3). However the universe was created, Christians believe that God, as omnipotent, created it. The world is also beautiful, which is evidence of his love (benevolence).

God as Judge

On the last day all of humanity will be brought before God to be judged. The judgement that God gives will be perfect because God is perfect. It will also be just (appropriate and right) because God is omniscient and knows not just the actions that people have performed, but also the thoughts and intents of their hearts.

The life of Jesus Christ

Jesus is the central figure of Christianity. Christians believe that Jesus is the Son of God, the Messiah (Christ) or 'anointed one'. With an understanding of his life it is possible to see its echoes in the lives of Christians today.

The Incarnation

As the Son of God, Jesus's birth is significant for Christians today. His birth is known as the 'Incarnation' but is more commonly known as the 'Nativity'. Incarnation means to receive flesh/body. Most Christians believe that at birth God was made incarnate (see John 1: 14). The events of the Nativity are familiar to most school children, they can be found in the first chapters of Matthew and Luke.

- The Annunciation: Angel Gabriel tells Mary that she is going to have the Son of God.
- She is overcome by the Holy Spirit.
- Joseph wants to send her away as he thinks she has been unfaithful to him.
- The Angel Gabriel visits Joseph in a dream and Joseph changes his mind.
- Joseph and Mary travel to Bethlehem.
- They are offered a stable to stay in when there is no room at the inn.
- A new star appears in the sky as the birth of Jesus occurs in a stable.
- The Angels announce the birth of the Messiah to the shepherds who then visit the child.
- Wise men from the east (not necessarily three) follow the star and visit King Herod.
- The wise men give Jesus gifts of gold, frankincense and myrrh.
- Fearful that Jesus would take his throne Herod orders all baby boys killed.
- To escape the slaughter Jesus is taken into Egypt.

The story is central to who Jesus is. One Christian has said:

> The Nativity is important to me because it is the story of the Incarnation. It tells me how God became flesh in order to save the world. The events are so miraculous it shows me that Jesus really is the Son of God.

A large number of Christians around the world celebrate this significant event at Christmas time.

The Baptism of Jesus

Before Jesus began teaching people as an adult he was baptised. When Jesus was baptised he was immersed in water by John the Baptist in the River Jordan. As Jesus came up out of the water the Bible describes the Holy Spirit descending in the form of a dove, and a voice from heaven being heard identifying Jesus as the Son of God (see Mark 1:

4–12). Jesus was baptised because it was a commandment from God. It is also a symbol of a new start, marking the beginning of his public ministry. A number of Christians will follow Jesus's example in being baptised (either as a child or an adult) to symbolise a forgiveness of sins and a new start within Christianity.

The temptations of Jesus

After Jesus was baptised he went and fasted for 40 days in the wilderness. During this time Satan tempted him with many things. Jesus is believed to be the Messiah, and the people at Jesus's time were expecting a great and powerful leader. These temptations show that this was not the Messiah that Jesus was. He was tempted to:

• turn stone into bread
• throw himself off the top of the Temple and be caught by angels
• bow down before the Devil and he would become ruler of the world.

Jesus did not give in to these temptations and used scripture to help him resist. This teaches Christians that Jesus was not going to be a worldly leader, and the importance of following God rather than their own desires. They also might believe that they should follow Jesus in resisting temptation. It could also help Christians to understand that everybody is subject to temptation but it is how a person responds that is important.

The miracles of Jesus

Throughout Jesus's ministry he performed many miracles. They were usually for one of three reasons:

1   Because he had compassion (felt the suffering of someone as his own).
2   Because of the person's faith (belief) in him.
3   To show he was sent from God as the Son of God.

There can be seen to be three major types of miracle:

1   A nature miracle, where he shows his command over nature, for example the calming of the storm.
2   Healing miracles, where people have been healed from an illness, including the Woman with Internal Bleeding (Matthew 9: 19–22); the healing of a paralysed man (Matthew 9:1–8); and the curing of a man with a withered hand.
3   The raising from the dead, such as Jairus's daughter or the raising of Lazarus.

Throughout Christ's ministry he taught the importance of helping other people, and showing them God's love through action. What is important for Christians is that Jesus did not just teach it but that he put that teaching into practice. One Christian has suggested that Jesus was different because he was able to say 'Do as I say and as I do' rather than the more common 'Don't do as I do, do as I say'.

Some Christians believe that God still performs miracles like these today. It is more likely, however, that Jesus will miraculously change a person's moral and spiritual character for the better either directly or through a human being.

The teachings of Jesus

Discipleship

Jesus taught many things about discipleship. The word 'disciple' means learner or follower. All Christians are invited to be Jesus's disciples. When Jesus heals a blind man in John's Gospel there can also be seen to be a message that Christians are spiritually blind until they become disciples. The blind man specifically goes through stages of realisation following his healing to the declaration that Jesus is the Messiah and that Jesus is the 'light of the world'. For Christians it is only possible to become truly enlightened when they understand who Jesus is and what it is to be a disciple.

The calling of the original twelve disciples provides an example for Christians today. When they were asked to follow Jesus they left their nets immediately and followed Jesus. This suggests that a disciple should not put anything else before the service of God. This service includes sharing the message of Christ and doing good to others (Mark 16: 15–18).

An important part of discipleship is sacrifice. Jesus told his disciples to take up their cross (see Mark 8: 34–36). The imagery of 'taking up the cross' might evoke images of people facing death for their Christian beliefs and practice. While this would have immediate relevance for the first disciples, the relevance today would be about the challenges and ridicule of being a Christian. The life of a Christian is not just 'tea with the vicar'.

Throughout the gospels other qualities of a disciple are taught by Jesus:

- Service (Mark 9: 35).
- Committed to Jesus (Mark 9: 40).
- Have faith and belief as a child (Mark 10: 14–15). Children accept teaching with great trust.
- Charity.

Some Christians may reject these as too demanding, but a large number would strive to live their life in such a way.

Parables

Jesus taught people in parables. These are stories with a meaning. Jesus used parables to make people think about what he was teaching, and also to disguise the truth from those people who would not accept it. Some parables offended people because they made them think about what they were doing, and maybe it was wrong. Parables that Jesus told include:

- The Two Debtors (Luke 7: 41–43).
- The Good Samaritan (Luke 10: 25–37).
- The Wise and the Foolish Men (Matthew 7: 24–27 Luke 6: 46–49).
- Parable of the Sower (Matthew 13: 3–9 Mark 4: 3–9 Luke 8: 5–8).

- The Mustard Seed (Matthew 13: 31–32 Mark 4: 30–32 Luke 13: 18–19).
- The Good Shepherd (Matthew 18: 10–14 Luke 15: 4–6).
- Parable of the Prodigal Son (Luke 15: 11–32).
- The Ten Virgins (Matthew 25: 1–13).
- The Talents (Matthew 25: 14–30 Luke 19: 12–27).
- The Sheep and the Goats (Matthew 25: 31–46).

Although these can be seen to be sanitised by familiarity of retelling over the past 2,000 years they still have importance for Christians today in exploring ways in which they should live; the demands of discipleship; the nature of the Kingdom of God and the treatment of other people. Consider the parable of the sheep and the goats, which asks Christians to help others, and in so doing they are helping Jesus. Jesus chose the hungry, naked and imprisoned to show there were no limits when it came to helping others. The implications for Christians today are challenging.

The Sermon on the Mount

The Sermon on the Mount (Matthew 5–7) is probably Jesus's most famous speech. A lot of Christians like to read its words and try to live their lives according to what it teaches. There are many teachings within the Sermon but all of them raise the standard expected. In the Sermon on the Mount Jesus 'fulfilled' Moses's teachings. For example, not committing adultery became not looking at someone with lustful thoughts; an eye for an eye became 'turn the other cheek', and not killing someone became not getting angry. Other examples of teachings from the Sermon on the Mount include the admonition to love your enemies and to not judge. The implications for the practice of an individual Christian are huge, and show the demands of living as a Christian.

Christians believe that by following Jesus's example they can receive God's grace and salvation. Christianity does not just give a purpose to life, but is also a structure for the realisation of Christians' ultimate goal of reconciliation and salvation. This structure involves the sacrifice of self to the will of God, and the service of others.

The Last Supper

Jesus spent the last week of his life in Jerusalem for the Jewish festival of Passover. On the Thursday evening Jesus had the Passover meal with his disciples. This has become known to Christians throughout the world as the Last Supper. It was the last evening meal before Jesus was crucified the following day. Events of the Last Supper include:

- Jesus washed the disciples' feet.
- He foretold his betrayal by Judas.
- He foretold the denial by Peter.
- He shared the bread and wine (Luke 22: 123).

The events of the Last Supper are of huge importance and are remembered across most of Christianity in worship that is sometimes termed the Eucharist, Communion, Mass, or the Breaking of the Bread. The bread and wine remind Christians of the death of Jesus, but also of his resurrection. Bread can represent life as the basic foodstuff and wine can represent joy as shown in the Resurrection. Some Christians see the emblems as a symbol, where the bread and wine represent the body and blood of Jesus. Anglicans generally believe in Consubstantiation (the view that the Christ is present within the bread but it is still bread). Many would want to say that it is more than just a symbol but this is the language that comes closest. In a non-conformist Church the focus is on the Bible, as the words of the Last Supper are read while the bread and wine are blessed. Some Churches will have leaders take the bread and wine around to the members of the congregation

Other Christians believe that Jesus is physically present in the bread and wine, and that it becomes his body and blood. This is the teaching of the Roman Catholic Church and is called transubstantiation. The Eucharist is the central event of the Mass.

Whatever their view of the bread and wine, Christians will generally feel that it is a thanksgiving meal that draws them closer to God. Some Christians believe that the Eucharist is so special its practice should be restricted. The Salvation Army do not have a Eucharist service, while Jehovah's Witnesses celebrate it annually. They may feel that frequent celebrations of the Eucharist in Christian worship may reduce its significance and impact for worshippers.

The Eucharist reminds worshippers of God's love in sacrificing his Son; as such it points forward to his death and resurrection.

The death and resurrection

The whole of Jesus's life is fulfilled in his death and resurrection. In the preparation for his death Jesus was able to show his submission to the will of his Father. Jesus was willing to sacrifice his life and take up his cross. Most importantly he was able to reconcile humanity with God. This was of far greater import than any of the healing miracles. Every event of his life pointed towards his death and resurrection. The events of the death and resurrection are summarised below.

Following the Last Supper Jesus went to pray in the Garden of Gethsemane, leaving some of his disciples to keep watch. While praying he prayed that the things he was about to do might be taken from him, but that he would submit to the Father's will.

On leaving he was met by Judas and the guards of the high priest. Judas kissed Jesus on the cheek to identify him to the guards who then promptly arrested Jesus. Peter tried to protect Jesus and chopped off one of the soldier's ears. Jesus stopped him and healed the soldier's ear.

Jesus was taken to the High Priest and Sanhedrin (the Jewish ruling council). Members of the Sanhedrin insulted him, spat on him and condemned him to death for blasphemy. The trial itself was illegal as it was held at night, the full Sanhedrin were not there and Jesus was asked a direct question, 'Are you the Messiah?', whose answer would condemn him to death.

The Sanhedrin was unable to enforce the death penalty because Judaea was part of the Roman Empire and so Jesus was taken to Pontius Pilate (the Roman Governor). Pilate questioned Jesus and found no fault in him. To try to placate the Sanhedrin he ordered Jesus to be flogged. As a part of this cruel punishment the soldiers clothed Jesus in a scarlet robe and crowned him with a crown of thorns to mock him as the 'King of the Jews'.

The Sanhedrin still demanded Jesus's death. Pilate again resisted by offering to set Jesus or Barabbas free – the Jews chose Barabbas. As an aside, Barabbas means 'son of the father' or 'son of a man'; the people reject the Son of God in favour of an ordinary man. Realising he would have to execute Jesus, Pilate washed his hands – to symbolise that it was not of his doing.

Jesus was forced to carry his cross to the hill Calvary (some Gospel accounts have him being helped by Simon of Cyrene). Jesus was nailed to the cross. Christians believe that Jesus was crucified for the sins of the world, as a sinless sacrifice offered to God on behalf of the world. In Old Testament times a lamb would be sacrificed to take away sin and guilt; now the 'Lamb of God' was being sacrificed as the great and last sacrifice.

While Jesus was on the cross (for the space of six hours) he said 'I thirst'; and he was given vinegar to drink from a sponge. He asked John to take care of his mother and the world went dark for three hours. His last words were 'It is finished'. To ensure that he was dead, the Roman soldiers stabbed him in the side with a spear.

Joseph of Arimathea, a Jewish leader who had also been a disciple of Jesus, asked Pilate for permission to take the body and bury it. And so Jesus was taken down from the cross and buried in the borrowed tomb. Jesus was crucified on the Sabbath day and so he was buried hurriedly.

On the Sunday morning (the third day) some women including Mary Magdalene went to the tomb to anoint the body with spices. When they arrived they discovered that the stone was rolled away and that Jesus's body had disappeared. The women were understandably upset thinking that the body had been stolen. They were told by an angel, or by Jesus himself, that he had risen from the dead (it is important to note that Gospel accounts of the resurrection differ in details). The women were amazed that Jesus was alive and quickly went to tell the disciples. The disciples did not believe them at first and so Peter and John went to look for themselves, only to find the tomb was empty.

The two disciples quickly rushed to tell the other disciples that they had seen Jesus. While they were telling them, Jesus appeared and the disciples thought he was a spirit. Jesus proved he was alive by letting them touch him, showing the wounds of crucifixion and eating some food.

These events are the most important that have ever happened in the history of the world (according to Christians). It was through these events that Jesus reconciled humanity with God. Without Jesus, humanity could not be forgiven for their sins, and would have no chance of eternal reward. It is only through Jesus that Christians believe true peace can be found. In addition, Jesus's resurrection shows the hope of an afterlife.

One Christian has shared his feelings about these events and their impact on his life:

Because Jesus died on the cross, I know I am able to be forgiven for the things that I do wrong. Even though I fall, I am able to pick myself back up again and through the love of my Saviour carry on. To take advantage of this I need to accept Him as my Saviour and show my love for Him and others. This means that through my life I should try my best to live my life in a good way to please Him. Also that if I expect Jesus to forgive me I must forgive other people. I know that He did these things, not for personal gain, but because of the love He has for all of us.

In addition to the celebration of these events in the Eucharist, these events are remembered each year by the majority of Christians during Holy Week and its culmination on the Sunday in the celebration of Easter.

Pentecost

Before Jesus died, he promised his disciples that he would always be with them through the Comforter – the Holy Spirit. This was to sustain, to help and to guide them. Pentecost is the time Christians remember when the Holy Spirit came to the disciples. Fifty days after Jesus's resurrection, the disciples were meeting in a room in Jerusalem. The Holy Spirit came upon them in the form of fire and changed them. Instead of being in hiding, the disciples became bold and spoke out about the effect Jesus had had on their lives with dramatic results. On the day of Pentecost the disciples spoke in tongues and 3,000 people became followers of Jesus. Pentecost is often referred to as 'the birth of the Christian Church'.

What happened to the disciples at Pentecost shows Christians that God is with them in the form of the Holy Spirit who will guide and sustain them as individuals and as the Church. In many Christian churches there is a rite known as confirmation where Christians receive the Holy Spirit.

The Life of Jesus as Central to RE teaching

Almost every Christian belief and practice finds its root or expression in the life of Jesus. Therefore, teachers of Christianity should have a thorough understanding of the events of his life and the importance for Christians. This will enable teachers to root their teaching of Christianity in the concepts that are most crucial to the religion. Why do Christians show their love to others? It is because of the love Jesus exemplified in his life. Why do they worship in the way that they do? It is because of the example of prayer, devotion and the Eucharist that Jesus showed in his life. Jesus's demands of discipleship are evidenced in the way that he lived and died. Although this chapter will explore other aspects of Christianity, there will be a large number of elements that will not have been explored. This is because an understanding of Jesus's life is central to teaching Christianity. The presentation may well have seemed to be a concept-cracking or phenomenological approach, but even if an ethnographic or experiential approach is adopted the teaching may not have its beginning in the life of Jesus but its ending will be there. Why is a Christian baptised? In the end it is because of humanity's relationship to God reconciled through the life and sacrifice of Jesus.

The nature of humanity

Within Christianity, humanity is seen to hold a preeminent place within creation. Humans are the pinnacle of creation. They are the only one of God's creations to be described as 'in his image' (Genesis). What this may mean differs from Christian to Christian, but agreement would probably be found in saying humans are the most important of God's creations. Humans have been endowed with a soul that enables them to communicate with God. Of the creation of Adam, Christians believe that he did not become living until he had received his soul (Genesis 2: 7). As a result of this, and the free will which it has been given, humanity can have a conscious relationship with God. The body is described by Paul as 'God's temple' (1 Cor 3: 16); suggesting that it houses part of God's nature or spirit. Thus the body is important, and the proper treatment of it is part of a Christian's responsibility. This links with the teaching about the sanctity of human life; most Christians believe that only God gives life and only he can take it away.

The soul makes it possible for humans to communicate with God. The soul that continues after death is different from a pure spirit. This is shown through the resurrection of Jesus when the disciples felt his wounds and saw him eat. The body and the soul remain integrally linked. Whatever form it takes post-mortally, most Christians would agree that the soul is what makes it possible to say that humans are created in God's image. God became human in order to reconcile humanity with God. Humans are uniquely called, by Christ, to a relationship with God, which represents their distinctive purpose.

Religious expression

There are many ways in which Christians express their beliefs and devotions through religious practices. For some their beliefs might be expressed through sacraments, others will worship in different ways. Some see the experience of living as a form of worship. The expression is however an outward expression of an inner commitment to a relationship with God and a belief in Christ. When exploring expressions of Christianity, this background of belief must be explored. The implications of such beliefs are debated within Christianity, and for this reason there are over 33,000 different Christian churches or groups. All of them have understood their relationship with God slightly differently but all would have Christ as the centre of their faith. In this way, exploring the importance and interpretation of the Bible, it is possible to see many different attitudes:

1   Some Christians see the Bible as the literal word of God, communicated through the human writers of scripture.
2   Others understand the Bible to be God's word but in human language that has been influenced by the writer's circumstances.
3   Some may argue that the writers may have unwittingly made mistakes and care should be taken against perpetuating them.

Which would in turn lead to different uses:

1   The Bible has ultimate authority. It cannot be wrong and should be used as such.
2   The Bible might have ultimate authority in matters of belief and conscience, but in other areas such as science and maybe morality it should be reinterpreted for today's society.
3   The Bible may have authority, in terms of matters of belief and conscience, but its message should be weighed against 'experience' and other sources.

Although there may be some efforts within traditions to establish both orthodoxy and orthopraxy, as teachers of RE it is necessary to explore these different expressions and have students develop informed opinions about them as expressions of faith. It would be an interesting task for pupils to begin with certain practices and, through the enquiry process, explore the theological justifications for them and whether the belief and expression are coherent.

References

Barrett, David B., Kurian, George T. and Johnson, Todd M. (2001) *World Christian Encyclopedia: A Comparative Survey of Churches and Religions in the Modern World* (2nd edn). Oxford: Oxford University Press.

'Credo' in *Catechism of the Catholic Church*. Available at: www.vatican.va/archive/ccc_css/archive/catechism/credo.htm (accessed 1 May 2014).

Education Reform Act (1988). Available at: www.legislation.gov.uk/ukpga/1988/40/contents/enacted (accessed 1 May 2014).

Holt, James D. (2004) Jehovah's Witnesses and the R.E. Classroom, *Resource*, *26*(2), 16–19.

Holt, James D. (2005) The frontiers of Christianity, *RE Today*, 22(2), 34.

Martyr, Justin (1999) 'The First Apology'. In R. Plantinga (Ed.), *Christianity and Plurality. Classic and Contemporary Readings*. Oxford: Blackwell (pp. 29–61).

Further reading

McGrath, A. (Ed.) (1995) *The Christian Theology Reader*. Oxford: Blackwell.

McGrath, A. (1997) *An Introduction to Christianity*. Oxford: Blackwell.

Macmillan, G. (2006) *Understanding Christianity*. Edinburgh, UK: Dunedin.

National Gallery (1999) *The Image of Christ*. London: National Gallery.

Wilson, B. (1999) *Christianity*. London: Routledge.

Woodhead, L. (2004) *Christianity: A Very Short Introduction*. Oxford: Oxford University Press.

Teaching Hinduism

.

What is Hinduism?

Hinduism could be seen to have more diverse beliefs and practices than any of the other world religions. In the unity of Hinduism there is much diversity. Nehru once attempted to describe Hinduism:

> Hinduism, as a faith, is vague, amorphous, many-sided, all things to all me. It is hardly possible to define it, or indeed say definitely whether it is a religion or not, in the usual sense of the word. In its present form, and even in the past, it embraces many beliefs and practices, from the highest to the lowest, often opposed to or contradicting each other.

(2002, p. 75)

This diversity is partly a result of the concept of 'Hinduism' being a western imperialistic construct. Hinduism began thousands of years ago. The name 'Hindu' was first used by Europeans to describe the people who lived near the River Indus in India – the word 'Indus' became 'Hindu'. Hinduism was not begun by any one person but developed gradually over thousands of years. This means that it has many different 'branches', and there are lots of different beliefs. Hinduism is a way of life as much as a religion. Hindus, while acknowledging the name 'Hinduism', might prefer to call it sanatana dharma. This means the eternal law or eternal religion. Hinduism is an umbrella term for a diversity of beliefs that have some shared points of contact: 'although Hinduism may not have a universally accepted core, it does have a family of distinctive concepts and social structures, and it also has certain tendencies in practice and belief' (Jackson and Killingley, 1988, p. 23).

In exploring Hinduism it is important to explore these overarching concepts while recognising their diversity of understanding and application within Hinduism.

The message of Hinduism

Within Hinduism, the central feature of a Hindu's life is dharma:

> The word itself comes from the Sanskrit root 'dhri', which means 'to sustain'. Another related meaning is 'that which is integral to something.' For example, the *dharma* of sugar is to be sweet and the *dharma* of fire is to be hot. Therefore a person's dharma consists of duties that sustain him [sic], according to his innate characteristics. Such characteristics are both material and spiritual.
>
> (Das, 2002, p. 24)

In living their dharma, a Hindu is seen to be developing positive karma, resulting in a positive reincarnation and eventual liberation (moksha) from the cycle of samsara and union with Brahman.

There are seen to be four paths to moksha, all of which have a spiritual underpinning and devotion:

- Karma-yoga: selfless action. Service to others and ultimately life as a service to Brahman.
- Jnana-yoga: spiritual knowledge. Can be seen to be world renouncing and focuses on the acquisition of wisdom, not just knowledge but the wisdom that comes through an awareness of the world as it really is and the elimination of desire.
- Raja-yoga: meditation. Passing through various stages of consciousness a person is able to attain moksha.
- Bhakti-yoga: devotional service. In essence, this is a combination of the other types of yoga. In its truest manifestation it is the selfless service and devotion to Brahman.

For some Hindus these are all parallel paths to moksha, while others would see one as more effective, and all of them as steps on the same path. However they are understood, it is through their practice that a person can receive moksha.

In living their dharma, a Hindu generally passes through four stages (Ashramas). Through fulfilling their duties within the Ashramas a Hindu is able to progress towards a positive reincarnation or moksha. The four stages are:

1   Student (brahmacharyi). Traditionally, this stage begins with the sacred thread ceremony and marked the beginning of study with a guru or priest. Yoga, scriptures, arts and sciences would all be studied alongside a simple and celibate life. Today, most Hindus in this stage will focus on the acquisition of knowledge and learning in whichever situation they find themselves. In the UK this would be by attending schools and learning at home and in the temple (mandir).
2   Householder (grihasta). On finishing their studies, a Hindu will marry and assume the responsibilities of a householder. Marriage is a part of Hindu's dharma as a way of sustaining social and religious obligations. The aspects of the householder stage are what would be expected in the running and maintenance of a home based on religious teachings and values. These would include: earning an honest wage; spending money wisely and for the benefit of the household and others; keeping the home clean; observing religious celebrations and so on.
3   Retirement (vanaprastha). When the children of a Hindu are grown and able to take responsibility for their own lives, a Hindu will enter the retirement stage of life. Anciently this would have meant becoming a 'forest dweller', to: renounce world concerns; devote time to quiet; study the scriptures; and meditate. These are generally no longer carried out in the forest but can be adopted in a home. People in the retirement stage are greatly respected.
4   Renunciation (sannyasin). A large number of Hindus will not enter this stage as it is the complete renunciation of material food and the devotion of the person's entire life to seeking moksha. In this stage a Hindu might become a wandering holy man.

A study of these stages by pupils will help them understand that even through seemingly mundane activities a Hindu is showing devotion to God. These stages may well include the practice of the aspects of yoga outlined before.

The final aspect of dharma that will be discussed here is that of caste or the system of the four varnas. Historically, the four varnas determined a Hindu's sense of identity and their role within society. A person is born into a varna (and within the varnas there are many different caste groupings). These are four main social groupings that were the basic structure of Hindu society.

1   The priests (Brahmins): the religious teachers who preserve and pass on the teachings of Hinduism.
2   The leaders/warriors (Kshatriyas): those who have responsibility for leadership, ruling society, defending the people from injustice and tyranny.
3   The merchants (Vaishyas): the business people in society; they are responsible for providing the wealth of society.
4   The servants/manual labourers (Shudra): those who do the physical and manual work and serve the needs of the other varnas.

Because some tasks were considered to be particularly unclean, especially those dealing with dead animals or rubbish, the people who performed them were thought to be so unclean as to be outside the caste system altogether. These people became known as untouchables, subsequently renamed Harijans or 'children of God' by Gandhi.

The caste a person is born into can be seen to be linked with their karma, and may therefore be a reflection of previous lives. There are certain rules associated with the caste system:

- A person cannot move out of their caste.
- A person cannot eat with or take food from someone of a lower caste.
- A person cannot marry someone from outside of their caste.
- It determines the job that will be performed.

The Rig Veda contains a hymn about the creation of humans from the first man, Purusha, who is split into the different varnas. Purusha's mouth was the Brahmins; his arms the Kshatriyas; his thighs the Vaishyas; and the feet the Shudra. This hymn could suggest that the priest's authority comes from the words he utters. The warrior's authority comes from his strength. The merchants and farmers support these two classes, just as the thighs support the body. The Shudra provide all the services to the other three varnas.

In today's society, and particularly in the UK, the traditional ideas of caste are breaking down. People see this structure as having served a positive purpose in the past but that it is no longer necessary. It may have provided structure and identity in the past, but in the modern world aspects of caste are seen to be rooted in history rather than religion. As such, it is possible that ideas of caste and a person's dharma with regard to caste can be fluid and developed rather than rigid and immovable. Some Hindus will continue to hold on to the dharmic responsibilities of caste, but its application and the importance of it differs significantly among Hindus. In offering a 'middle' view of caste, Mark Tully has suggested:

> It would lead to greater respect for India's culture, and indeed a better understanding of it, if it were recognised that the caste system has never been totally static, that it is adapting itself to today's changing circumstances and that it has positive as well as negative aspects. The caste system provides security and a community for millions of Indians. It gives them an identity that neither Western science nor Western thought has yet provided, because the caste is not just a matter of being a Brahmin or a Harijan; it is also a kinship system. The system provides a wider support group than a family.

(1992, p. 7)

It is this function as kinship that might continue within Hindu society today. In exploring concepts of caste within the classroom it will be difficult for pupils to understand. However, if it is taught within the concept of dharma it becomes a lot more understandable. If a Hindu is seeking moksha, fulfilling their duty in its different forms is crucial.

The Nature of God

An uninformed view of Hinduism presents it as a polytheistic religion; however this view is based on the experience of seeing Hindus worship different 'gods' such as Vishnu, Shiva, Ganesh and so on. A story explores this dichotomy of expression within Hinduism:

A Hindu child asked:
'Grandmother, how many gods are there?'
'There are as many gods as there are creatures, so there must be 300,000,000 gods.'
'Grandmother, how many gods are there really?'
'3000 my child.'
'Grandmother, how many gods are there really?'
'300 my child.'
'Grandmother, how many gods are there really?'
'30 my child.'
'Grandmother, how many gods are there really?'
'3 my child.'
'Grandmother, how many gods are there really?'
'One my child, really.'

(in Voiels, 1998, p. 21)

This conversation shows that Hindus have no difficulty in accepting that god is one and yet has many different forms. Hindus believe that there is one universal spirit (god) called Brahman, which is present throughout the entire universe and is symbolised in the symbol AUM (OM). This symbol consists of the three sanskrit letters A, U, and M and is considered to be the sacred sound or vibration that is made by the life-giving power of the universe or Brahman. It is symbolic of Brahman as he is present within everything and everyone, all life is interconnected and contains a spark of the divine. Hindus believe that Brahman dwells in all creatures as the innermost spirit or true self. This belief of the interconnectedness of nature and all living things can be used as a basis for the teaching of ahimsa or the injunction not to harm any living thing.

This theological monotheism may seem at odds with the traditional or experiential view of Hinduism that people hold. For example, a person may visit a temple (mandir) and see statues of many 'gods' and different people making offerings to the different ones that are within the temple. Indeed, some would view Hinduism as an idolatrous religion as the focus of their worship appears to be statues of the gods (murtis). Some Hindus may hold this belief themselves, and not think theologically about the symbolism that these expressions are of the sacred.

Brahman is one, but is known through many forms. In essence, there is a manifestation of Brahman according to specific role and purpose. This may be explained for some through the Hindu concept of illusion (Maya). Maya explores the concept that the material world is a mask for the spiritual truth that lies behind everything. Thus, the manifestations of God that are worshipped are truly Brahman himself, and as such when any deity is worshipped the devotee is actually focusing their attention on Brahman; similarly, when a murti is a seeming object of devotion it is actually Brahman rather than the material that is being worshipped. Various different explanations can be used to explore this belief; for example, a woman who is at the same time a mother, daughter, sister, aunt and grandmother. The people who approach her approach her as the 'role' they associate her with; thus a child will seek her in a different way from her mother.

It may be that a Hindu will go to a particular manifestation of Brahman if they need particular help; for example Ganesh is the remover of obstacles (among other things). On the other hand, a family may have a particular manifestation that is particularly close to their heart, and as such most of the devotion will be focused around this deity. As all deities are manifestations of Brahman, the devotion offered to different manifestations could be seen to be serving the same purpose.

The three main manifestations of Brahman are known collectively as the Trimurti:

- Brahma the Creator
- Vishnu the Preserver
- Shiva the Destroyer.

Brahma

Brahma is the creator. He created the world and everything that is on it. In pictures and murtis he often appears seated on a lotus and is shown with four heads facing the four directions. This symbolises that he created the entire universe. Other objects in representations of him might include Vedas (Holy Books) in his hands, which helped him create the universe. The rosary or mala (beads) he holds help people to meditate. His vehicle is a swan (Hans), which is known for its judgement between good and bad. Brahma's consort is Saraswati, the Goddess of Learning. While very important in Hinduism, Brahma has few worshippers as his work has been done, the world has been created.

Vishnu

Vishnu, as the preserver, makes sure that the universe stays safe. His colour is blue to indicate he is as endless as the sky. His vehicle is the swift-flying bird Garuda. Vishnu's consort is Lakshmi, the Goddess of Wealth. He is depicted with four hands, which could show that he is ruler of all four corners of the universe. In his hands he holds:

- a conch shell, which indicates the spread of the divine sound 'Aum';
- a discus, which reminds devotees of the wheel of time, and to lead a good life;
- a lotus, which is an example of existence and a symbol of beauty and purity;
- a mace, which indicates the power and punishing ability of Vishnu if discipline in life is ignored.

Vishnu is often shown sitting on a large snake called Ananta (endless) with many heads.

He has come many times to the earth to save it and protect it from evil. He is seen to have taken upon himself human form to come to earth; these are known as avatars (some Hindus would recognise these avatars as material, others as a spiritual form). Sometimes Vishnu's avatars are worshipped independently – like Krishna and Rama; indeed, some Hindus may see them as manifestations in their own right.

The nine main avatars through which Vishnu is known to have come to the earth to preserve the truth are:

- Matsya the fish who saved all the creatures of the world from being drowned in a great flood.
- Narasimha, half man and half lion. He killed a demon that was attacking devotees of Vishnu.

- Krishna the cowherd is loved by humans for his beauty, love and sense of fun. He is the main protagonist in the Mahabharata.
- Kuma the tortoise helped the gods live forever.
- Vamana the beautiful dwarf defeated the demon king Bali.
- Buddha the teacher is revered by Hindus as well as Buddhists, because of his focus on ahimsa.
- Varaha the boar rescued the earth when it fell from its place.
- Parasurama the warrior put an end to war itself.
- Rama the king showed how to rule justly and live simply and is the main figure in the Ramayana.

It is believed that Vishnu is to come to earth once more as Kalki the slayer who will come to bring this age to an end and destroy all evil. This list may not be comprehensive as other avatars may be accepted by different Hindus; some Hindus accept Jesus as a manifestation of Vishnu as one example of a further avatar. Vishnu, and his associated avatars, is one of the deities within Hinduism that has the most devotees. Worship of Vishnu and his avatars forms the largest group within Hinduism, known as Vaishnavism.

Shiva

Shiva, as the destroyer, destroys and recreates the universe. He is the object of devotion for the second largest Hindu group within India: Shaivism. Shiva's consort is Shakti the mother goddess, sometimes known as Parvati. Shaktism is another form of Hindu devotion, which focuses devotion on the mother goddess in her forms of Shakti, Parvati, Durga and Kali. Shaktism is often seen as complementary to Shaivism as the subjects of devotion are Shiva's consort. Shiva's vehicle is Nandi the Bull.

Shiva has many different ways of being depicted but the three main murtis are:

- Shiva Nataraja
- Shiva Yogiraj
- Shiva Lingum.

As Nataraja, the Lord of the dance, he is shown dancing to demonstrate his creative energy to create the world and his power as the destroyer. In his four hands he:

- Holds a drum to represent the pulse of time and the bang that began the universe.
- Has flame symbolising destruction.
- Has one raised in blessing of protection to his devotees.
- Has one pointing towards his foot symbolising rising above the demon dwarf, Apasarmara Purasha, who represents ignorance.

As Yogiraj or Maha-Yogi, Shiva is depicted in a meditative pose with his eyes half closed indicating perfect inner peace attained through liberation (moksha) achieved through yoga and mental discipline. The River Ganges is seen to flow out of his hair, remembering a story when Shiva saved the Ganges. Other symbols associated with Yogiraj include:

- A third eye to symbolise insight and wisdom.
- A trident as a symbol of asceticism.
- A serpent draped around his neck showing Shiva's ability to control desires.

The Shiva Lingum is used to symbolise fertility and show Shiva's power to create life.

It could be interesting to utilise the 'Similar and Different' template (see Figure 6.3) in exploring the Trimurti or, indeed, the three manifestations of Shiva explored here.

Other manifestations of Brahman

There are many other manifestations of Brahman within Hinduism that can be objects of devotion. Each of these has a specific role, specific symbols and often a vehicle similar to the Trimurti and their consorts. The symbols associated with a deity are an effective way of exploring their role and importance. For example the symbols associated with Ganesh are:

- His vehicle is a mouse or rat; a symbol of ignorance that he overcomes.
- A bowl of sweets/jewels as a reward for the faithful.
- A mark on his forehead (tilak) to symbolise his position as a follower of Shiva (being his son).
- A goad, which elephant drivers use to guide the elephant; showing Ganesh is a guide for his devotees.
- An axe, which can be used to destroy ignorance.
- A snake tied around his waist to show his conquering of desires.
- A single tusk to show his single-mindedness.
- A trunk with which obstacles can be removed.

An enquiry approach within the RE classroom might use murtis as a starting point to explore the importance of the various manifestations of Brahman and why they might be worshipped.

Other deities include:

- Hanuman, a major figure of the Ramayana, who is the provider of courage, hope, knowledge, intellect and devotion. He has no known vehicle but is a powerful warrior. He often holds a mace (gada), which is a sign of bravery, and sometimes has a picture of Rama on his chest, which is a sign of his devotion.
- Kartikeya, the god of war. His vehicle is a peacock, which is able to destroy harmful serpents. Stories surrounding Kartikeya show extraordinary courage and heroism in saving the world. He destroys the wicked and protects the virtuous. He carries a spear called sakti, symbolising the destruction of negative tendencies in humans. His other hand is used to bless devotees.

- Saraswati, the goddess of learning, arts and sciences whose vehicle is a swan. She holds sacred scriptures in one hand and in her second hand is a lotus symbolising knowledge, purity and virtue. Her other two hands are used to play the music of love and life on the violin.
- Durga the warrior or mother goddess. Her vehicle is a tiger or lion. Stories are told of her defeating Mahisha. Mahisha changed form many times during the fight, finally becoming a buffalo, a symbol of death. Durga slit the buffalo's throat and cut off the demon's head as he emerged from within. Following this the gods were able to return to heaven. Durga often has ten arms and carries a sword.

Rasamandala Das (2002, p. 53) identifies a further category of deity, which he describes as 'administrative gods' who are charged with specific roles in the functioning of the universe:

- Indra: the King of Heaven and the god of rain. He is also considered to be in charge of the East.
- Agni: the god of fire. He is also considered to be in charge of the South East.
- Yama: the god of death. He is also considered to be in charge of the South.
- Surya: the god of the sun. He is also considered to be in charge of the South West.
- Varuna: the god of water. He is also considered to be in charge of the West.
- Vayu: the god of the wind/air. He is also considered to be in charge of the North West.
- Kuvera: the god of wealth. He is also considered to be in charge of the North.
- Soma/Chandra: the god of the moon. He is also considered to be in charge of the North East.

The nature of humanity

The body is a temporary housing for the real, non-material self, sometimes called the soul or atman. This atman is the life giving force and the true self; this is unchanging and inhabits different bodies and life forms through the cycle of samsara and reincarnation. Das suggests that the idea of humanity possessing a soul is a misconception; he suggests that 'on the contrary, Hindus believe that we, like all living beings, are the soul and possess a body' (2002, p. 9). The atman contains a spar of divinity and it is through the atman that Brahman gives life and is within every living thing. All life is therefore sacred. The goal of a Hindu is to escape this material world of reincarnation that reflects the four problems of birth, disease, old-age and death.

Within Hinduism it is seen that all living things, including humans, have three basic qualities (gunas). These gunas are positive, creation or goodness (sattvic); neutral, sustaining or passion (rajasic); and negative, destructive or ignorance (tamasic). The interactions of these gunas make up the living things. Das suggests that the gunas are like colours and that 'By mixing the three primary colours … we create an almost infinite range, such as we see in a colour chart for paints. Similarly, from the interaction of the three gunas emerges the entire range of life forms' (2002, p. 14). As such, humans can have a prevalence of each of the gunas, which determines what type of person they are. A focus on the development of positive gunas contributes to a person's state of mind at death and has some impact, along with karma on the next reincarnation.

Recognising the temporality of life is an important facet of Hindu teaching and will influence how a Hindu follows their dharma. It is only within human form that karma, and as such 'lower' forms of life, are influenced by instinct only. On an animal's reincarnation the karma accumulated within a previous human life will determine the next phase of existence: 'The soul passing through lower species doesn't create any new "karma". He [sic] only works off the karmic reactions generated whilst in the human form and gradually rises towards another human birth' (Das, 2002, p. 13). Decisions and actions made while in human form are thus central to a Hindu's path to moksha.

Scripture

Within Hinduism there are seen to be two types of scripture:

1   What is heard or what is revealed by God (sruti). These deal 'with eternal principles' (Prinja, 2003, p. 129).
2   What is remembered (smruti). These deal 'with the practical application of eternal principles' (Prinja, 2003, p. 129).

There are numerous Hindu scriptures, some of which are outlined in Table 11.1 below:

Table 11.1 Hindu scriptures (see Prinja, 2003, pp. 129–130)

Type of scripture	Main writings/groups	Subdivisions
Sruti	Rig Veda Yajur Veda Sama Veda Atharva Veda	Each split into two sections: 1. Karma Kanda consisting of hymns and prayers (Samhitas) and descriptions of rituals (Brahmanas). 2. Jnana Kanda, which contains the Upansihads (to sit down near) consisting of conversations between a teacher and their pupils. These provide a philosophical interpretation of the Vedas.
Smruti	Upa Vedas	Ajur Veda (medicine) Dhanur Veda (military science) Gandharva Veda (music) Shilpa (mechanics/ architecture)
	Vedangas	Shiksha (phonetics) Chanda (prosody) Vyakrana (grammar) Nirukta (Vedic glossary) Jyotisha (astronomy) Kalpa (household/religious duties)
	Darshanas (philosophy)	Nastika (atheistic) Charvaka (materialism) Astika (theistic)
	Dharma Shastras (law codes)	Niti shastras (Chanakya, Vidhur, Shukra) 18 Smrutis (e.g. Manu) Kautilya shastra (economics, politics, law)
	Puranas	46 Upa Puranas 18 Main Puranas

Table 11.1 (continued)

Type of scripture	Main writings/groups	Subdivisions
	Itihasas/Epics	Ramayana
		Mahabharata (including the Bhagavad Gita)
	Agamas	Shakta
		Shaiva
		Vaishnava
	Modern	Swaminarayana – Skikshapatri
		ISKCON – Teachings of Chaitanya
		Arya Samaj – Satyarth Praksah

Focusing on the Vedas and the Epics could be a way to approach Hindu scriptures in the classroom.

The Vedas

The Vedas, to some degree, can be seen to be the unifying feature of Hinduism; they are the source of all the other scriptures of Hinduism in that all of the others could be seen to be interpretations or developments of the message of the Vedas. '[T]o Hindus the truths of the Vedas were first revealed by God at the beginning of human creation for the benefit of humankind, and they are timeless and eternal truths' (Voiels, 1998, p. 53). The Vedas are used today as the basis of all religious ritual and practice. The four Vedas are:

1   The Rig Veda. A collection of 1028 hymns of praise and devotion. These hymns are usually directed to deities.
2   The Yajur Veda. In essence this is a priestly handbook.
3   The Sama Veda contains melodies and chants to be used during worship.
4   The Atharva Veda contains hymns that fall outside of the aspects of the Yajur Veda and touches on aspects of scientific knowledge.

The Upanishads as a priestly discussion and use of the Vedas are very important within Hinduism. It would be of interest within the RE classroom to explore the implications of aspects of the Vedas and Upanishads on the life of a Hindu today. One example of this might be how they are used as the source of, and in the celebration of, the samskaras. The samskaras are rituals that mark various important stages in life. The exact number suggested or mentioned in the Vedas is debated, but there are commonly seen to be 16:

1   Conception (Garbhahana): usually at the first day of menstruation for a new bride following her wedding.
2   During the second or third month of pregnancy (Pumsavana).
3   Between the sixth month of pregnancy (Simanatonnayana).
4   Birth (Jatakarma).
5   Naming ceremony (Namakarana).
6   Child's first outing at approximately four months (Nishkramana).
7   Child's first solid food (Annaprashana).
8   Child's first haircut (between one and three years old) (Chudakarana).
9   Child's ears are pierced (Karnavedha).
10 Sacred Thread ceremony (Upanayana).
11 Beginning of child's formal education (Vidyarambha).

12 End of studies (Samavartana).
13 Marriage (Vivaha).
14 Retirement (Vanaprastha).
15 Entering the sanyasa stage.
16 Death rites (Antyeshti).

The Epics

Das notes that 'For popular purposes in the UK, the Ramayana, the Mahabharata, the Puranas and the Bhagavad Gita are most commonly used' (2002, p. 123). As such, even without further discussion the Epics would be worthy of focus within the RE classroom. As stories that are used throughout Hinduism in many different ways these are arguably the scriptures that most Hindus will be most familiar with. They are stories that teach people important moral lessons and how to behave, and show the application of Vedic principles in the lives of the gods and others. These scriptures can often be seen in carvings on temples, comic books or picture stories and thus are accessible to all people whatever their level of literacy. The Ramayana was serialised on television in the 1980s, and when it was shown 'life in cities, towns and villages came to a standstill. It was estimated that over 80 million people [in India] watched it – in a place where most people don't own televisions' (Dyson, 2009, p. 16). Within Hinduism some see these stories as depicting real events; others as allegories. However they are understood, they are extremely important in the transmission of Hinduism and the way to live.

The Ramayana

The Ramayana tells the story of Rama, an avatar of Vishnu, and his wife Sita, an avatar of Lakshmi. In a very brief summary of aspects of the story, the following points can be highlighted:

- Rama is banished from his kingdom because of his jealous step mother. His brother refuses the throne and leaves a pair of sandals on the throne to symbolise that Rama is the rightful King.
- He sets up home in the forest accompanied by his devoted wife Sita, and servant Lakshmana.
- Rama rejects the advances of the evil King Ravana's sister, who returns to her brother to seek revenge.
- Rama and Lakshmana go hunting. While away Rama requests that Sita stay within a circle of protection.
- Sita is tricked into helping an old man, who is really Ravana in disguise. Sita is kidnapped by the evil King Ravana.
- Rama and Lakshmana search for Sita with no success.
- Hanuman, Jatyu and others offer to help.
- Hanuman finds Sita by leaping over the ocean to Lanka.
- They build a bridge across the sea to Ravana's kingdom.

- A battle takes place. Rama kills Ravana.Rama and Sita are reunited.
- Rama tells Sita he cannot take her home with him because people may think she is impure.
- Sita passes through fire unharmed to prove she is pure, and they return home.

This brief summary does not adequately convey the important messages of the Ramayana, but the examples of Rama, Sita and Lakshmana as models of living can be easily seen. The overcoming of evil by good is also an important concept that is developed within the story. There are, however, many more ways in which the story can be used within the classroom as a beginning to the study of Hinduism.

The Bhagavad Gita

The Gita is two chapters of the much larger Mahabharata. It is a record of a conversation between Krishna (an avatar of Vishnu) and his charioteer Arjuna as they sat between two armies that were about to go to battle. Arjuna initially refused to go to battle on seeing friends and family on both sides of the battlefield. Krishna explained the concepts of the atman and the importance of self-realisation through the various stages of yoga culminating in bhakti. Krishna also explains the gunas and service to God. On the completion of the 'sermon' Arjuna was determined to fight.

As an exploration of Hindu beliefs the Gita is incredibly important, and the implications for an individual can be clearly seen in the response of Arjuna.

Religious expression

There are many ways in which Hindus express their beliefs and devotions through religious practices. While aspects have been explored in various parts of this chapter, it can do little more that function as a starting point to explore the implications of these beliefs and concepts for Hindu practice. In understanding the basic concepts and beliefs of Hinduism it is hoped that the pupils can be prepared to explore the implications for practice. The diversity of expression within Hinduism would be a good template for exploring other religions also, as while it might be more noticeable within Hinduism it is just as evident in the other religions of the world.

References

Das, Rasamandala (2002) *The Heart of Hinduism. A Comprehensive Guide for Teachers and Professionals.* Aldenham, UK: ISKCON Educational Services.

Dyson, Janet (2009) What's the Use of Stories? Exploring the Place of Personal Stories and Grand Narratives in RE (and Life in General). *REsource,* 32(1), 14–17.

Jackson, Robert and Killingley, Dermot (1988) *Approaches to Hinduism.* London: Murray.

Nehru, Jawaharlal (2002 [1945]) *The Discovery of India.* New Delhi, India: Oxford University Press.

Prinja, Nawal K. (2003) *Hindu Dharma. A Guide for Teachers* (2nd edn). Thornton Heath, UK: Vishwa Hindu Parishad.

Tully, Mark (1992) *No Full Stops in India.* New Delhi, India: Penguin.

Voiels, Veronica (1998) *Hinduism. A New Approach.* Abingdon, UK: Hodder and Stoughton.

Further reading

Bowen, P. (1996) *Themes and Issues in Hinduism*. London: Cassell.

Demariaux, J.-C. (1995) *How to Understand Hinduism*. London: SCM.

Flood, G. (1996) *An Introduction to Hinduism*. Cambridge: Cambridge University Press.

Kanitkar, V. P. and Cole, W. O. (1995) *Teach Yourself Hinduism*. London: Hodder.

Knott, K. (1999) *Hinduism: A Very Short Introduction*. Oxford: Oxford University Press.

Shattuck, C. (1999) *Hinduism*. London: Routledge.

Chapter 12

Teaching Islam

Chapter outline
What is Islam?

- The challenge of extremism

The message of Islam
The nature of humanity
The Articles of Faith (Iman)

- Belief in Allah as the one (Tawhid)
- Belief in angels
- Belief in the holy books
- Belief in the prophets
- Belief in the Day of Judgement
- Belief in predestination

The Five Pillars of Islam

- Statement of Faith (Shahadah)
- Prayer (Salah)
- Almsgiving/Charity (Zakah)
- Fasting (Sawm)
- Pilgrimage (Hajj)
- The Five Pillars

What is Islam?

In a similar way to other religions of the world, Islam is both a unified and a diversified religion. The worldwide community of Muslims (the ummah) provides a sense of community and belonging, and places the responsibility for Muslims to strengthen one another. It is a way of life that strives to have the individual and family live in submission to the will of God (Allah). Its modern roots can be traced back to the life and example of the Prophet Muhammad (pbuh)[1], who lived from 570 CE–632 CE and is seen by the vast majority of Muslims as the last of the messengers of God. There are various traditions of Islam and care should be taken not to establish a particular expression as normative, and others as schismatic. Some groups will be rejected and outside of Islam by others. The articles of faith would usually be unifying beliefs within Islam, but there are different nuances and emphases according to the tradition represented. The two major expressions of Islam are Sunni and Shi'a:

- *Sunni*: Following the death of Muhammad, Sunni Muslims see the leadership of the Muslim community as passing to Abu Bakr, the first of the Rightly Guided Caliphs. Sunni is usually divided into four schools of law: Hanifa, Shafi, Hanibal and Malik. They constitute a large majority of Muslims around the world. Within these schools of law are different groups, for example the Wahhabi who might be seen as part of the Hanibal school of law with distinctive practices and aims.
- *Shi'a*: The Jafri school who constitute a minority within Islam. Shi'a Muslims believe that the successor to Muhammad should have been his cousin/son-in-law, Ali. Their leaders tend to promote a strict interpretation of the Qur'an and close adherence to its teachings. Some Shi'a believe in 12 heavenly Imams (perfect teachers) who led the Shi'ites in succession. Shi'ites believe that the twelfth Imam, the Mahdi (guided one), never died but went into hiding and is waiting for the appropriate time to reappear and lead humans.

Ismaili Muslims are a group of Muslims who split with Shi'a after the death of Ja'far al-Sadiq (the sixth Imam of Shi'a and fifth of Ismaili). Ismailis feel the successor was Isma'il ibn Jafar with the leadership of the ummah continuing, for some until today, in the family line of the Prophet Muhammad. The Naziri school of Ismaili Islam is led by the Aga Khan.

Sufi Islam, while sometimes identified as a third group, is a tradition in which followers seek inner knowledge directly from God through meditation and ritual and dancing. It developed in the late tenth century CE as a reaction to the formalism and laws of the Qur'an. There are Sufis to be found within the Sunni and Shi'a groups. Sufi Muslims emphasise personal union with the divine. In the Middle East, some Sufi traditions are considered to be a separate school of Islam.

These, however, are not the limits of denominations within Islam. Groups such as the Nation of Islam are rejected by 'mainstream' Islam but still consider themselves to be Muslim. The unifying feature is found in the oneness of God, and the prophetic calling of Muhammad.

The challenge of extremism

At the beginning of the twenty-first century, Islam presents challenges to RE teachers that are not faced with other world religions. The challenges are provided by the experience that pupils have of Muslims as presented in the media. Whether it be a discussion of 9/11, the Taliban in Afghanistan, the abduction of 200 school girls in Nigeria, or the supposed desire of some for Shari'ah law in the UK. Each of these is perpetrated by a small minority of Muslims but the headlines and reporting would sometimes suggest that these events reflect the attitudes of the vast majority of Muslims. RE teachers teach that Islam means 'peace' and 'submission' and, as such, the aim of Islam is to achieve peace. This is at odds with the one-sided and caricatured view of Islam that is presented in many areas of the media and an approach that ignores the media representation is not going to meet the needs of pupils. Sarah Smalley has articulated this concern:

> How can we teach about Islam in a positive way, yet one which is realistic and does not duck the difficulties posed by the existence of extreme Islamist groups or of values which seem to be in conflict with those of the social and religious majorities?
>
> (2005, p. 5)

In teaching the 'chocolate box' view, it might be useful to use elements of the ethnographic approach where Islam is experienced through the eyes of a child and the impact it has on them. Similarly, enquiry could be used to explore the implications of beliefs, and whether the practices would be supported by Islamic beliefs. In this presentation of Islam, the authentic voices of British Muslims are needed to combat the loud and vociferous voices given an arena by the media. Consider the school that holds an annual Iftar meal to which the entire school community is invited. Muslims and non-Muslims heard a respected Muslim speaker talk about fish and chips being a Muslim food, about jeans being Muslim clothes. Making the point that accepting large elements of the existing British culture does not oppose Islam, and can make a person more prepared to face the challenges faced in the world today. These are the voices that need to be heard in the classroom. It is important that more Muslims become involved in this important task – both in schools and other places – so that the negative view of Islam is challenged, not by teachers who 'have to' but by Muslims who will reflect the true essence of Islam in their conversation and actions.

The message of Islam

The message of Islam is that humanity should live in submission to God, and only through such living can a person hope to find peace. Islam is a word that means 'peace' and 'submission'. A Muslim is therefore someone who submits to the will of God. Every aspect of a person's life is to worship God; as such, God is seen to be the source of all life and creation. The will of God is made known through revelation to his prophets, especially the message to the Prophet Muhammad that is found within the Qur'an. This 'book' holds a pre-eminent place in Islam as it reflects the will of God for humanity. On this book is based all law and practice.

The nature of humanity

Within Islam, humanity is a special creation of God being given a soul, freedom to choose and a conscience. All of these qualities are important in explaining what it means to be a human within Islam. Humans are the only part of God's creation that can consciously worship him. The most important part of their life is to worship God and to live in submission to his will, because they are the only species that is capable of doing so.

Most Muslims believe that 120 days into a pregnancy a foetus receives its soul (ensoulment). This 'soul' is the 'real' person with all the character, personality and sacredness of the individual. It is inextricably linked with the body. At birth, human beings are born innocent and good, with the potential to do good or evil. Every person is believed to be born in a state of submission to God, and as such could be considered Muslim. For this reason 'converts' are termed 'reverts' within Islam.

The greater struggle (jihad) of this life is to do good and to bring the soul into submission to God. Although born innocent, there is a belief within Islam that teaches that aspects of the soul have a downward dimension (nafs). Geaves suggests that nafs can refer to 'impurities such as anger, greed, jealousy, hatred and lust' (2007, p. 44). The purpose of life is to overcome the downward nafs. When this mastery is attained a person is prepared for paradise.

A further aspect of the soul is the heart (qalb) which is the spiritual nature of humanity and has a link with the physical heart. It is capable of learning both good and evil. And, as such, a person's life becomes a battle for the mastery of the heart between God and the devil (shaytan). The outward behaviours of a person reflect the purity of a person's qalb. As a person gains wisdom and performs good deeds then the person is prepared to receive paradise. The purification of the qalb is made possible by worship of, and submission to, God.

The Articles of Faith (Iman)

It is common to see the Five Pillars explored within the RE classroom, but to some extent the grounding in the beliefs of Islam is missed if the Articles of Faith are not explored. These are the underpinning beliefs, the message of Islam that has been delivered by all of the prophets. A Hadith reports:

> A man came up to the Prophet whilst he was sitting with some of his companions. He asked Muhammad ... 'What is iman?' The Prophet replied, 'Iman is to believe in Allah, His Angels, His Books, His Prophets and in the Day of Judgement; and to believe in what has been ordained whether it is good or evil.' The man responded again, 'Correct, you have spoken the truth.'
>
> (in Geaves, 2005, pp. 121–122)

Belief in Allah as the one (Tawhid)

Islam is a monotheistic religion, and the belief in one God (Allah) is central to all belief and worship. The most important concept about God to Muslims is Tawhid, or the unity of God.

> Say: He is Allah, the One and Only; Allah, the Eternal, Absolute; None is born of Him, nor is He born; And there is none like Him.
>
> (sura 112)

To a Muslim this shows that Allah is unique, there is none other like him. He has no partners nor is he born or is anyone born of him. The greatest sin in Islam is shirk or the ascribing of partners to God. God is without form or substance, is not anthropomorphic in any way and is not male or female. The first chapter of the Qur'an (Sura al-Fatihah) explores the various beliefs about God within Islam:

> In the name of Allah, Most Gracious, Most Merciful.
>
> Praise be to Allah, the Cherisher and Sustainer of the worlds;
>
> Most Gracious, Most Merciful;
>
> Master of the Day of Judgment.
>
> Thee do we worship, and Thine aid we seek.
>
> Show us the straight way;
>
> The way of those on whom Thou hast bestowed Thy Grace, those whose (portion) is not wrath, and who go not astray.

The beliefs in Sura al-Fatihah are the fact that God is creator, sustainer, judge, merciful, the object of worship and guide. The Qur'an outlines other characteristics of God that help Muslims understand who God is and their relationship to him. These characteristics are known as the 99 Beautiful Names, which include: The All-Hearing, The All-Seeing, The Light, The All-Aware, The Merciful, The Guide, The Creator, the Sustainer, The Truth, The Forgiving, The Just.

All forms of idolatry, whether of God or of material things, are rejected and for this reason no images are used, but the beautiful names are an important element of learning about Allah and may be used as an exploration of the nature and role of God.

In presentations of Islam it is possible to focus on a very legalistic and external relationship with God. However, it should be noted that for a number of Muslims, particularly Sufis, a personal and spiritual relationship with God is at the centre of their faith. One Hadith reports: "'Tell me about ihsan?" The Prophet replied, "Ihsan is to worship Allah as though you see Him for it is certain that He sees you"' (in Geaves, 2005, pp. 121–122).

Belief in angels

Within Islam angels are creations of God; he created the angels from light prior to creating humans from clay. Just as with all of God's creation the angels submit to the will of God. Without a body, angels never tire of worship and do not need any of the sustenance associated with humanity. There are many different angels within Islam of different status and role.

There are more 'commonplace' angels who assist humanity in many different ways. These are evidence of God's will for humans, and will assist in drawing people into submission to, and a relationship with, God. Believing in angels helps a person understand his magnificence in the multiplicity of creations.

Within Islam there is no concept of fallen angels; rather there are Jinn who were created from smoke. One of these Jinn 'Iblis' rebelled against God; he leads the rebellious Jinn (Shaytan) who roam the world with free will seeking to draw people to hell where they will reside. The Jinn will be judged at the last day and assigned to either paradise or hell, thus not all Jinn may be followers of Iblis. While Jinn are able to see humans, the opposite is not true.

> Examples of angels include:
>
> • Jibra'il: the messenger of God who revealed the Qur'an to the prophet Muhammad. He, like other angels, is able to take on different forms and did so. Jibra'il is also the angel who visited Mary in the form of man to announce her pregnancy.
> • Munkar and Nakeer: test people in the grave about their faith.
> • Azra'il: the angel of death.
> • Mika'el : sustains creatures, and is one of the most important angels.
> • Ridwan: watches over Heaven.
> • Malik: watches over Hell (assisted by nine other angels).

A belief in angels shows the struggle that is evident within a person's soul. In seeking to do good a person may be aided by angels but will be hindered and tempted by shaytan. In exploring the practices of Islam, it is important to discuss how the influence of these beings could be found within the life of an individual.

Belief in the holy books

Linked with belief in the prophets/messengers of God, is the belief in the holy books associated with these prophets. A Muslim believes in all the revelations of God to his prophets as they were originally given. Thus a Muslim would believe in the Torah as originally revealed to Moses, the Psalms as originally given to David and the message given to Jesus. However, these scriptures do not exist in their original form today. While the 'people of the book' are respected, it is important to note that their books (the Bible and TeNaKh) are not the original revelation and have changed the original message.

Within Islam the supreme authority is the Qur'an. Muslims believe the Qur'an to be the word of God, which was given to Muhammad through the Angel Jibra'il (or Gabriel). Jibra'il made Muhammad learn it by reciting it (repeating it out loud) and so at first it was not written down. The Arabic word Qur'an means recitation. The giving of the Qur'an is a miracle and provides evidence of God's existence and concern for humanity. When Muhammad first received the Qur'an he was commanded to read, or recite, by the Angel Jibra'il. He refused because he could not. Miraculously, despite his illiteracy he was able to read the words that Jibra'il presented to him.

Muhammad recited the messages to his followers who memorised it and later wrote it down. Following Muhammad's death the revelations were collected together into the Qur'an. The structure and order of the 114 chapters (suras) is believed to have been given to the Prophet Muhammad and is retained. The chapters are in turn divided into verses (ayahs). (The message of the Qur'an is central to a Muslim's faith and belief.)

The words that the Qur'an contains have remained unchanged since the time of Muhammad; consequently, there are no different versions of the Qur'an. Although the Qur'an has now been translated into many different languages, Muslims still try to learn its contents in the original Arabic to discover the nuances and intended original message.

As the direct word of God, the Qur'an is both sacred and authoritative to Muslims. It is the best guide that people can have for living. The Qur'an describes itself as 'the Book, wherein is no doubt, a guidance to the god-fearing' (Sura 2:2). The Qur'an is central in all forms of instruction and education within Islam, as it forms the basis of all Muslim law (Shari'ah). As outlined earlier, the purpose of a Muslim's life is to praise God and to live in submission to his will. The Qur'an teaches a Muslim how to live in submission and shows praise and glorification of God in every chapter.

Belief in the prophets

Prophets (rasul) in Islam are messengers sent to speak to people in all the countries to deliver the message of God. They were specially chosen people for certain times and places to reveal God's will. Each prophet delivered the same message, including the oneness of God and the afterlife. Some prophets are also found within Judaism and/or Christianity. Examples include:

Adam	Jacob (Yaqub)	Solomon (Sulayman)
Enoch (Idris)	Joseph (Yusuf)	Ezra (Uzair)
Noah (Nuh)	Lot (Lut)	Elisha (Al-Yasa)
Abraham ('Ibrāhīm)	Job (Ayub)	Zechariah (Zakariya)
Ishmael (Ismā'īl)	Aaron (Harun)	John (the Baptist) (Yahya)
Isaac ('Ishāq)	Moses (Musa)	Jesus (Isa)

Although these prophets may be seen to have taught things that might be in opposition to the Qur'an, this is as a result of the corruption of their message after they have died. For Muslims, Jesus would not have taught that he was the Son of God, rather he would have taught the oneness of God and his role as messenger of God. The stories of each of the prophets from the Qur'an are interesting to compare with those in the respective holy books in that the outworkings of the differences are important. One specific example comes in the story of Abraham. In the Bible and TeNaKh, Abraham is asked by God to sacrifice his only son Isaac; perhaps indicating Ishmael's mother Hagar as an inferior wife and thus her offspring not receiving inheritance. Within the Qur'an, the child that is to be sacrificed is Ishmael, reflecting his status as a full son of Abraham. The outworkings of this story are crucial when exploring the promise made to Abraham to possess the land of Canaan forever. Should this land be inherited by the descendants of Isaac (the Jews) or those of Ishmael (Arabs)?

These prophets' messages were for a specific time, and it was known by God that their messages would become diluted or corrupted. The final prophet, Muhammad, and the message of the Qur'an were, and are, to be protected so that the message is never corrupted. Muhammad is important as the 'seal of the prophets'; meaning that the message he delivered will not be added to and he completed the work of those who came before him.

Muhammad's importance as a prophet is shown in the prominence given to his sayings (Hadith) and actions (Sunnah), which are used as an example of how to put the teachings of the Qur'an into practice and live in submission to God. Muhammad is seen by Muslims to have lived his life in perfect obedience to the Qur'an; as such, he sets an example to all Muslims in how to be a faithful servant of Allah. His life also shows the involvement of God in human history. It is counterintuitive that an illiterate orphan should rise to be the founder of a world religion except that he was blessed by God.

It is only possible to provide a brief overview of the life of the Prophet Muhammad here:

- Muhammad was born in Makkah in 570 CE. Prior to his birth, his father died.
- Stories are told from Muhammad's childhood that foretell his importance; for example, trees spontaneously coming into bloom.
- His mother died when he was six, and he went to live with his uncle. At different points in his childhood Muhammad lived with a desert tribe, tended sheep and camels, and travelled with his uncle on journeys through Arabia to Syria.
- He began working for a wealthy widow, Khadijah. He later married her at the approximate age of 25.
- When a flood damaged the Ka'ba, Muhammad was selected to place the sacred black stone back into place. This shows his respect among the people.
- Muhammad often spent time praying in a cave at Mount Hira, concerned by the state of society.
- At age 40 he had a vision of the Angel Jibra'il, which began the revelation of the Qur'an.
- His wife Khadijah, and his cousin Ali, were the first to believe his message.
- His message was rejected by many and he was forced out of Makkah. He escaped to Makkah with his life being miraculously protected by God. The journey to Madinah is known as the Hijra; this took place in 622 CE and marks the beginning of the Muslim calendar.
- He established the first Muslim community in Madinah and built the first mosque.
- After a series of battles he returned to Makkah in victory in 630 CE. He forgave the people of Makkah and destroyed the pagan idols in the Ka'ba, prayed there, and made it a mosque (place of prostration). The Ka'ba is seen by Muslims as the first place of worship on the earth built by Abraham.
- In 632 CE Muhammad delivered his final sermon in Makkah.
- Muhammad died later that year.

Belief in the Day of Judgement (Akhirah)

Muslims believe that they will be judged after they die by God, whether they have performed good or bad deeds during this life. When life is over, it is not possible to change the impending judgement as the test has been completed. Those who did not believe in God may beg for a second chance or the opportunity to return to warn those that they loved – but there is no second chance. The souls of those who die before the Day of Judgement are taken by Azra'il, the angel of death, and will wait in the grave. This waiting period is called barzakh. There are different interpretations of what barzakh is; the majority of Muslims would describe it as a waiting place for the soul while the body is in the grave. Some believe that the deeds and beliefs of this life will have an influence on the nature of the waiting period. Those who were bad may be punished for their deeds in their past life while a person will receive the blessings from God in response to their good deeds and beliefs. Interestingly, in elements of Sufi Islam, barzakh is also the place that is visited during dreams.

On the Last Day, all graves will be opened and the dead will be resurrected with the soul and body brought back together. Two angels will question each person about their life. The deeds of everyone are weighed in Allah's balance and judgement will be passed as God hands a book over. If this book is placed into the right hand, the person enters into paradise (Jannah). If it is placed in the left hand, they pass into hell (Jahannam).

Paradise

Muslims believe that all those who believe in God and have done good deeds will go to Paradise. The Qur'an describes it as like a garden with green plants, the sound of running water and birds singing. There is no pain or suffering, it is a state of bliss.

Hell

Muslims believe that unbelievers and those who have done bad deeds go to hell. This is a place of scorching fire under the earth's crust. The descriptions of hell in the Qur'an suggest a place where people are in a state of suffering being chained up with hot winds, boiling water and black smoke around them. They stay in hell forever.

The belief in the afterlife and particularly the judgement will have an impact on the way a Muslim will live their life. It is possible to suggest that the decisions a Muslim makes will be weighed up in light of the will of God, but also their eventual destiny. Akhirah is one reason why a Muslim will strive to live their life in submission to God and it will also help them think of others and be generous while they are on earth. Within the classroom, when considering a Muslim's ethical response to an issue, the belief in akhirah should be an aspect of belief to be explored.

Belief in predestination

Predestination (al-Qadr) is a central teaching of Islam and is found within the Qur'an. God's omniscience for Muslims means that his knowledge does not just extend backwards but also extends into the future. As such, God knows what a person is going to do before it happens. The Qur'an teaches that all of the events of the universe are already recorded by God.

> The first thing He created is the pen, He said to it: 'Write'. It said: 'What shall I write?' He said: 'Write what will take place until the Day of Judgment.' Whatever is to strike a human being will never miss him, and whatever is to miss him will never strike him. The pens had been dried and the scrolls had been folded as Allah, The Glorified, The Exalted, said: 'Did you not know that Allah knows (all) what in heaven and earth? Verily, all put down in a record. Indeed, that is very easy of Allah.'
> (Sura 22:70)

Nothing happens unless it is the will of God: hence, the phrase 'if it is God's will' (inshallah). 'God wills it' is common within Islam and recognises that whatever happens is from the will of God. This could suggest a lack of free will; however, most Muslims would argue that free will is an important part of what it means to be human. God's knowledge of what each human will choose does not take away freedom to act independently. God's knowledge is such that he knows his creation so well that he is able to know the decisions and actions that will be taken in every circumstance. Humanity remains free to act without interference or compulsion from God; if it were not so, this life as a test would be unfair. The reward/punishment associated with this life is based on a righteous judgement as it reflects a person's conscious and free choices.

The Five Pillars of Islam

Muslims believe that their faith is supported by the living of five basic duties. These are commonly known as the Five Pillars: just as pillars hold a house up, so these five pillars hold up a Muslim's faith. A Hadith reports:

> A man came up to the Prophet whilst he was sitting with some of his companions. He asked Muhammad, 'Tell me about Islam?' The Prophet replied, 'Islam is to bear witness that there is no god but Allah, and that Muhammad is His Prophet; to perform the prayer; to pay zakat [the poor tax]; to fast in the month of Ramadan; and to undergo the Hajj if it is possible.' The man replied, 'Correct, you have spoken the truth.'
>
> (in Geaves, 2005, pp. 121–122)

These are the most often talked about aspects of Islam, but when they are explored within the classroom it is important that they are contextualised within the framework of the articles of faith and a Muslim's relationship with God. All are designed to show submission to his will and remind a Muslim of the different aspects of their faith. In the other chapters of this book the various practices of religions are not explored in this depth, but the pillars' place within existing arrangements in schools necessitates their inclusion here.

Statement of Faith (Shahadah)

To become a Muslim, a person must believe and repeat three times the statement:

> There is no god but Allah and Muhammad is His prophet.

This is a statement that is repeated throughout a person's life; its words are the first words that a Muslim child will hear when they are whispered into their ear after their birth. Similarly, they should be the last words that are said by a Muslim prior to death, either by the person or on their behalf. To become a Muslim, a person must believe and recite the Shahadah three times in front of witnesses. It can thus be seen to be the beginning and end of a person's faith. It is the most important statement because it is the basis of all that Muslims believe. There two beliefs expressed in the Shahadah:

1   There is only one God.
2   Muslims believe that Muhammad is the messenger of God, and the seal of the prophets.

The two beliefs come together in the message of God written down in the Qur'an. The beliefs associated with these two beliefs, and the centrality of the Qur'an, are explored in the Articles of Faith section above; but they lay the basis for every other aspect of Muslim belief. The two beliefs together are an important declaration and delineator of Islam to and from other religions.

Prayer (Salah)

Submission to God is nowhere more evident in the practices of Muslims than in prayer. Muslims generally pray five times a day. During the prayer, the Muslim will go through different movements, i.e. standing straight, bowing, prostrating before Allah (forehead, nose, hands, knees plus feet on the floor in the way that a servant will bow before a king). The action of prayer shows that a Muslim submits to God and his will. With Islam meaning submission (obeying), through prayer a Muslim shows that they are submitting their will to God.

There is a strength that comes with praying as a community and, as such, men are asked to pray in mosques. Women can also pray in mosques but it is not compulsory. For prayer outside of the mosque a Muslim may pray anywhere that is clean; hence the use of a prayer mat (musulla). A prayer is always towards the Ka'ba in Makkah (a compass points the way). Children are taught to pray from the age of seven and would be expected to be participating in all prayers by puberty.

Prayers:

- are always said in Arabic (just as Muhammad (pbuh) did).
- are offered at dawn, soon after midday, mid-afternoon, just after sunset and at night.
- are made up, if missed through unavoidable circumstances. Some mosques suggest a prayer time, which gives a broad window where prayer could be offered rather than limiting it to a specific minute.
- consist of cycles (rak'a). In the morning prayers there are two rak'as, the sunset prayer has three, and the midday, mid-afternoon and evening all have four.

The procedure of the prayer would usually be as follows:

- An official of the mosque (muezzin) will call people to prayer. In Islamic countries he will stand on a pillar of the mosque; in Britain he will stand inside the mosque. This call to prayer (adhan) consists of seven short statements (in Arabic):

   Allah is most great (repeated four times).
   I testify there is no god but Allah (repeated twice).
   I testify that Muhammad is the messenger of Allah (repeated twice).
   Come to prayer (repeated twice).
   Come to success (repeated twice). In the call to morning prayer the statement, 'Prayer is better than sleep' is inserted after the fifth statement.

Allah is most great (repeated twice).
There is no god but Allah.

- A Muslim will perform ablutions (wu'du), during which they will wash – including hands, face, arms and feet.
- The cycle of prayer begins. In a standing position with hands by the side of the head (takbeer), a Muslim will say that God is most great.
- In a standing position, the person folds their right arm over their left arm (woquoof) and recites the first chapter of the Qur'an (and verses from the Qur'an).
- While saying God is most great three times, the worshipper will go into a bowing position with hands on knees and back parallel to the floor (Rukoo). They then praise God in this position.
- In a standing position, they praise God again.
- The worshipper will prostrate themselves (sujood), saying 'God is most great, glory to my Lord, the highest' three times.
- Sitting (tashahhud), a Muslim will rest for a few moments then repeat the prostration.
- The Muslim will then get up, saying 'God is most great' (end of the cycle).
- Prayer is finished in the sitting position by turning the head first to the right, saying 'Peace be upon you' (As-salaamu alaikum), and then by turning the head to the left and saying 'Peace be upon you'.
- A Muslim may offer their own prayers with their own concerns (du'a). These may also be said anywhere and at any time and can be said in the vernacular. These can also be said during the prostration cycle of prayer.

Once a week there is a special Friday afternoon prayer (al j'umah) that all men should attend; it is a requirement of faith to attend the congregational prayers. Women may also attend; this prayer is normally performed in a mosque but can be done in other places such as at school. This prayer also involves a sermon (khutbah) by the imam. Praying together gives a greater sense of community, and strengthens the ummah.

Almsgiving/charity (Zakah)

Muhammad experienced times of hardship during his life. His father (Abdullah) died before he was born and his mother (Aminah) died when he was only six years old. This made him aware of human suffering and taught him compassion. He instructed his followers that they should always help others, especially the poorest members of society including orphans, widows and the sick. Giving to charity follows the example of the Prophet but it also recognises God as the source of all that a Muslim has. In giving to charity a Muslim is acknowledging that God should be a person's first consideration; there should be nothing that is placed in front of their submission to him. To place riches before their duty to God is to commit the sin of shirk, in making something equivalent to, or more important than, God.

Zakah is given at the end of the month of Ramadan and should be 2.5 per cent of a Muslim's savings or surplus wealth. Paying Zakah is a spiritual act. The word 'Zakah' means to purify or clean; and, as such, the wealth that a person has, and perhaps the person themselves, is purified through the willing gift of Zakah.

> **The money that is given can be used to help other Muslims in a number of situations:**
>
> - To look after refugees or stranded strangers.
> - To help the poor of your community.
> - To ransom hostages or prisoners of war.
> - To relieve people from debt.
> - To support converts (reverts) to Islam.

The use of Zakah only for Muslims reinforces the centrality and importance of the worldwide community of Muslims (ummah). A Muslim's first responsibility is to God, then to their family and from there to the ummah. Zakah reminds a Muslim of their responsibility to contribute to the building of the ummah in supporting and strengthening fellow Muslims.

Fasting (Sawm)

Sawm is an expression of a Muslim's belief in God and of living their lives in submission to his will. God is the source of everything in life and in providing for the world he has given the good things to all believers to enjoy. However the month of Ramadan is set aside for fasting, a time when Muslims do not eat or drink anything during daylight hours. This has been a practice since the time of Muhammad and is required by the Qur'an (See Sura 2:183–186). The Qur'an also details the timings of the fast from dawn until darkness (see Sura 2:187).

> **Every Muslim must fast during Ramadan in submission to the will of God. The only people who are excused are:**
>
> - the very old.
> - those under the age of puberty.
> - those who are ill (mentally or physically).
> - those who are expecting a baby or breast-feeding one.
> - those who are travelling.
>
> Apart from the first two groups, the others are expected to make up the fast as soon as possible. There are many reasons why a Muslim will fast during Ramadan:
>
> - It is commanded by God in the Qur'an.
> - It prevents greed and builds up self-control.

- It reminds Muslims of what it is like to be poor and hungry. This then encourages Muslims to fulfil the command to give more charity in this month.
- It develops a greater awareness of God during Ramadan; it is a time of great spiritual devotion. One Muslim has said of fasting that: 'It is a time where I feel closer to God. Without reference to worldly desires I am able to concentrate on God and where I stand in relation to his will'.

Fasting is a more spiritual time for Muslims as it is linked with the giving of the Qur'an to the Prophet Muhammad. During the month of Ramadan many Muslims will read the Qur'an each evening; for this reason the text is split into 30 sections in all Arabic editions of the Qur'an. The recitation of the first revelations from God through Jibra'il came during the last ten days of Ramadan. The exact night is known to Muslims as the Night of Power. This is a special night when Muslims are encouraged to perform extra worship to receive greater forgiveness of sins.

Pilgrimage (hajj)

A Muslim should complete the pilgrimage to Makkah (hajj) at least once during their lifetime if they have the health and wealth. The hajj enables the Muslim to put to one side the worries of their normal life, to draw closer in submission to God. Hajj is performed during Dhul Hijjah, which is the twelfth and last month of the Islamic calendar on specific days. Muslims can go on another extra pilgrimage at other times of the year, which is not compulsory, but this does not fulfil the requirement of hajj. Each year at pilgrimage time an estimated two million Muslims from all over the world travel to Makkah. So sacred is Makkah that non-Muslims are not allowed inside the city.

Activities of the hajj include:

- The clothing in simple white robes (ihram). Women can wear ordinary clothes whatever the colour, though a lot of Muslim women would also wear white as well. This reflects the unity and equality of all within the ummah and in the sight of God. Malcolm X referred to this aspect of the hajj:

They asked me what about the Hajj had impressed me the most ... I said, 'The brotherhood! ... It has proved to me the power of the One God ... All ate as one, and slept as one. Everything about the pilgrimage atmosphere accented the Oneness of Man under One God.

(Malcolm X, 1968, pp. 452, 443)

- The pilgrims walk around the Ka'ba seven times praising God, and asking for his forgiveness and assistance. As they pass the black stone, pilgrims will raise their right hand towards it.

- Pilgrims will perform two cycles of prayer at the station of Abraham and drink some water from the zam zam well.
- The pilgrims walk seven times between two hills very near to Makkah. When Abraham left Hagar and Ishmael, he ran between two hills seven times, looking for water. Ishmael found the zam zam spring by putting the heel of one of his feet into the ground. Pilgrims will collect bottles of this holy water, which they believe is good for healing.d a ram instead. Animals will be sacrificed, eaten and given to the poor.
- Pilgrims spend the night in Mina.
- Pilgrims will pray on the plain of Arafat (20 km away) and may spend the entire day there asking Allah for forgiveness. It is believed that Adam and Eve were forgiven on Arafat.
- Pilgrims say evening prayers and camp in the village of Muzdalifah. They may collect very small stones here.
- In Mina pilgrims throw stones at three stone pillars. These mark the places where the devil tempted Abraham to disobey God. Muslims believe that Abraham drove away the devil by throwing stones at him. Following Abraham's example is a way for pilgrims to show that they reject evil and wish to follow Allah.
- In Mina, the festival of sacrifice (Id-ul-adha) is celebrated. On this day animals are sacrificed. Abraham had been willing to sacrifice Ishmael; when he was spared, Abraham sacrifice
- The pilgrims will remove the ihram; have their hair cut and go around the Ka'ba again seven times (tawaf) and run between the two hills seven times.
- Some may afterwards go to Madinah to visit the Prophet's mosque.

All of these events indicate to Muslims the importance of the prophets and the examples that they set by living in submission to God's will.

In exploring the Five Pillars, a teacher might explore the varying commitments that a pupil makes throughout their lives in contrast to Islam. A Muslim will have a choice and belief that underpins all they do (Shahadah); one they perform every day (prayer); once a year (almsgiving); for a period of time once a year (fasting) and once in their lifetime (hajj).

The Five Pillars

1   Write down your beliefs that relate to each of the Pillars of Islam in the third column of the table below.

2   Write down the similarities and differences between the two in the middle column.

Table 12.1 The Five Pillars: Links with pupils' beliefs

Pillar	Links, similarities and differences	My beliefs
Shahadah – Muslims believe that there is no God but Allah, and Muhammad is his prophet.		I believe that:
Salah – Muslims pray five times a day.		I believe that:
Sawm – Muslims fast during daylight hours during the month of Ramadan to remember the poor.		I believe that:
Zakah – Muslims pay 2.5% of their savings to help the poor.		I believe that:
Hajj – Muslims go on pilgrimage once in their lifetime to Mecca.		I believe that: (clue: is there anywhere people should go?)

Note

1   'pbuh' is an acronym of 'Peace be upon him'. This is a sign of respect for the prophets and will be repeated by Muslims when speaking or writing about the Prophets. In this book, it is acknowledged here but is not used throughout the rest of this chapter. No disrespect is intended.

References

Geaves, Ron (2005) *Aspects of Islam*. London: Darton, Longman and Todd.

Geaves, Ron (2007) 'A Reality Without a Name':A Repositioning of Sufism From the Margins, *World Religions in Education. Journal of the SHAP Working Party*, XXX, 42–44.

Smalley, Sarah (2005) Teaching about Islam and Learning about Muslims: Islamophobia in the Classroom, *Resource*, 27(2), 4–7.

X, Malcolm (1968) *Autobiography of Malcolm X*. London: Penguin.

Further Reading

Burckhardt, T. (1990) *An Introduction to Sufism*. Wellingborough, UK: Crucible.

Elias, I. J. (1999) *Islam*. London: Routledge.

Esposito, J. (1994) *Islam, the Straight Path*. Oxford: Oxford University Press.

Ruthven, M. (1996) *Islam: A Very Short Introduction*. Oxford: Oxford University Press.

Chapter 13

Teaching Judaism

.

Chapter outline
What is Judaism?

- Who is Jewish?
- Orthodox
- Reform
- Conservative/Masorti Judaism
- Kabbalah

The nature of the Almighty

- The Shekinah
- The story of the Exodus

The nature of humanity
The Law/Halakhah
Scriptures

- The Torah (Law)
- The Prophets (Nevi'im)
- The Writings (Ketuvi'im)
- The Talmud

Anti-Semitism including the Shoah/Holocaust
Religious Expression

What is Judaism?

Judaism can be seen to begin with Abraham in about 2000 BCE; and it developed from the religion of Abraham and his descendants, often called the House of Israel (Abraham's grandson Jacob changed his name to Israel). Judaism started in the land now called Israel, but for the past 2,000 years most Jews have lived in other countries. These Jews who live outside Israel are said to be part of the Diaspora. Many Jews believe that they have been chosen by G-d to be His people. This 'chosenness' has its roots in a covenant that the Almighty made with Abraham. Abram (later to be called Abraham) was born about 4,000 years ago in Ur near the Persian Gulf. He grew up to be a wealthy man, and like everybody else he worshipped many gods. At some point he began to believe in one God, and began to teach his family to believe the same things. This change in Abram's life marks the beginning of Jewish faith. Abraham came to believe in the G-d who controlled all of creation. This same G-d wanted to enter into a covenant (b'rit) with Abraham (see Genesis 12).

The Almighty promised Abraham the land of Canaan as a perpetual inheritance with circumcision being the sign of the covenant. In response to the covenant, Abraham took his family to Canaan. As part of the covenant Abraham had been promised that his descendants would become a great nation. This worried Abraham because he was well into his old age and did not have any children. Deciding to take steps to make God's promise work out, and in accordance with the custom of the time, Abraham had a son with Hagar, who was Sarah's (his wife's) servant – they called this son Ishmael. The promise, however, was that Sarah would have a son and when both Sarah and Abraham were very old, they had a son called Isaac – from whom Jews believe they are descended. This means that all the promises given to Abraham's family are given to all Jews. Abraham is the 'Father' or 'Patriarch' of Judaism, his name, Abraham, means 'Father of the nations'.

Who is Jewish?

This may seem like a straightforward question to answer – a Jewish person is someone who goes to synagogue and keeps the laws of Judaism. This answer would only be partially true – these people would be religious Jews of which there are different types. There are also many people who identify themselves as Jewish, but in some cases only by lineage or heritage; these might be termed secular Jews. To be considered Jewish a person usually has a Jewish mother. These Jews may not practise or follow their faith. They may not celebrate the Jewish festivals, observe Shabbat or attend worship in the synagogue. Secular Jews cannot entirely turn their backs on being Jewish. They remain Jewish and many are proud to do so.

Ehrlich (2010) has identified that 'Judaism has three essential elements: God, Torah and Israel' (p. 6). The Torah refers to the Law given to Moses and Israel can be seen to be a land but also includes 'an historic political entity, a people, a nation, a belief system, a social group and a culture' (Ehrlich, 2010, p. 7). These elements are not isolated from one another; aspects of the history of Israel will be explored below in a discussion of the Almighty. Elements of both the Almighty and Israel will be explored in the discussion of the Law. Every element of Judaism interlinks with others to form the religious experience of the Jews.

There are various groups within Judaism; and care should be taken not to present one expression as normative. The two major groups of Judaism are Reform/Progressive and Orthodox, though these are not monolithic, and there are other groups such as Chasidic (Hasidic), Conservative and Kabbalah.

Orthodox

Modern Orthodox Judaism began in the late eighteenth/early nineteenth century in Europe as a reaction against some reforming tendencies within Judaism. It was felt that a focus on the traditional laws and teachings of Judaism was important to maintain their religious identity. The term 'Orthodox' was first applied to the traditional Jews by some elements of the Reform movement as an insult suggesting that they were rigid and stuck in the past. However, the name is fairly apt as Orthodox Jews would tend to see themselves as practising the correct and normative expression of Judaism. Orthodox Jews believe the entire Torah was given to Moses by God at Sinai; the Talmud is also authoritative and both remain a source of guidance and structure for life in the modern world.

There are many different types of Orthodox Judaism; in addition to the movement described, there are older groups of Jews who would be considered Orthodox. Hasidic Jews are possibly the most visible expression of Orthodox Judaism within the UK today. Hasidism arose in Eastern Europe in the eighteenth century within a very close knit community. In combining a scholarship of the Talmud and a mystical expression and living of the mitzvot, the Hasidic Jews are most noticeable by a very conservative form of dress, sometimes very reminiscent of the fashions of eighteenth-century Eastern Europe. In assuming that this group is the only expression of Orthodox Judaism, a person will miss many of the other expressions that are different in their expression of faith. Other expressions include:

• Sephardi Jews who have their origin in Spain and the Iberian Peninsula. Sephardi Jews would perhaps not be seen as a separate expression, rather as an expression within Orthodoxy.
• Ashkenazi Jews who have their origins in Central and Eastern Europe around the end of the first millennium CE. It is estimated that the majority of Jews killed in the Holocaust were Ashkenazi.

All have slightly different emphases but would accept the Torah as authoritative, and utilise the teachings of different scholars and rabbis.

Reform

Reform Judaism generally teaches that the beliefs and practices of Judaism should be updated for the modern world. Within the UK such groups might be described as either Reform or Progressive. The Torah and the Talmud are used as guides rather than as a strict set of guidelines that must be adhered to. The most obvious manifestations surround the place of women within Judaism, with the introduction of bat mitzvahs for girls, the seating together in the synagogue and female rabbis. The reforms are not solely linked with the place of women however. Jewish laws about Shabbat may be developed to allow for certain restrictions on Sabbath activities to be removed. This may mean that Reform communities are more disparate than elements of Orthodox Jews who tend to walk to synagogue, in contrast to Reform Jews who would generally have no problem with transport on Shabbat. Reform Jews would tend to consider the possibility that some of the laws were meant for a specific time and place, were maybe influenced by the physical and social context and as such are subject to change.

Conservative/Masorti Judaism

Modern Conservative Judaism has its roots in Europe in the late eighteenth century. While the modern Reform and Orthodox movements were developing, an expression of Ashkenazi Judaism arose that at a very basic level offers a middle way between them both. A number of American Conservative Jewish Groups expressed a codified statement of Conservative Jewish beliefs in 1988. It is summarised below:

1   God is Creator; humanity is created in his image and given free will. The Torah is the representation of God's will for Jews revealed through the prophet Moses.
2   The authority of the Law (the Halakhah) is recognised but it can grow and change in different times and circumstances.
3   Judaism entails the right to a freedom of inquiry and a right of dissension.
4   The later halakhah and philosophical writings of Judaism are rich resources to bless the spirituality of Israel and the wider world.
5   The law and practices of Judaism emphasise the ethics in Jewish living.
6   Israel is a symbol of the unity of the Jewish people throughout the world. It should be used to bless the communities of Jews throughout the world.
7   Jewish law and tradition when it is properly understood will be an enriching influence for Jewish living and the world as it draws closer to the Kingdom of God (see The Jewish Theological Seminary of America et al., 1988).

Thus Conservative Judaism strives to strike a balance between a respect for the traditions of Judaism and a need to reinterpret aspects for the modern world.

Kabbalah

Kabbalah is a school of Jewish mysticism that began nearly 2,000 years ago. Kabbalah was textualised in the Yalkut Re'uveni by Reuben Hoeshke in 1660, but is not restricted to an esoteric group. Aspects of Kabbalah can be seen in prayer books, popular customs and ethics in the different expressions of Judaism. The focus of the Kabbalah is transcendence and immanence of the Almighty and a person's exploration of their place in regard to him.

The Nature of the Almighty

Every morning and evening in the synagogue and in the home Jewish people say the Shema (Deuteronomy 6: 4–9):

> Hear, Israel, the Lord is our G-d, the Lord is One.

This declares the Jewish belief that there is only one G-d. Judaism is a monotheistic religion. There is no limit to the Almighty's power. He has created everything in nature and it is all under his control. The nature of the Almighty is summarised in Maimonides' 13 principles of faith. Written in the twelfth century CE, these could be seen to be as much a statement of belief as a reaction to the beliefs of Christianity and Islam. A summary of these beliefs is:

1   The Creator is the creator and guide of everything. Only he creates.
2   The Creator is a perfect unity.
3   The Creator has no body, is incorporeal and cannot have a physical comparison.
4   The Creator is the first and the last.
5   The Creator is the only one to whom should be prayed.
6   All of the words of the prophets are true.
7   Moses is the most important and chief of all of the prophets.
8   The Torah as now constituted is the same as was given to Moses.
9   The Torah will never be changed or replaced.
10 The Creator knows all the thoughts and deeds of humans.
11 Those who keep the commandments will be rewarded; those who break them will be punished.
12 The Messiah will come.
13 The dead shall be raised at a time decided by the Creator (see Birnbaum, 2005, p. 157f).

When Jews pray to G–d they may call 'him' Adonai, which means Lord, as the name of G–d is so sacred that other names are used in its stead. Jews use Adonai with great respect and would never use it carelessly. Jews also believe that G–d is eternal, that he is always present, that he knows everything and that he cares about the world that he has made. This idea of care means that Jews believe that the Almighty can be experienced through the entire world.

The Shekinah

The Almighty is not separate to the world. He does not simply live in heaven. The almighty is close to everything and everyone that he has made; he is omnipresent. Throughout the scriptures the Almighty's involvement with the people of Israel is very evident and shows the concern that he has for his people. Jews would see that this closeness is evidenced today in the lives of Jewish people around the world. The word to describe this closeness of God is Shekinah. This simply means that God is present everywhere.

Examples of Shekinah from the scriptures include the deliverance of the Hebrews from Egypt under the leadership of Moses; or Esther who saved the Jewish people from persecution and death in Persia. These events are remembered today in the festivals of Passover and Purim respectively. There are many more examples throughout the TeNaKh (Jewish holy book) of the Almighty preserving his chosen people. There are also examples of the people of Israel forgetting the Almighty and suffering because of this; to remember him and be delivered. The story of the history of Israel is told allegorically in the book of Hosea in the TeNaKh. Hosea has a wife, Gomer, who seems to be regularly unfaithful but after a period of suffering on the part of Gomer Hosea seeks her out and becomes reconciled. Hosea is the first of the prophets that uses marriage as a metaphor for the Almighty's relation to Israel.

The story of the Exodus

The story of Moses and the Exodus highlights for Jews the role that the Almighty has in the preservation of Israel. Moses is also seen as a pre-eminent prophet. A classroom version of the story of Moses is below.

When Moses was born the Pharaoh was very worried about the number of Israelites and ordered all Israelite baby boys to be killed. Moses's mother placed him in a basket on the River Nile and asked the Almighty to protect him. He was found on the banks of the river by the Pharaoh's daughter who brought him up as her own son.

When he had grown up a 'Prince of Egypt', he saw a slave being mistreated by an Egyptian slave master. To protect the slave, Moses killed the abuser. Fearing for his life, Moses was forced to flee across the Red Sea and into the desert, where he worked for a man called Jethro as a shepherd, and married Jethro's daughter, Zipporah.

Forty years later, Moses had a vision of the Almighty in which a bush was on fire, but did not burn. God spoke to him, telling him that he had seen the suffering of his people in Egypt. God told Moses to return to Egypt and lead the people of Israel into their own land of Canaan. Moses asked how the Almighty wanted to be known. The Almighty replied:

> I AM what I am. Tell them that I am has sent you to them. You are to tell the Israelites that the god of their ancestors, the Lord, the God of Abraham, Isaac and Jacob has sent you to them.

Moses did as the Almighty told him. He returned to Egypt and asked the Pharaoh to set the slaves free. The Pharaoh refused. To persuade him, God sent a plague, which turned the River Nile to blood. The Pharaoh agreed to release the slaves, but after Moses took this 'plague' away the Pharaoh changed his mind. This happened eight more times with eight worsening plagues on Egypt.

- A plague of frogs invaded Egypt.
- Gnats attacked both people and animals.
- Swarms of insects covered Egypt.
- All of the Egyptian livestock died.
- People were afflicted with boils.
- Hail and fire fell down on Egypt from heaven.
- A plague of locusts covered all Egyptian land.
- The land of Egypt was covered by total darkness for three days.

It was the tenth and final plague that enabled the Israelites to escape Egypt. The Israelites were to kill a lamb and paint the blood on their door posts. This would mean that the final plague would pass over the Israelite homes. This final plague was the most brutal; the Angel of Death killed the firstborn son in all the Egyptian homes. This terrible event and the preceding nine convinced the Pharaoh to let the slaves go.

After the Israelites had left Egypt, the Pharaoh changed his mind about letting them go. His army caught up with the Israelites on the shores of the Red Sea. With the power of the Almighty, Moses parted the waters, which allowed the Israelites to pass safely through. The waters then came together and the whole Egyptian army was drowned. The Israelites were now safe to make their way to the Promised Land and reclaim their covenant.

When Moses and the people of Israel arrived on the banks of the Red Sea they may have felt that their troubles were at an end. The threat from the Egyptians had lessened but there were many more trials to be faced.

The people of Israel needed to be prepared to enter the Promised Land. The journey that they did – called the Exodus – helped them learn more about themselves and their relationship with the Almighty. They were not without their moans and groans though. Even when miracles happened they sometimes forgot the things the Almighty had done for them.

For safety, when they had crossed the Red Sea the Almighty sent a pillar of smoke to guide them by day, and a pillar of fire to guide them by night. The Israelites moaned that they were thirsty. Moses struck a rock with his stick and water came gushing out. They also complained that they were hungry, and so the Almighty sent manna (sweet food) overnight. This would last for one day, except on the Sabbath when they were to gather twice as much the day before so they would not have to work. The Israelites even complained that there was no variety in this food.

The camp of Israel was also infested by snakes. Moses told people to look upon him and the staff the Almighty had given him, and they would be saved. But because this seemed so easy, many people did not look and were poisoned.

Moses reached Mount Sinai and went up to speak with the Almighty. He was gone for quite a while. While he was gone the Israelites forgot the Almighty and began to worship a Golden Calf. Moses came down from speaking on the mountain and was angry with the Israelites – so angry he broke the tablets on which were written the commandments from the Almighty. The Israelites repented and Moses went and received new tablets with the law on.

The Israelites were travelling for 40 years. Near the end of the 40 years 'Moses went to be with God', and it was left to Joshua to lead them into the Promised Land.

Within this story there are many aspects that could be explored by pupils with careful design and questioning by them. Its applicability for the life of a Jew today is significant: as one of the chosen people how do they react to the struggles and blessings that they experience in life? How can the Almighty help them in their lives? And many more.

The nature of humanity

The TeNaKh teaches that humanity is created in the image of the Almighty (see Genesis 1–2). This does not mean literally, as God is incorporeal, rather this phrase is a simile, meaning that humanity has senses that enables perception and action. The Almighty perceives and acts, and in this sense humanity is in his image.

Although humanity is seen to be created in the image of the Almighty, in distinction from him human nature is essentially twofold. Human nature is made up of good inclinations (yetzer haTov) and evil inclination (yetzer haRa). In this a human has free will to choose one or the other; the purpose of life thus becomes seeking to overcome the evils in the world. Individuals should recognise that their deeds can push the whole world towards good and evil. Just as Adam's decision to partake of the fruit in the Garden of Eden had repercussions for the world, so too do the decisions that individuals make.

This reward is vague within Judaism as the focus tends to be on this life, rather than the afterlife. There is a concept of the afterlife (Olam Ha-Ba) but this has a lot of flexibility in how it can be understood. Traditional interpretations highlight a resurrection to a place of reward (Gan Eden) or punishment (Gehinnom); though this punishment may only be for a short period of time. There are some Jewish people who would accept reincarnation in certain cases. What is important about life after death is that it should not be a motivator for action. Rather the focus is on the proper living of the law and performance of good acts in this life.

The Law/Halakhah

In common with other religions, Judaism is more than a belief system; it is a way of life. The word halakhah, which is usually translated as Jewish law, might be more accurately rendered as 'the path one walks'. This suggests that Judaism is that path that affects every aspect of life. An understanding of the law is crucial to understand why a Jewish person will live the way that they do; an observance of the law is a spiritual expression of a person's relationship with the Almighty in even the most mundane, or every day, acts. Each of these tasks takes on a spiritual significance.

There are three sources of the laws:

1   The Torah. These are the unchangeable 613 commandments (mitzvot) that are given in the books of Moses. Examples include the mitzvah to not stand by idly when someone is in danger (Lev. 19: 16), or to place a mezuzah on the door post (Deut. 6: 9). The various mitzvot cover many different topics and circumstances such as G-d, the Torah, Prayer and Blessings, Love and Brotherhood, Marriage, Divorce and Family, Forbidden Sexual Relations, Dietary Laws and many more. Some are unable to be lived in today's world, such as those surrounding the observance of rites in the Temple, and agricultural laws only apply in Israel.

2   Laws given by Rabbis. They are seen by some Jews as being as binding as the mitzvot in the Torah. There are two different types of laws given by the rabbis:

   i.   Gezeirah: These laws are given to stop people accidentally breaking mitzvot from the Torah. For example, not holding an agricultural tool on Shabbat in case they forget the day and use it without thinking.

   ii. Takkanah: These are laws with no link to the Torah but were created by the rabbis for the benefit of the people. One example is the mitzvah to light candles on Chanukah. These will vary from community to community, dependent on rabbis accepted as authoritative.

Table 13.1 Books of the TeNaKh

Ketuvi'im	Nevi'im	Torah
	Jewish History Former Prophets	Jewish Law
	Joshua	Genesis
	Judges	Exodus
	Ruth	Leviticus
	1 Samuel	Numbers
	2 Samuel	Deuteronomy
	1 Kings	
	2 Kings	
	1 Chronicles	
	2 Chronicles	
	Latter Prophets	
	Malachi	
	Zechariah	
	Haggai	
	Zephaniah	
	Habbakuk	
	Nahum	
	Micah	
	Jonah	
	Obadiah	
	Amos	
	Joel	
	Ezekiel	
	Lamentations	
	Jeremiah	
	Isaiah	
	Ezra	
	Nehemiah	
Poems and Songs		
Song of Songs		
Ecclesiastes		
Proverbs		
Psalms		
Job		
Esther		

3   Custom. These can also be seen to be a third type of law given by rabbis, but they are not arrived at through reasoning and discussion, rather it is a custom that has been followed long enough to become accepted. One example is the two days associated with some festivals; this developed so that people outside Israel did not accidentally break a mitzvah because they were unsure of the date. While having no basis in any law it just became an accepted law. This type of law could also differ from place to place as different customs are accepted into religious practice.

While seemingly legalistic, it is important for people to understand that every aspect of the Jewish law is carried out in devotion to the Almighty and is an expression of a deeply held belief.

Scriptures

The Jewish Scriptures are a collection of books in what is commonly called the TeNaKh. This is split into three sections: The Torah, the Nevi'im and the Ketuvi'im.

The Torah (Law)

The Torah is the five books of Moses and is very important to Jews because it tells the story of how God chose them and gave them their laws and land. It contains the stories of creation and the Plagues of Egypt, as well as the laws such as the Ten Commandments. It is divided into 54 sections and one is read each Shabbat. More about the Torah has been explored above in relation to the law and rules (mitzvot).

The Prophets (Nevi'im)

The Prophets were God's spokesmen. Their writings are amongst the most beautiful in the TeNaKh. The Prophets gave warning messages to the people of the time about things they were doing wrong and the consequences they would face. There are three long books in the Prophets – Isaiah, Jeremiah and Ezekiel – and many shorter ones. Readings from the Prophets accompany those from the Torah in synagogue services.

The Writings (Ketuvi'im)

Although these writings are not so important as the Torah and the Prophets they do contain the Psalms. They also contain stories, histories and poems. These help Jews to know how to live their lives, and with their relationship with God. These are used regularly in synagogue worship. Readings from the Writings are usually given on festival days.

The Talmud

The Talmud is not scripture but rather the accumulated wisdom of Judaism interpreting the Torah. For centuries a great number of judgements and opinions based on the Torah were passed by Jewish teachers. They were all to do with the way that the Jews were expected to behave. These were passed down by word of mouth until around 200 CE when they were collected together into one book – the Mishnah.

People then began to discuss the Mishnah in addition to the Torah. Soon there was more material forming a commentary on the Mishnah. This was collected together into the Gemara. The Mishnah and the Gemara were brought together to form the Talmud. It still has a great effect on the way that Jewish people live. Jewish people and leaders will refer to it to try to work out how they should behave in certain situations.

Anti-Semitism including the Shoah/Holocaust

> Open your eyes … and gather your inner strength; what you will see here may put your mental sanity and moral quest in peril. You will see here all that cannot be seen anywhere else: the infinite ability of tormentors and also their victims' endless agony. How could human beings first imagine then commit such inhuman actions against other human beings?
>
> (Wiesel, 2014)

Elie Wiesel is here describing the Shoah or Holocaust; the act of genocide against the Jews during the Second World War. The Holocaust was perhaps the worst example in a long history of anti-Semitism throughout the ages. Examples trace back to Manetho in the third century BCE, and include events such as the massacre of Jews during the Crusades; the expulsion of Jews from England in the thirteenth century, which was not rescinded for 350 years; and the presentation of Shylock in Shakespeare's *The Merchant of Venice*. There are many modern examples of anti-semitism in society. One such example is the discussion among Tottenham Hotspur fans and the wider media over the self-identification in a chant on the football terraces using an offensive epithet describing Jewish people; or swastikas sprayed within areas that may be seen as mainly Jewish. This is not to suggest that anti-Semitism is the default position, in today's pluralistic society it is much less prevalent, and positive examples are shown in documentaries and in the media.

However, anti-Semitism, and in particular the Holocaust, raises issues when considering the concept of shekinah. If the Almighty is intimately involved in the history of Israel and its people how could such an atrocity happen? In light of the story of Hosea earlier, some might suggest it as a punishment; but punishment on such a horrific scale would be rejected within Judaism. A person cannot fathom the mind of the Almighty and as such the question should perhaps be asked about a person's response to this suffering rather than the thoughts of the Almighty. These questions are struggled with by survivors:

> For more than twenty years, I have been struggling with these questions. To find one answer or another, nothing is easier: language can mend anything. What the answers have in common is that they bear no relation to the questions. I cannot believe that an entire generation of fathers and sons could vanish into the abyss without creating, by their very disappearance, mystery which exceeds and overwhelms us. I still do not understand what happened, or how, or why. All the words in all the mouths of the philosophers and psychologists are not worth the silent tears of that child and his mother, who live their own death twice. What can be done? In my calculations, all the figures always add up to the same number: six million.
>
> (Wiesel, 1968, p. 182)

However, the answer the Almighty gives might be silence; there are no answers that can be given by humanity. This does not take away a Jew's responsibility to learn from the events. Such events give all people the opportunity to respond positively and as such part of this response is to continue to believe in the Almighty and his wisdom. Victor Frankl suggested three ways to respond with a 'tragic optimism' to such evil by:

> (1) turning suffering into a human achievement and accomplishment; (2) deriving guilt from the opportunity to change oneself for the better; and (3) deriving from life's transitoriness an incentive to take responsible action.
>
> (2004, p. 140)

To provide a theodicy for such evil is perhaps impossible, but the reaction of Jewish people and the contribution of anti-Semitism to their identity and faith cannot be overestimated.

Religious expression

There are many elements of Judaism that have not been explored in this chapter, but hopefully the grounding of the various concepts developed will provide an impetus to further study. One aspect that is particularly evident within schools is that of worship within Judaism, however, it should be evident that while there is formal worship in the synagogue Jewish people will worship and express their devotion in everyday living. While there may be differences in application, the centrality of the Almighty and the history of Judaism provide an identity that is both religious and cultural. To be Jewish is more than belonging to a religion but following a way of life.

References

Birnbaum, David (2005) *Jews, Church & Civilization, Volume III*. Manhattan, NY: Millennium Education Foundation.

Ehrlich, Carl S. (2010) *Judaism*. New York, NY: Rosen Publishing.

Frankl, Victor (2004 [1946]) *Man's Search for Meaning. The Classic Tribute to Hope from the Holocaust*. London: Rider.

The Jewish Theological Seminary of America, The Rabbinical Assembly, United Synagogue of America, Women's League for Conservative Judaism, Federation of Jewish Men's Clubs (1988) *Ve'em unah: Statement of Principles of Conservative Judaism*. USA: The Jewish Theological Seminary of America, The Rabbinical Assembly, and The United Synagogue of America.

Wiesel, Elie (1968) *Legends of Our Time*. New York, NY: Holt, Rinehart, Winston, Inc.

Wiesel, Elie (2014) 'Message from Elie Wiesel' in *Shoah*. Available at: www.yadvashem.org/yv/en/exhibitions/pavilion_auschwitz/wiesel.asp (accessed 1 May 2014).

Further reading

Aylett, E. (1991) *The Jewish Experience*. London: Hodder.

Cohn-Sherbok, D. (1999) *Judaism*. London: Routledge.

Cohn-Sherbok, L. and Cohn-Sherbok, D. (2001) *Judaism: A Short Reader*. London: One World Publications.

de Lange, N. (2000) *An Introduction to Judaism*. Cambridge: Cambridge University Press.

Isaacson, S. (1999) *Principles of Jewish Spirituality*. London: Thorsons.

Solomon, N. (1996) *Judaism: A Very Short Introduction*. Oxford: Oxford University Press.

Chapter 14

Teaching Sikhism

Chapter outline

What is Sikhism?

The Nature of God

The Nature of humanity

The Gurus

- Guru Nanak
- Nanak's successors
- Guru Gobind Rai/Guru Gobind Singh
- Guru Granth Sahib

Service

Equality

The Nishan Sahib

Religious expression

What is Sikhism?

Sikhism is the youngest of the six world religions, beginning with the life of Guru Nanak who was born on April 15, 1469 CE in India. It can be overlooked in a discussion of the world's religions. For example, Prothero, in his book *God is not One*, explores the eight major world religions, of which Sikhism is not one (2010). This could be because of the American context within which Prothero writes, but it suggests a wider ignorance of aspects of Sikhism. Also, Rodney Stark, in discussing the rise of Mormonism in the nineteenth century, suggests that Mormons:

> will soon achieve a worldwide following comparable to that of Islam, Buddhism, Christianity, Hinduism and the other dominant faiths.... Indeed, today they [Latter-day Saints] stand on the threshold of becoming the first major faith to appear on earth since the Prophet Mohammed.

> (Stark, 1984, pp. 18–19).

Again, Sikhs are omitted from the list of dominant faiths, perhaps because of their relatively small numbers in the USA.

The Sikh Code of Conduct (Rahet Maryada) defines as a Sikh anyone who believes in:

- One God,
- the ten Gurus,
- the Guru Granth Sahib,
- the words of the ten Gurus.

And:

- has faith in Amrit, the initiation ceremony of the Khalsa,
- does not follow any other religion.

In a school environment it is possible that the only aspects of Sikhism that are explored are the life of Guru Nanak, the ten Gurus and perhaps the Five Ks. If this is the case then the presentation of Sikhism misses the exploration of some of the key beliefs behind these expressions.

Sikhism is built on various principles including:

- Simran – a remembrance and meditation on the name of God.
- Sewa – selfless service.

In addition to Three Pillars that underpin Sikh morality and ethics:

1. Contemplating God's names (Naam Japo) to control and subjugate the Five Thieves (see below).
2. Work diligently (Kirat Karo) to earn an honest living.
3. Sharing with others (Vand Chhako).

In doing this, a Sikh is able to develop aspects of the Five Virtues:

1. Truth (Satya)
2. Contentment (Santosh)
3. Compassion (Daya)
4. Humility (Namrata)
5. Love (Pyaar)

Enabling them to avoid the Five Thieves:

1. Lust (Kaam)
2. Anger (Krodh)
3. Greed (Lobh)
4. Attachment (Moh)
5. Pride (Hankaar)

These will be explored in detail with regard to the Nature of God, the Nature of humanity and the importance of service within this chapter.

While Sikh means learner or follower, those who subscribe to the Rahet Maryada would be considered a part of Sikhism. The different types of Sikh are usually described by levels of commitment and practice. However, there are some small groups who would consider themselves Sikh but whose origins pre-date the organisation of the Khalsa by Guru Gobind Singh. Other divisions may be geographical and cultural. While there is a unity within Sikhism, there are Sikhs who prefer to worship in a gurdwara that they are familiar with; this does not suggest a difference of practice, just a preference for company and leadership.

The Nature of God

The Nature of God is outlined in the Japji, which is the beginning of the Guru Granth Sahib (consisting of 38 verses in addition to the Mool Mantar and a final verse) and was given by Guru Nanak. The first section of the Japji is known as the Mool Mantar (or Mantra):

> There is only One God. Truth is His Name. He is the Creator. He is without fear. He is without hate. He is timeless and without form. He is beyond birth and death. The enlightened one. He can be known by The Guru's Grace.

The teachings outlined in Sikhism identify Waheguru (the true guru, or wonderful Lord) as the creator, incorporeal and indescribable. He is further described as being without gender, with no offspring, is not created. God can be found within everything and desires the salvation of all of humanity. The Japji is repeated every morning as the meditation on the name of God enables a person to become in a closer union with God. This is one of the pillars of Sikhism.

The Nature of humanity

Within Sikhism, humanity has a soul, which is a part of God. As a general rule, humans seem to be unaware of the divine presence within themselves and are therefore unaware of the purpose of life. The purpose of this life for Sikhs is to become aware of their relationship to God and seek union with him. In order to do this a person needs to become aware of the illusion (maya) through which they see the world. The world is real, it is not an illusion, but their perception of it is skewed by the Five Thieves as they reflect the search for material and worldly pleasure. In succumbing to these Thieves a person removes themselves from any possibility of a relationship with the divine.

As such, a person should, through hard work and effort, seek to develop the Five Virtues. Gobind Singh Mansukhani has described the process that a person will go through in seeking union with God, based on the teaching of Guru Nanak in the Japji:

> The first stage: is in the region of duty – *Dharam Khand* – here, man does act and reaps the consequences. Those who carry out their duties sincerely and honestly, enter the second region – the region of knowledge – *Gian Khand*. Here a devotee may obtain a knowledge of God and the Universe. He learns of his own human limitations, the omnipotence of God and the vastness of His creation. He may then realise that there is some further purpose behind God's creation. He then enters the

third stage – the region of effort – *Saram Khand* – here his mind and understanding are purified. He endeavours to act according to the instructions of the Guru. Such efforts may lead him to the next region – the region of grace – *Karam Khand*; here the selfless devotee may find divine grace and develop spiritual power. Finally, only with God's grace he may enter the next stage – the region of truth – *Sach Khand* – where he may unite with God. Such is the progress of man from the spiritual place. Undoubtedly, being moral is a great help to spiritual progress.

(2007, p. 71)

The nature and purpose of humanity is to overcome the physical urges of the self and seek union with God through morality, service and a meditation on God. Through this a person is released from the cycle of reincarnation.

This life can, therefore, be seen as a test through which experience, knowledge and wisdom are gained through hard work and dedication. God seeks the union of all of humanity with him; as such, this process may take many lifetimes to achieve, but it is eminently possible.

The Gurus

God has revealed the truth of existence to his Gurus. Guru is a word that means teacher but can be seen to have other etymological roots, though these interpretations are not accepted by all. 'Gu' is a Punjabi word that means 'darkness' and 'ru' can be seen to mean 'light' or 'shatter' (or even 'heavy' but that does not quite fit here). In essence then a Guru is someone who takes a person from darkness to light, or shatters darkness. Either of these explanations gives an insight into the role of the Guru in Sikhism; a teacher who brings God's light to humanity and shatters the darkness caused by an illusory view of the world. There are ten human Gurus within Sikhism.

Guru Nanak

Guru Nanak is the founder of Sikhism, and as the first Guru is very important as he expresses God's will and message to Sikhs. Guru Nanak was born to a Hindu family on April 15, 1469. His father was an accountant. During his childhood Nanak was friends with both Hindu and Muslim children and was concerned about spiritual matters including the meaning of life. At the age of six he started school and learned quickly. When he was 13, as a Hindu, Nanak was to receive sacred thread but he refused it saying that he believed the spiritual thread of mercy, contentment and continence was the thread he wished to wear as these would never perish.

While working as the family cowherd Nanak would often meditate and discuss religion with holy men. Noting Nanak's distractions his father tried to get him to settle down by finding him a wife. He was married at the age of 16 to Sulakhani, daughter of a merchant. Nanak saw no need for married life to stop him searching for answers and he had a happy marriage. Nanak and Sulakhani had two sons, Sri Chand (1494) and Lakshmi Chand (1497).

To support his family Nanak worked as an accountant for the Muslim governor of Sultanpur. When he was not in work Nanak would meditate and sing hymns with a Muslim friend, Mardana. One early morning in 1499 Nanak went to the river Bain to bathe. After going under the water Nanak disappeared and he was thought to have drowned. Nanak was actually communing with Waheguru.

When he returned after three days he taught people that he had learned: 'There is no Hindu, no Muslim'. Guru Nanak travelled far and wide to teach God's message to people through hymns, which he felt people would be able to understand. He established local groups called manjis, where his followers could congregate to sing hymns and meditate.

After 12 years Guru Nanak returned home but immediately set off on another journey. On his return from this journey he founded a settlement known as Kartharpur (the home of God) on the banks of the river Ravi. When he taught he always wore the clothes of both Hindu and Muslim holy men. He was often asked whether he was a Hindu or Muslim. His response repeated that there was no Muslim or Hindu just people who worshipped God as he is within the whole universe.

Nanak was once taken prisoner by the Mughal Empire. Guru Nanak sang a hymn about the killing of innocent people by the Mughals while he was imprisoned. The King recognised Guru Nanak as a great teacher and asked him for forgiveness and set him free.

As he got older, Guru Nanak settled in Kartharpur with his wife and sons. Many people came to hear him teach and sing hymns. He established a society without divisions of caste, inheritance, religion or gender. Here he established the langar.

Recognising that Guru Nanak was about to die, some of his followers that were Hindus and Muslims argued about whether Nanak should be buried (according to the rites of Islam) or cremated (as in Hinduism). Guru Nanak instructed them to place flowers on either side of his body: Hindus on the right, Muslims on the left. Those whose flowers remained fresh in the morning would know that was how his body was to be treated. He asked his followers to pray and lay down while covering himself with a sheet. On September 22, 1539, in the early hours of the morning, Guru Nanak died and became one with God. In the morning his followers found nothing except the flowers still in bloom.

Nanak's example and teaching form the basis of Sikhism. The majority of his teachings focused around God, service and the equality of all people. One story relates the importance of earning a living through honest living. When Guru Nanak visited Saidpur in the West Punjab he stayed with Lalo, a carpenter of low caste. The chief of the town, Malik Bhago, who was wealthy, invited Nanak to a feast for all the holy men. Nanak refused the invitation preferring to eat the simple food prepared by Lalo. On hearing this Malik Bhago was angry and had the Guru brought before him. Malik Bhago asked Nanak why he had refused his sumptuous feast. In response Nanak asked for some of the food served by Malik Bhago and some of the food he was sharing with Lalo. He held each in one of his hands and squeezed them. Malik Bhago's food dripped with blood while milk came out of Lalo's. Nanak taught that Malik Bhago's wealth was earned through the blood of others while Lalo offered the milk of his own hard work.

There are many stories from the life of Guru Nanak that can be used as a starting point for the exploration of Sikh belief and practice.

Nanak's successors

Guru Nanak appointed and prepared Lehna (later Angad) to be his successor. His name 'Angad' means 'my limb', which suggests that the new Guru and his message were an extension of Nanak. Sikhs believe that the Gurus taught the same truth about God and are seen as exemplars of living life in devotion to God. Each of the ten Gurus is important to Sikhs but each achieved different things in the development of Sikhism. The nine human Gurus that came after Guru Nanak are:

- Guru Angad (1504–52 CE) – was responsible for the establishment of the Gurmukhi script, and collected together Guru Nanak's hymns.
- Guru Amar Das (1479–1574 CE) – his teachings on equality and women's rights were a central aspect of his teaching.
- Guru Ram Das (1534–81 CE) – was the founder of the city of Amritsar.
- Guru Arjan (1563–1606 CE) was responsible for the Golden Temple (Hari Mandir) at Amritsar and compiled the writings of the previous Gurus into the 'Adi Granth' (First Collection). Guru Arjan was the first Guru to be martyred.
- Guru Har Gobind (1595–1644 CE) – spent a large amount of his time fighting to protect Sikhism. He introduced the two swords representing worldly authority (meeri) and spiritual authority (peeri).
- Guru Har Rai (1630–1661 CE) was a kind Guru who distributed medicines. Sewa (selfless service) was shown as he helped those who fought against his father, Guru Har Gobind.
- Guru Har Krishan (1656–1664 CE) – died at the age of eight from smallpox, which he caught whilst helping those suffering in Delhi.
- Guru Tegh Bahadur (1621–1675 CE) – tried to live a life of peace and teach the words of the Gurus. He was martyred.
- Guru Gobind Singh (1666–1708 CE) – the last human Guru who established the Khalsa (and appointed the Guru Granth Sahib as the 'living Guru' after his death).

Guru Gobind Rai/Guru Gobind Singh

Guru Gobind Rai (later Guru Gobind Singh) is an important figure within Sikhism as he established the Khalsa (the pure ones). The Khalsa was established on the celebration of Vaisakhi in 1699. The events of the day are an essential part of learning about Sikhism and recognising the devotion that a Khalsa Sikh has to God. A summary of the story is below.

- Guru Gobind Rai asked Sikhs to congregate at Anandpur for Vaisakhi.
- The Guru addressed the congregation and reminded them about the commitment necessary to follow the Sikh path.
- At the end of his address he asked who would be willing to give something up for their faith.
- People offered many different things including money, time, and many other things.
- Raising his sword he asked who would be willing to give up their own life.
- After a period of silence a man stepped forward declaring that he would die for his faith.
- The Guru took him into a tent.
- There was a thud and blood seeped out from under the tent; the Guru came out with a sword covered in blood.

- He asked for another who would be willing to die for their faith.
- Another man stepped forward, and he was taken into the tent and the thud and blood were repeated.
- This happened again another three times.
- After some time the Guru emerged from the tent with the five men alive behind him.
- Some consider this to be a miracle, while others suggest the Guru was beheading animals to test people's faith.
- The Guru declared the men as the Beloved Five (Panj Piares).
- He invited all present to become Khalsa.
- The people who became Khalsa went through the Amrit ceremony, which involved a bowl of water with sugar crystals (amrit).
- He sprinkled it on the crowd as a symbol of community, devotion and commitment.
- He then sprayed himself with the amrit.
- He declared that each person would have new names; men would add 'Lion' (Singh) to their names, and the women would add 'Princess' (Kaur).

This ceremony is repeated today for Sikhs who wish to become Khalsa Sikhs. The initiation ceremony takes place with five other Khalsa Sikhs to represent the Five Beloved ones and a bowl of amrit that has been stirred with a double-edged sword. The amrit is drunk and sprinkled on the eyes and hair. During the ceremony, those being initiated recite the Mool Mantar and are told the rules of the Khalsa, which were given by Guru Gobind Singh. These rules are:

- Worship only the Waheguru. There should be no worship of idols or human beings.
- Only believe in the Guru Granth Sahib as a holy book.
- Wear the 5Ks.
- Add 'Singh' (lion) or 'Kaur' (princess) to their name.
- Never remove hair from any part of their bodies.
- Drugs, smoking and alcohol are forbidden.
- Do not eat that which has been killed in the name of another god.
- There should be no ear or nose rings.
- Women will not wear a veil.
- Earn an honest living.
- Give generously to the poor and the needy.
- No stealing or gambling.
- Dress simply and modestly.

The devotion to Waheguru is evident in all aspects of living as a Khalsa Sikh. They enable the Sikh to think less of themselves and more of the spiritual aspect of life as they strive for union with God.

The Five Ks (panj kakke)

As an expression of Sikh spirituality and identity the 5Ks will be briefly explored here, especially in light of their common use in teaching within the classroom.

1   Uncut hair (kesh): Hair is believed to be given by God. To keep their long hair tidy, men often, and women sometimes, wear turbans.
2   Comb (kangha): By looking after their hair, they are showing respect to God. It would be disrespectful for a Sikh to let any part of their body, as a gift from God, become untidy or dirty.
3   Steel bangle (kara): This may have developed from a piece of forearm armour used when the Khalsa fought the rulers of India. It reminds Sikhs of unity, the eternal nature of God and the need to defend their faith.
4   Undershorts (kachera): These remind Sikhs of the struggle of their faith and of soldiers for whom the shorts provided great freedom when fighting.
5   Sword (kirpan): They are only to be used in self-defence. In the UK most Sikhs wear a small decorative version. It reminds them of their responsibility to fight for those who are less fortunate.

Guru Granth Sahib

Prior to his death, Guru Gobind Singh declared that there were to be no more human Gurus, but the Guru Granth Sahib would be the 'living Guru'. In essence it is a collection of the words of the Ten Gurus and is seen to contain God's words through them. The Living Guru occupies the same status as a human Guru if they were on the earth. As such, it is treated with respect, has its own resting room including a bed and is awoken each morning. It is placed at the front of the prayer hall in the Gurdwara (door of the Guru) and is a focus for worship. Sikhs bow before the book when they enter the temple and make offerings of money or food to it, as they would have done to the human Gurus in the past. Services are held in the presence of the book and the hymns, prayers and sermons are all taken from or based on the Guru Granth Sahib. Rites of passage within Sikhism take place in the presence of the Guru Granth Sahib.

The words of the Guru Granth Sahib are important as the Gurus reflected the divine in the way that they lived their lives. As such, use of the Guru Granth Sahib to praise God and learn of him is essential to overcome illusion, and to lead the mind away from the Five Thieves. The contemplation of the name of God (simran) provides focus for the Sikh to find peace and overcome the selfishness and ego. It may seem to observers that when a Sikh worships they may be listening to the words of the Guru for guidance, and while this may be true, it only tells part of the story as the contemplation of God's name enables progression towards union with the divine. This contemplation must, however, be combined with service (sewa) for a balance to be found and Sikhism to be lived effectively and the purpose of life to be fulfilled.

Service

The life and work of the Gurus teach Sikhs about the concept of selfless service (sewa) which helps a Sikh live the virtues of compassion, humility and love; while avoiding the

Thieves of greed, attachment and pride. Sewa is central to all Sikhs living and is integral to the path to union with God. Examples from the lives of the Guru include when Bhai Kannayya provided water to injured Mughal soldiers who were fighting Sikhs. Sikh soldiers took Bhai Kannayya to Guru Gobind Singh as a traitor. When the Guru asked him for the reasons why he had helped the enemy, he replied that the Guru had told people to see the Divine in everyone, so he focused on the Guru's face and saw it in everyone he came across. The Guru asked him to not just provide water but also medical care to the injured soldiers.

Guru Nanak established the langar for all people. This reflected his teaching that all were equal and Waheguru lived in all of humanity. His creation of the langar put into practice his message of inclusion, service and friendship in direct opposition to concepts of caste and untouchability in the prevailing Hindu culture in India. This message is lived out in Gurdwaras all over the world today. In every Gurdwara there will be a Guru's kitchen where the communal langar meal will be eaten as part of Sikh worship. As outlined earlier, simran and sewa are the two integral parts of a Sikh's search for the divine; this is evidenced in their worship that would begin by listening to the Guru Granth Sahib and conclude with the serving and sharing of the langar meal.

The eating of the meal signifies equality but the preparation, provision, service and cleaning up of it evidences sewa in a very practical sense. The food in the langar is provided by Sikh families, and is usually served by male members of the community. Participation in the provision of the langar meal is considered to be a privilege by Sikh families as an expression of faith and belief. The langar meal is not the only expression of sewa within Sikhism today. Any act of selfless service shows devotion to the divine and enables a person to fulfil more of the purpose of life.

The combination of sewa and simran is exemplified in the life of the Gurus. It would be a very interesting task for pupils to trace the two elements and see whether a balance is achieved. This might also be carried out through focusing on the practices of an individual Sikh today.

Equality

Guru Nanak's message was radical in the social, cultural and religious context in which he found himself. He advocated a totally egalitarian society with no distinctions between people in terms of caste, gender, religion or birthright. All are equal in the sight of God, and therefore all should be equal in the sight of his people. This type of equality was expressed by others of the Gurus in their actions. For example, Guru Amar Das promoted equality by having women in senior religious positions. In the twenty-first century the equality of all is taken for granted as all are seated on the floor for langar, men and women work together in the Gurdwara and many other examples; but some Sikhs suggest that this safe equality misses the radical message of the Gurus. The Gurus opened up the equality of opportunity for all people; it was not just that they could do the same things as each other, it was that there was no restriction on the opportunities that were open to them.

A story is told of an eight-year-old Guru, Gobind Singh, and his white hawk. Going on a hunting trip one day on his horse, the Guru came to a big garden just outside the city of Ambala and met a local leader called Pir Amir Din who had a black hawk. Amir Din wanted the Guru's white hawk and challenged the Guru to a fight between the two hawks. Recognising Amir Din's intentions, the Guru refused but suggested he have sparrows fight Amir Din's hawk. To much laughter from Amir Din, the Guru called to two sparrows that were sitting on a nearby tree. The sparrows fought bravely and injured the hawk, which then fell to its death. The message of this story is not about the fight but the potential that everybody has to do things that might seem extraordinary. The equality of all beings is no longer a radical concept within the world, but Sikhs are called to make the most of this equality as they seek for union with the divine.

The Nishan Sahib

The Nishan Sahib is a saffron flag that can be seen flying outside every Sikh Gurdwara. Guru Har Gobind first introduced the use of the Nishan Sahib. In the centre of the Nishan Sahib is the Khanda, a symbol of Sikhism, which shows:

- A circle
- Two swords (kirpan)
- A double-edged sword.

Each of these reflects aspects of a Sikh's beliefs.

- The two kirpans reflect the Sikh teaching of worldly and spiritual riches (meeri-peeri), which is also reflected in the balance in the identity of the Sikh as a Saint-Soldier – someone who seeks for spiritual knowledge, but in doing so is willing to fight to protect others. In the history of Sikhism, and particularly at the time of Guru Gobind Singh who introduced the concept of Saint-Soldier, this was a very real possibility. Today, while this may happen, more likely is the struggle to help others spiritually and physically.
- Circle (or chakra (quoit)) reflects the belief that God is without beginning or end and also that he is not born and does not die.
- The double-edged sword reflects that God is One while being able to combine two opposing descriptions, e.g. God is Justice and God is Mercy.

The use of the Nishan Sahib to begin an exploration of Sikh beliefs, or to reflect on the learning that has taken place would be an important part of a study of Sikhism.

Religious expression

Sikhs would perhaps not identify Sikhism as a religion; rather it might be seen to be a path or way of life, indeed, maybe even a community. Eleanor Nesbitt has suggested that to codify it into a neatly packaged religion would be to lose its vitality as a 'fluid tradition, pulsing with life and difficult to pin down' (2005, p. 2). Recognising its radical nature and its place in the world of religions is crucial to a proper understanding of Sikhism.

Being the newest of the major world religions, Sikhism has developed in a world in which its message and revelation have had to take account of the other world religions. While not discriminating against other world religions, it is possible to identify aspects of Sikh belief that stand in contrast to the teaching of the other religions. For example, the rejection of meat killed in a specific way stands in distinction to Islam; the rejection of caste distinguishes it from the Hinduism practised at the time, and others. This may be an aspect of Sikh expression that would be interesting to explore in the classroom.

References

Mansukhani, Gobind Singh (2007) *Introduction to Sikhism* (14th edn). New Delhi, India: Harkunt Press.
Nesbitt, Eleanor (2005) *Sikhism: A Very Short Introduction*. Oxford: Oxford University Press.
Prothero, S. (2010) *God is not One*. New York, NY: HarperOne.
Stark, R. (1984, 26 September) The Rise of a New World Faith. *Review of Religious Research*, 18–27.

Further reading

Cole, W. O. (2004) *Understanding Sikhism*. Edinburgh, UK: Dunedin Academic Press.
Cole, W. O. and Sambhi, P. S. (1995) *The Sikhs: Their Religious Beliefs and Practices*. Brighton, UK: Sussex Academic Press.
Kalsi, S. S. (1999) *Simple Guide to Sikhism*. Folkestone, UK: Global Books.
Mann, G. S. (2004) *Sikhism*. Upper Saddle River, NJ: Prentice Hall.

Index